*f***P**

Shirley A. Mason

SYBIL EXPOSED

The Extraordinary Story Behind
the Famous Multiple Personality Case

DEBBIE NATHAN

FREE PRESS

New York   London   Toronto   Sydney   New Delhi

Free Press
A Division of Simon & Schuster, Inc.
1230 Avenue of the Americas
New York, NY 10020

Copyright © 2011 by Debbie Nathan

First Free Press hardcover edition October 2011

FREE PRESS and colophon are trademarks of Simon & Schuster, Inc.

For information about special discounts for bulk purchases,
please contact Simon & Schuster Special Sales at
1-866-506-1949 or business@simonandschuster.com.

The Simon & Schuster Speakers Bureau can bring authors to your live event.
For more information or to book an event, contact the Simon & Schuster
Speakers Bureau at 1-866-248-3049 or visit our website at www.simonspeakers.com.

Designed by Carla Jayne Jones

Manufactured in the United States of America

10   9   8   7   6   5   4

Library of Congress Control No.: 2011009164

ISBN 978-1-4391-6827-1
ISBN 978-1-4391-6829-5 (ebook)

To my own blessed sisterhood:
Anita Nathan Beckenstein
Barbara Nathan Katz
Miriam Nathan Lerner

CONTENTS

CONTENTS

I felt a clearing in my mind
As if my brain had split;
I tried to match it, seam by seam,
But could not make them fit.

—Emily Dickinson

INTRODUCTION

W HAT ABOUT MAMMA?" THE WOMAN psychiatrist asks her patient, another woman, who is lying on a divan in the early 1960s. "What's mamma been doing to you, dear? I know she's given you the enemas," the psychiatrist continues. "And filled your bladder up with cold water, and I know she used the flashlight on you, and I know she stuck the washcloth in your mouth, cotton in your nose so you couldn't breathe. . . . What else did she do to you? It's all right to talk about it now."

"My mommy," the patient answers groggily. She is in a hypnotic trance, induced with the help of the psychiatrist.

"Yes."

"My mommy said I was bad, and . . . my lips were too big like a nigger's . . . she slapped me . . . with her knuckles . . . she said don't tell Daddy. She said to keep my mouth shut."

"Mommy isn't going to ever hurt you again," the psychiatrist answers. "Do you want to know something, Sweety? I'm stronger than mother."[1]

The transcript of this long ago conversation is stored at John Jay College of Criminal Justice, in New York City. The college's library houses a cramped room called Special Collections, whose walls are adorned with lithographs of a gangster jumping to his death from a window on Coney Island, and prisoners rotting in cells at Sing Sing. Not far from the lithographs hangs a black-and-white photograph of John Jay's staff in the 1960s, peopled by over two dozen men and five women. One of the women wears a serious expression and a plain, woolen coat. "Interesting, that coat," comments a librarian. "It's from before she got rich. Afterward, it was nothing but mink for her. Full-length mink."

The woman who got rich was Flora Rheta Schreiber, author of *Sybil*, the blockbuster book from the 1970s about the woman with sixteen personalities. *Sybil* first went on sale in 1973, and soon it was moving off the shelves as briskly as the Bible. Within four years it had sold over six million copies in the United States and hundreds of thousands more worldwide. A television adaptation was broadcast in 1976 and seen then by a fifth of the American population. The book is still in print and the TV drama has become a classic. Both versions were instrumental in creating a new psychiatric diagnosis: multiple personality disorder, or MPD. Sybil also created a new way for millions of people—most of them women—to think about their memories, their families, and their capabilities, even when they were psychologically normal, without a hint of MPD.

To create the book which caused this phenomenon, Schreiber collaborated with Dr. Cornelia Wilbur, the psychiatrist in the transcript who asks, "What about mamma?"—and with Wilbur's patient, whose real name Schreiber changed in her book to the pseudonym Sybil Dorsett. The two women helped Schreiber by giving her records of Sybil's therapy, including thousands of pages of treatment notes, patient diaries, and transcripts of sessions that had been tape-recorded over a period of eleven years. Schreiber was a pack rat who never threw away a scrap. After she died in the late 1980s, her papers, including the Sybil therapy material, were archived at John Jay.

For a decade after Schreiber's death, Sybil's real name and whereabouts were unknown to the public, and to protect her privacy, librarians sealed her therapy records. But in 1998, two researchers accidentally discovered a piece of paper that revealed her real identity and, following up on that information, they learned that she was dead. The John Jay papers were unsealed, and today researchers can find disturbing conversations in them, such as the hypnotherapy session just cited. Many describe how Sybil's mother perpetrated sexual assaults and other atrocities on her when she was as young as three years old—traumas so horrible that the little girl was said to have pushed them out of her consciousness for decades, until she saw a psychiatrist. "Mamma was a bad mamma," Dr. Wilbur declares in the transcripts. "I can help you remember."

But countless other records suggest that the outrages Sybil recalled never happened at all. Dr. Wilbur had helped her patient do *something*, these records suggest, and for a very long period of time. But whatever that behavior was, it can hardly be called remembering. What was it, then? And why did it enthrall not just psychiatrists in charge of creating new diagnoses, but ordinary people all over the world—and especially women?

Is there anyone in America who does not remember what started it all? Just in case, here is the abridged version of *Sybil*.

One cold day in winter 1956, a shy and painfully anorexic graduate student in the pre-med department at Columbia University stands outside her chemistry classroom waiting for the elevator. The next thing she knows, she is on a freezing, snow-swept street in a city she doesn't recognize. Eventually she figures out it's Philadelphia, and that between the elevator and the snow five days have passed, days which for the young woman—whose name is Sybil Dorsett—are an utter blank. Sybil catches a train back to New York to see Dr. Wilbur, her steely but superbly kind and caring Park Avenue psychoanalyst. Dr. Wilbur mothers, medicates, and hypnotizes her patient, tirelessly attempting to dredge up memories of the forgotten childhood trauma which she assumes provokes Sybil's flights to other cities.

The Philadelphia trip is not the first time Sybil's mind has shattered. Though she doesn't realize it, she is possessed by so many inner personalities that they need a family tree to keep themselves straight. There are a whimpering toddler, a depressed grandmother, a pair of unruly, prepubescent boys, and two saucy grade school girls named Peggy Lou and Peggy Ann. With unpredictable frequency, these "alters" take turns suppressing Sybil's main personality as they emerge to control her behavior in chilling ways. A young female personality keeps trying to commit suicide—which would, of course, kill Sybil. The toddler cowers under furniture, sobbing with incoherent terror.

This psychic splitting has been going on since Sybil was three, but no one around her realized it, though the little girl's behavior was often puzzling. In fifth grade she suddenly forgot how to do arithmetic. She doesn't know it, but she forgot her multiplication tables because an alter personality named Peggy Lou took over her body at age nine and attended school in Sybil's place. Then, two grades later, Peggy Lou suddenly vanished, leaving Sybil ignorant of everything her alter had learned.

At the time the book begins, Sybil has no idea she has alters. All she knows is that she dissociates—or "loses time," as she puts it. She ends up in strange places without the slightest idea how she got there. She discovers dresses in her closet that are not her style and which she does not remember buying. She finds herself chatting intimately with people she has no recollection of ever having met.

Dr. Wilbur decides that the cause of this puzzling illness is some terrible thing done to Sybil during childhood, the memory of which she walled off into other personalities so that she would not have to deal with the pain. But what, exactly, happened? That's what, together, they need to figure out so that Sybil can "integrate" her personalities and be whole again. The only way to do that is for Sybil to remember the trauma, and Dr. Wilbur must help.

Dr. Wilbur puts Sybil into drug-induced and hypnotic trances that finally cause her to remember. The trauma she suffered as a young child turns out to have been abuse—barbaric, gothic, grotesque beyond imagination—inflicted by her psychotic mother, Hattie Dorsett. Hattie once tried to suffocate four-year-old Sybil by locking her into a box filled with grain. Other times, she made her daughter watch as she defecated on neighbors' lawns, held lesbian orgies in the woods with teenagers, and fondled the genitals of babies. If all this weren't enough to destroy a child's psyche, Hattie regularly hung preschooler Sybil by the ankles above a kitchen table, raped her with household utensils, gave her ice-water enemas, and tied her under the piano while banging out crazed versions of Beethoven and Chopin.

Could these nightmare memories, recovered so many years after the crimes supposedly happened, really be true? Yes, says the book—undoubtedly. One chapter has Dr. Wilbur interrogating Sybil's quiet, colorless father about the family's past. Mr. Dorsett admits that his wife—by now long dead—was a "nervous" woman. Hemming and hawing, he allows that Hattie could have tortured her daughter without his or anyone else's noticing.

Now, decades after the abuse and the psychic splitting, Sybil's only hope for cure is her kindly psychoanalyst. Dr. Wilbur does not disappoint. After eleven years and hundreds of pages of heroic ministrations, she convinces all the alter personalities to integrate into a united self. As Sybil lies on Dr. Wilbur's couch, hypnotized, the babies, little boys, and teenagers all grow into adults within minutes, and they dutifully fold back into Sybil's consciousness, promising never to "come out" again. The grown-up alters make a similar pact. Sybil's broken mind is mended; she vanquishes the hell of her mother's mistreatment and finally becomes a whole person. End of story. Except that after the integration, Dr. Wilbur introduces Sybil to New York City writer Flora Rheta Schrieber. The three women decide to write a book together, the better to help others cope with their mental health problems.

When *Sybil* first came out, fewer than two hundred people worldwide had ever been identified with conditions that today would be labeled multiple personalities. They were so rare that they were considered medical curiosities, like Siamese twins and giants. Most sufferers possessed only one or two alter selves, and no one knew what had caused the splitting. Bad experiences could have induced it. But among those experiences, severe child abuse was never mentioned by the patients or their doctors. Instead, by the early twentieth century, people who exhibited dual consciousness were thought to be suffering from repressed sexual urges, which they denied by imagining that those desires belonged to other selves. Such people were diagnosed as hysterics.

Sybil was something completely new. Her history of sadistic incest and her enormous number of alter personalities made her brand of multiplicity unprecedented. After a tiny fraternity of psychiatrists became fascinated with the condition and started hunting for new cases, that brand turned into an epidemic. In 1980, multiple personality disorder was listed as an official psychiatric illness. Soon, mental health practitioners in America were diagnosing thousands of cases a year.

Almost all were female, and when they first entered therapy most had no alter personalities that they knew of. Nor did they remember being raped and brutalized as children. But during MPD treatment they developed just as many alter personalities, and just as many horrific abuse memories, as Sybil had—if not many more.

Many of these patients began filing lawsuits against their parents for having hurt them so terribly. They went on television talk shows to discuss their suffering, and celebrities joined the fray. Every MPD story unleashed more cases and claims of abuse.

Then a new group of patients surfaced, complaining they'd been wrongly diagnosed and suing their therapists for malpractice. In tandem with these lawsuits, thousands of hurt and angry parents said they were being falsely accused by adult children in therapy. Some brought suits against the therapists.

As a result of this backlash, which crested in the early 1990s, the media did a 180-degree turn from their former credulity about MPD. "Is it real or is it fake?" became the new question. Were the patients, and the therapists who treated them, honest and inspiring? Or were they liars and hustlers?

Some commentators, mostly scholars, tried to square the circle of these questions. It clarified nothing, they said, to argue about whether MPD was real or a hoax. A more useful way of understanding the phenomenon was to recognize that the feeling of being inhabited by other selves has very deep roots in our culture and history. Look at the Middle Ages, they pointed out. Many Catholics then complained of being possessed by Satan; Jews, meanwhile, suffered from invasion by dybbuks. Prayers and exorcism were the treatment then. And now, for people convinced they harbored alter personalities, the cure was supposed to be psychotherapy.

Scholars also pointed out that everyone is prone to "dissociate," to focus so much attention on one event or idea that everything else falls by the wayside, unseen, unheard, unremembered. Think of what happens while watching a really good movie. You are aware of nothing around you, least of all the other people in the theater. Think of "highway hypnosis," driving a habitual route and arriving at your destination without remembering that you exited from the interstate. That is dissociation. It is common and perfectly normal.

But some individuals experience a far more intense kind of dissociation, focusing on one thing so intently that they behave as though in a trance, spending long periods doing and saying things they often don't remember later. In many cultures, people are thought to be visited by benevolent or evil spirits when they display these behaviors. Anthropologists have a term for them: "idioms of distress." Idioms, because trance behavior is considered to be a kind of language. Distress, because what's being communicated, albeit in a masked way, is feelings of pain. The pain may be emotional or it may be physical. Either way, sick people feel possessed because possession states are their society's idiom of distress.

But how, in modern America, could an educated person in distress come to feel she was possessed? How could Sybil have learned to feel and act as though she had multiple selves, when no one else in her world was doing this? An explanation was provided in the early 1990s by a prominent, elderly psychiatrist who had known Dr. Wilbur years earlier and had sometimes treated Sybil when Wilbur was out of town. The old doctor remembered Wilbur telling him that she wanted to write a book about multiple personality disorder. He also remembered Sybil mentioning to him that Wilbur wanted her to act as though she had different selves inside her. He speculated that Wilbur—who had once boasted to her patient that she was "stronger than Mother"—had pressured and coaxed Sybil to develop alter personalities.

In light of this accusation, even more questions arose. What had gotten Dr. Wilbur, herself, so interested in the idea of multiple personalities? And if *Sybil*—the basis for the modern MPD diagnosis—was a product of therapist suggestion, what about all those tens of thousands of patients who had walked into the offices of other mental health practitioners and walked out thinking they had several beings living inside them? And what about all of us book readers and TV watchers? Why had we found the Sybil story so credible?

I remember when *Sybil* first came out. I was in my early twenties, and my girlfriends and I wondered if multiple personalities could invade us. "Could you, like, just be walking around minding your business?" we would ask each other. "And all of a sudden five days have passed and it turns out that different people were inside you the whole time? People who act devil-may-care when you're usually shy and cautious, who tell jerks to go to hell though you were raised to be polite, who converse in foreign languages that you never learned well—even people who are men instead of women? Could this actually happen?" The prospect was terrifying—and irresistible.

In the early 1990s, I was a journalist writing about child-sex-abuse panics: day care teachers falsely accused of molesting preschoolers, and women in therapy recovering memories of tortures too bizarre ever to have happened. I thought about Sybil again, of course. I wondered what her real story was.

Almost twenty years after that, I finally got a chance to find out. In 2008, while browsing on the internet, I was surprised to learn that *Sybil* author Schreiber's papers were archived at John Jay College, a quick subway ride from where I live in Manhattan. I also learned that the papers are open for public inspection, and I made an appointment to take a quick look.

What I found was shocking but utterly absorbing. The papers revealed that Sybil's sixteen personalities had not popped up spontaneously but were provoked over many years of rogue treatment that violated practically every ethical standard of practice for mental health practitioners.

Dr. Wilbur had approached Sybil's health problems with a predetermined diagnosis that brooked no alternative explanations. In her therapy she had made extravagant, sadistic use of habit-forming, mind-bending drugs. And she had treated the patient day and night, on weekdays and weekends, inside her office and outside, making house calls and even taking Sybil with her to social events and on vacations. She fed Sybil, gave her money, and paid her rent. After years of this behavior, the archives revealed, the two women developed a slavish mutual dependency upon each other. Toward the end of their lives they ended up living together.

I also learned that I was not the first researcher to examine the incriminating papers. A professor of comparative literature on the West Coast had teamed up with an assistant and visited John Jay almost a decade before I laid eyes on the material. Afterward he had written several pages about the archives in a book criticizing psychoanalysis. But he'd written in French, and the book was published in Paris. Practically nobody in America read it.

And even if they had been able to, the French book offered little insight into larger questions that were beginning to fascinate me. Why, for instance, when *Sybil* was first published, had so many millions of people like myself, most of us young and female, so fervidly embraced as truth a story whose mythic qualities should have immediately made us skeptical? How had we been so naïve?

The answer, I realized as I read more files, lay in the lives of the women who had created Sybil: not just the patient, but the psychoanalyst and the author. They were my mother's and grandmothers' ages, from earlier generations than mine. Yet I suspected that the frustrations they'd endured as ambitious women in a prefeminist age, and the struggles they'd mounted regardless, had infused the Sybil story with a weird yet potent appeal for young women like myself who were being whipped back and forth by new ambitions and anxieties. To understand myself and my friends, I wanted to know more about the three pioneers: Dr. Wilbur, Flora Schreiber, and Sybil.

All were long dead, but I began using census and other historical records to reconstruct their childhoods, young adulthoods, and experiences as professional women in the 1930s, 1940s, 1950s, and beyond. I tracked down relatives, friends, and colleagues who were still alive. I interviewed these people by phone and traveled through North America for face-to-face meetings. Periodically, I took my notes and returned to John Jay. Comparing the archival material to what I'd found outside the library yielded new insights and lines of inquiry.

All this work deepened my sense that *Sybil* was as much about the conflict between women's highest hopes and deepest fears as it was about a medical diagnosis. Women during the later decades of the twentieth century were aflame, not just with analyses of sexism but also with a great yearning for the freedom to play new roles in life. Taking jobs once held only by men yet going home at night and still being saddled with housework. Postponing childbirth or avoiding it altogether but being told that the goal was still motherhood. Exploring sex outside of marriage (including with women), but worrying about being "sluts." These dilemmas were so new and so acute in the 1970s—the decade when *Sybil* came out—that sometimes young women felt as though alien inner beings were doing their behaving, and not the women themselves. The idea of "multiple personalities" seemed not so strange an idea.

Seeking psychotherapy was not strange, either, even for people deeply critical of the idea that marrying and having babies was the only way to be normal, especially for women. Officially, American psychoanalysis had pushed that notion for years. Unofficially, many therapists had more enlightened ideas. In the 1950s, one of them encouraged budding poet Allen Ginsberg to explore and celebrate his homosexuality. In her book *The Feminine Mystique*, Betty Friedan quoted a psychiatrist reminiscing about a woman patient who was having dreams about being a teacher. Her real problem, the doctor realized, was not penis envy but the fact "that it was not enough for her to be just a housewife and mother." He encouraged her to become a teacher.

Dr. Cornelia Wilbur had always thought that she, too, was helping her female patients, my research revealed. She unfailingly pushed them to follow their dreams, even though the therapy she used on them was bizarre, requiring as it did that they become multiple personalities in order to receive her care. That was a stringent demand from a doctor. But Dr. Wilbur saw herself as a nurturer. She was a maternal figure writ large, and in the 1970s, when young women were rebelling against the conservatism of their own families, the Sybil story gave them a symbolic, modern mother.

Flora Schreiber, the author of the story, never seemed motherly. But she, too, perceived the heroine of her book as a woman in flux, moving from the backwardness of rural life and religiosity to the independence and reason of New York City. Like Cornelia Wilbur, Flora struggled to do transformative work during a time when women's efforts to change the world were still laughed at. *Sybil* was her attempt to do serious nonfiction—even though, in order to be taken seriously, she resorted to making up "facts."

Then there was Sybil herself. Even if she'd never been diagnosed with multiple personality disorder or horrific child abuse, my research revealed, she still would have struggled terribly in life. She would have fought to escape a milieu that discouraged her artistic abilities. She would have felt sad, angry, anxious, and confused about who she was. She might have made art that expressed these feelings, art that could have reached a high degree of professionalism if she had spent her time perfecting her drawing and painting skills rather than languishing for years in psychotherapy.

With competent medical care, she might also have learned a physical cause of her troubles, then received effective treatment instead of broadcasting the pain in her mind and body through the "idiom of distress" of MPD.

But none of that happened. Instead, the woman who became Sybil fell in with a psychiatrist and a journalist, and the three saw their project, a pathbreaking book about female mental suffering, burst upon the world with perfect timing. They were a blessed sisterhood.

This being America, however, they were also a business, and in one box of Schreiber's archives at John Jay College I found the records of their enterprise. They named it Sybil Incorporated, and the contract they signed designated a three-way split of all profits and spin-offs from their book, including *Sybil* movies, *Sybil* board games, *Sybil* tee shirts, *Sybil* dolls, and a *Sybil* musical.

On paper Sybil Incorporated looked industrious and optimistic. But in the real world it was conflicted and Faustian. The three parties made money and for a while changed the course of psychiatry. But to do so, one had to give up her friends and become a recluse. Another lost control of her success and ran through her fortune and reputation. A third used her medical credentials to aggressively promote a diagnosis that, ultimately, hurt women far more than it helped them, defining their conflicts as pathological, curable not by living more actively in the world, but by taking to their beds and swooning with trance and medicine.

How was it that the three women did not foresee the risks? Why had an otherwise reputable psychiatrist helped to concoct sixteen alter personalities in a patient? What made a seasoned journalist charge ahead with her writing even as she realized that the story she was crafting contained more falsehoods than truth?

And what about Sybil? How, exactly, did she take on that parade of personalities? If she used them to speak an idiom of distress, what, exactly, was she trying to *say*? After the best-sellerdom and the Emmy-winning movie and the glitz and brouhaha, did it bother her that no one knew her true identity? What kind of emotional shape would she have to have been in that she would go along with anything a doctor and a journalist cooked up for her? Did she understand the full implications of what they were cooking? How did she help stir the pot?

Sybil affected millions of readers, thousands of psychotherapists, and the tens of thousands of people they diagnosed. It spurred the writing of hundreds of articles and scores of medical texts, and resulted in dozens of movie, television, and book spin-offs. The three women behind this amazing proliferation each had a life and a self full of conflict.

What follows is a cautionary exposé of their—and our—grand and disordered multiplicity.

PART I

SYMPTOMS

CHAPTER 1

SHIRLEY

MANY YEARS LATER, THE WORLD would come to know her as Sybil. But in 1933, the little girl with the colored pencils in her hand was simply Shirley Ardell Mason, a sensitive and confused fifth grader in the tiny town of Dodge Center, Minnesota. She was quiet and slender back then, with crisp clothes, dark hair trimmed in a Dutch-boy bob, and skin so milky that the veins stood blue on her forearms. She had no brothers or sisters so she spent hours alone, playing with baby dolls and paper dolls. In her bedroom she tended an enormous collection of large matchboxes, ordered precisely in stacks. Sheets of paper lay on the floor, and she drew chickens on them in crayon and painted rabbits in water colors. To all who knew her, she seemed like a pleasant, well behaved girl. But young Shirley felt like a hopeless sinner.

She was a sinner because she loved to pretend, and pretending was the work of the Devil. It was forbidden by her family's fundamentalist religion, which also banned the novels and short stories that Shirley loved to read and write. Art done in strange colors was evil, too, yet she adored making her chickens purple and her rabbits green. Her mother warned her to use yellow for her chickens and to stop inventing phantom playmates. To do otherwise was an affront to God, Mrs. Mason said. Hearing this, Shirley's eyes grew wide. She squeezed them shut in church and prayed for strength to abandon her wayward imaginings. But God did not answer. He left her struggling with her stories, her art, and her sin.

Shirley's family were Seventh-Day Adventists. As the religion's name implies, members mark the Lord's day of rest not on Sunday, the first day of the week, but on the last one, Saturday. When Shirley was a child, Adventists met all day on Saturday and prayed. During Shirley's youth in the 1920s and 1930s about a hundred thousand members of the denomination lived in the United States and four dozen resided in the Dodge Center area. The whole town had eight hundred people.[1]

Dodge Center back then was a muddy depot for southeastern Minnesota farmers shipping their crops to the city. It was like thousands of other towns in the Midwest: Each burg had a raggedy main street, usually named Main Street. Each had a dairy cooperative, a grocery or two, a gas station, and a clothing store. Each was filled with churches, church ladies, church gossip, Masonic orders, tea parties, ministers, and young people buying railroad tickets to St. Paul, Chicago, and New York: one way only, please. Barely two generations had passed since the founding of these toiling, pious towns. Already the youth wanted out.

Shirley's grandfather, Neill Mason, was an Adventist, and so was his mother—which made the Mason family pioneering members of this mystic, all-American faith. Adventism goes back to a barely educated farmer named William Miller, a devout Baptist who lived in upstate New York in the 1820s. He had a passion for arithmetic, and as a young man he began to study the numbers in the Bible. These sacred figures, he felt, could predict God's plan for the future.

Miller found a sentence in *Daniel*: "Unto two thousand and three hundred days; then shall the sanctuary be cleansed."

Miller decided that "the sanctuary" actually meant the world. He changed 2,300 days to 2,300 years. He reckoned further and finally landed on 458 B.C., when King Artaxerxes of Persia approved the rebuilding of the Temple in Jerusalem. Miller subtracted 458 from 2300, adjusted for the modern calendar, and determined the year Jesus Christ would make his Second Coming to earth, resulting in the Apocalypse.

That year was 1843.

Miller began spreading his End Time prediction to the Protestants of the northeastern United States. He held meetings with the young farmers and shopkeepers who had streamed west from New England after the American Revolution, in search of land to be gotten from driving out the Indians. To the frontier these newcomers brought religion that turned enthusiastic, even ecstatic during mass revivals where thousands of people fell down together, writhing and singing to the glory of God. Their excitement made it feel as though anything was possible, not just in the everyday world of America, which was moving toward perfection, but also in the firmament of Heaven. Time would cease when Salvation came, they believed, but until that happened, it was imperative for the devout to fix their minds on Time. Those who neglected to do so, by distracting themselves with mundane things and fantasy, would never enter Heaven.

When William Miller first foretold that the world would end in 1843, believers left their crops unharvested, closed their businesses, and quit their jobs. But 1843 turned into 1844. Disillusioned, many Millerites left the fold, but others pressed on, doing more math and fixing new dates. By summer 1844 they had settled on October 22. That day dawned and they climbed hills together, wide-eyed and trembling to await Heaven's parting. When Heaven stayed closed they wept piteously. This non-event would go down in American religious history as The Great Disappointment.

Miller's disappointed spent weeks trying to understand what had gone wrong. Then, Ellen Harmon, a sad-faced teenaged girl from Maine, received a divine answer.

For years Ellen had been a sickly but highly devout girl. By late adolescence she had become an excited Millerite, given to entering trances and communicating with God. One day in December 1844, just weeks after the Great Disappointment, Ellen bent low in fervent prayer. Suddenly she felt bathed in light, and she saw "Advent people" in the sky, traveling on a path toward Heaven. The Lord told her the Millerites had not mistaken the date of the Coming—they'd only misinterpreted it. Jesus really had descended on October 22. But instead of coming all the way down, he had stopped off in a "sanctuary" of heaven. He planned to stay there a while before proceeding to earth.

When He finally came, God told Ellen, the Savior would fashion a New Jerusalem, a paradise. First, though, God and Christ would deal with the wicked—with people who had sinned and defiled their minds. Along with Lucifer, they would be incinerated in a vast, lava-filled lake, boiling with fire and brimstone.

When would this holy cataclysm occur? No one knew exactly. Still Christ *would* come soon. The faithful must remain devoted and focused on time and not get distracted with the glitter of Satan's fiction and make-believe.

After Ellen developed her theology she married a man named White and took his last name. As Mrs. Ellen G. White, she became the leader of a new religious movement. It adopted Saturday as the Sabbath and called itself Seventh-Day Adventism.[2]

Shirley felt bad about her make-believe art. But at least she was painting chickens, and even if she used impossible colors, chickens were real. The stories she made up, though, were not. Jesus was the Son of God and he walked by the side of Christians, but imaginary mortals, like her friends Vicky and Sam, walked nowhere except through a falsifying mind that should be thinking about God's truth instead of characters forged from fancy. No doubt about it, Shirley's stories were fictions. They were displeasing to the Lord and they might evict her from the grace of eternal life. How could she save herself?

She got an idea. She would do writing that wasn't really writing. And she would do it in secret.

Genuine writing required a pencil or pen, but there were other ways to fashion words. All Shirley needed were her parents' old magazines, her paper dolls, and her matchboxes. Her father, Walter, was away from home all day working. Her mother, Mattie, ran errands. The maid went to the grocery and the boarders left for their jobs. Shirley took advantage of her solitude by spending hours cutting single letters from the magazines. She scissored hundreds of A's, B's, C's, D's, F's—all the way to the end of the alphabet. She snipped words, too, like a kidnapper preparing a ransom note. She stuffed the clippings into her matchboxes and covered them with paper dolls. She labeled the boxes with dolls' names—Anna or Alice or Arlene for the letter A and words starting with A; Barbara or Bonnie for B; Peggy Ann for P; and so on and on, to fool the adults into thinking the names on her boxes stood for dolls' names, not letters and words for writing fiction.

When Mattie and the others left, Shirley dumped out the matchboxes. Lining up letters on the floor, she formed long, snaking stories about the exploits of her imaginary friends, Vicky and Sam. At the first sound of footsteps, she collapsed the snakes and crammed the print back in the matchboxes under the paper dolls, to be sorted and used another time in different stories.

Then she sat dreamily in the sun, on the porch steps of the Masons' house. On good days she glowed with pleasure at how she'd created her fictions on the sly, without even writing. On bad days, she knew the angels had seen her even if Mattie and Walter hadn't. When the Second Coming arrived and all the righteous Adventists ascended heavenward, she would be one of the bad ones left behind, burning to ash in the Holocaust flames of His reckoning against the sinful.[3]

In Dodge Center, the Adventists had a small, white building with rude chairs and walls so bare that not even a cross was hung. Neill Mason had started attending services when he was in his thirties, with his wife, Mary. Their son, Walter—Shirley's father—had taken baptism as a teenager in the 1890s.

The Masons did not go to church just on Saturdays. They also attended "testimonies" on Wednesday nights, where the faithful confessed their latest sins and recounted recent miracles. (As one elderly Adventist from the rural Midwest remembered recently, testimonies consisted of statements such as: "I was working on my combine and lost the header bar, then I knelt down and prayed to Jesus and found it." "Praise God!" the congregation would shout. "Isn't Jesus wonderful?")[4] In addition to attending church, Adventists regularly traveled to camp meetings where hundreds of families lived in tents and listened to preaching in the open air. Neill became an aggressive Adventist proselytizer. He ranted to his Methodist and Baptist neighbors about the coming time of trouble such as the world had never seen before. Throughout America, he proclaimed heatedly, Protestants and Papists were conspiring to make people work on Saturday. This conspiracy was part of the run-up to a series of plagues that would precede the Second Coming. Before the plagues poured down, God would smite the bad people.

Walter Mason had not always been so passionately devout. At one time, he had rebelled completely against Adventism. As a young man he'd spent one year at a denominational college, but his father had insisted the Second Coming was imminent, so Walter dropped out at age nineteen to prepare himself. The Coming did not come. Disappointed with his religion and his father, he left the church.

When he was twenty-six he met Mattie Atkinson. She was a year older and lived in another farming community, Emmetsburg, Iowa. Mattie's family was Methodist and had minimal interest in the End Time or the perils of fiction.

Mattie was slender, with an aquiline nose and hair she pulled back tight to show off a delicate face. She had a good education for a small-town girl: at seventeen she was still in school, and she'd used her years of study to memorize "Evangeline," "The Village Blacksmith," and dozens of other poems. She was flamboyant, moving in a flurry and rushing from room to room. Sometimes she talked loudly, and her laugh came out shrill, like a cackle. She loved reciting verses and occasionally, in a driven mood, she repeated a word from someone's conversation then rattled off syllables that rhymed with that word. Mattie was nice, people thought. A little strange, but nice.

When she met Walter he was tall and wiry, with a full head of hair, a thoughtful face, and a quiet voice. The couple married in 1910 and Walter became an architect and a contractor in Dodge Center. By the 1920s the Masons were one of the little town's most respected couples. They lived in a small but handsome two-story wooden house that Walter had designed himself in the middle of town, just across the alley in back of Main Street. The house boasted built-in cabinets and a room off the dining room with a deck of windows facing south. Beneath the windows was a built-in bench for sitting and basking in the natural light. In the bleakness of Minnesota winters, the sunroom was magical.

Mattie wanted children but kept miscarrying. She had health problems: her hips hurt, she tired easily, she sometimes got nauseated and lost weight, her body twitched, and she felt nervous. The brand new Mayo Clinic was fifteen miles east of Dodge Center, and in 1912 Mattie went there to find out what was wrong. A doctor diagnosed cardiac damage from the rheumatic fever she'd had as a child. The old illness caused the hip pains and body spasms, the doctor said. But Mattie had two additional problems, he concluded: anemia and asthenia. The second term was synonymous with neurasthenia, a word also applied to people in the early twentieth century who felt tired, discouraged, and anxious. Asthenia was supposed to come from overworked nerves. Though not as serious as hysteria, it was thought to be related. Mattie worried that her bad health would keep her from becoming a mother. She longed for sons and daughters to fill the house and the cheery sunroom.[5]

In 1923, when she was almost forty—old enough to be a grandmother, and with hair that was prematurely and strikingly white—one of Mattie's pregnancies finally went to term. Shirley was born in January. She was a small baby, just under six pounds, but lively and healthy. Mattie should have felt overjoyed, but instead she fell into a severe, postpartum depression. Grandmother Mason and women hired by Walter cared for Shirley for four months until Mattie rallied.[6]

She began thinking she should convert to Seventh-Day Adventism. Walter had returned to the church four years earlier, but Mattie, still a Methodist, had resisted joining. For the three years that followed her birth, Shirley was the child of a mother and father who were "unequally yoked"—the Adventists' derisive term for a couple in which one spouse was not a member of the faith. But when Mattie finally took baptism as an Adventist, the Masons started putting things right. Walter became active in church affairs and Mattie joined the women's group. She tried to become devout.[7]

The Masons started sending Shirley to Sabbath School. About a dozen boys and girls attended each Saturday morning. Back at home after church, Walter and Mattie probably also took out *Bible Readings for the Home Circle*, a popular book among Adventists in the 1920s. It featured Bible verses, followed by questions that parents and children were supposed to answer together. "And I stood upon the sand of the sea," went one verse, "and saw a beast rise up out of the sea. Having seven heads and ten horns. And upon his horns ten crowns, and upon his heads the names of blasphemy."

Family members of all ages took turns answering the questions which followed these frightening readings—questions about the hated Catholic church, which celebrated Sabbath on Sunday, and about the end of the world. Shirley had trouble concentrating. She fussed and squirmed until Mattie scolded her with "Land sakes!" and "Stand still!" To relax, Shirley emptied her head of beasts and horns. In their place she conjured tales based on stories in Adventist children's books—stories their authors swore were true, about mischievous kitty cats and winsome little girls and boys who often misbehaved but were usually forgiven by Jesus. Soon imaginary friends started visiting Shirley—Vicky, whose family was Catholic but gentle and honest, and little Sam, whose name came from Shirley's initials: S.A.M. Immersed in fantasies, she forgot the long, grim hours of her family's day of rest.[8]

While still in her fantasy world, she often heard scolding outside. It came from Mattie, who was angry that Shirley had just done or said something objectionable. Shirley came to, unable to remember doing anything wrong. "I did *not!*" she would protest, and Mattie grew angrier. "I stood right there and heard you, young lady!" she would yell, and warn Shirley about "talking back to your mother like that." Shirley would slink off, confused and angry. Her parents would laugh at her "pouting."[9]

In the bleak little Adventist meeting house, fights would break out about who was devout and who was reprobate. Someone yelled once at Shirley's grandmother Mary for not being sufficiently faithful. Mrs. White taught that even Adventists would be barred from Heaven unless they scrupulously controlled their bodies and their baser instincts. Sex was strictly for procreation, and even married couples should indulge only moderately. Masturbation—the "solitary vice" and "secret vice," Mrs. White called it—was a horrible sin for boys and men, worse than fiction reading. For women and girls it was virtually unforgiveable.[10]

To keep sex temptation at bay, Adventists followed a radical, vegetarian diet related to the health reform movement, which was tremendously popular in America in the nineteenth century, among many groups besides Adventists. The people who developed the menu included Sylvester Graham, a Presbyterian minister who obsessively feared masturbation and excessive sex. Graham blamed this degenerate behavior on meat, gravy, butter, jam, eggs, pastry, white bread, coffee, pepper, tobacco, tea, beer, and liquor. These substances inflamed the nerves and the genitals, he believed, and he invented a flat biscuit to replace the offending foods. He named it the graham cracker.

Adventists came up with other products: peanut butter, soy milk, Granola, and Kellogg's corn flakes, invented by John Harvey Kellogg, who was raised in an Adventist family. Today's widely available veggie burgers from companies such as Worthington, Loma Linda, and Morningstar Farms also have an Adventist legacy.

As part of the health reform movement, Americans during the nineteenth century also gave themselves "internal baths"—known nowadays as enemas. Many believed constipation caused sexual excitement in males and nymphomania in females. John Harvey Kellogg gave himself several enemas a day, and by the early twentieth century, Americans of all classes and faiths were enthusiastically flushing their bowels, even giving enemas to their children. Mattie had an enema bag hanging over her shower in Dodge Center that she probably used on Shirley.[11]

Mattie tried to be a good wife, mother, and member of the community. Usually she functioned quite well. With extraordinary energy she did volunteer work for the church, collecting money for missionary work and taking minutes at meetings of the women's society. She made house calls to the town's less fortunate. She yelled greetings to people on the street and laughed her odd laugh. Following the recipes in Adventist cookbooks, she kneaded dough from wheat flour, then washed and washed it until the starch was rinsed out, leaving a wad of glutinous plant protein. She mixed the gluten with ground peanuts and tomato sauce, pressed it into tin cans, baked it, and sliced it into rounds of substitute meat.

But then she would slow down and turn worried, snappish, and distant, confusing her daughter terribly. After weeks of laughing with Shirley and playing dolls with her, she would ignore her, or worse, call her names. Mattie labeled her moods "the blues." Sometimes they got so bad that she would sit motionless in a chair for hours.

Mattie got the blues in 1927, after she miscarried a male fetus. It was so well developed that she and Walter named it Willard before they buried it.[12] If losing the baby was not upsetting enough, the Masons had to move five miles out of town that year, to a piece of farmland they owned. The only habitable building was a one-room structure originally intended as a chicken house. The move apparently was made because of bank failures in the Dodge Center area, which wiped out Walter's capital, and because of Walter's lackadaisical business sense even when times were good. He would buy lumber and cement on credit, then build barns and houses in spring and summer without yet being paid by his clients. He would wait till fall to collect, when the farmers got their crops in. But if the harvest turned out badly, he was in trouble.

It seems that Walter had problems with creditors, and to hide from them he moved his family to the chicken house. Mattie was devastated. Her home in Dodge Center boasted a piano in the parlor, heirloom china in polished cabinets, and light streaming through the sunroom. The chicken house had none of these luxuries, and Mattie got the blues so bad that she spent days barely moving.

The Masons left the farm in spring 1928 to enroll Shirley in kindergarten. The Adventists had their own school, which all their children were supposed to attend, to protect them from what the Adventists called the "polluting, corrupting" influence of secular education. Virtually all parents supported the denominational facility, but not the Masons: For reasons unknown, they chose public school for Shirley. They may have felt they could not afford the church's modest tuition. More likely, they were venting their own conflicts about Seventh-Day Adventism through their daughter.[13]

Shirley's matriculation took the Masons out of the chicken house and back to town, where Mattie had not only her nice furnishings but also her women's magazines. She had subscriptions to *Ladies' Home Journal* and *Good Housekeeping*. The magazines' lavishly illustrated pages celebrated the latest in home appliances, interior decorating, and the season's hats from Paris and New York. And there was more. They carried short fiction with seductive teasers on the cover: "Another Glamorous Story of the Theater by Booth Tarkington," "A New Hollywood Series by Frederick Collins." These stories, with their focus on actresses, vanity, and romance, were poison for Adventists.[14] Mattie knew the faith's warnings about such material but could not help loving it. She read even on Saturday and tried to keep her habit under wraps.

Shirley knew, and she had her own secrets. On Saturdays she stared at her paper dolls, wondering: Is it OK to dress them on the Sabbath?[15] She certainly couldn't ask, especially not on the sacred day of the week. So she only *thought* about doll clothes. But angels could read minds. According to Adventist theology, they took information about people's bad ideas to Heaven, where—as one of Shirley's children's storybooks warned—they jotted the information into a holy record book. Shirley squirmed.

She felt bad about other things, including Mary Mason, her paternal grandmother. Mary was an easygoing, affectionate woman who had helped care for Shirley when she was a baby but suffered a stroke when her granddaughter was four, and by then also had cancer of the cervix. Grandma Mary sometimes lived on the second floor of the Mason house with Grandpa Neill. Her room was filled with fascinating objects: paintings she had done on panes of glass; little pots she'd helped Shirley pinch from clay dug out of the riverbank; big, farm-supply-store calendars with paintings of cows. But as the cancer worsened, Mattie began timing Shirley's visits to conserve her mother-in-law's ebbing strength. She seldom allowed Shirley's to stay upstairs for more than half an hour.[16]

After Grandma Mary died in 1931, Shirley stopped eating and lost weight. The third grader appeared distracted in class. When the teacher called on her, she sometimes seemed in a daze. Her teachers noticed but hardly intervened. As children they, too, had seen death, and adults seldom asked them how it felt. Shirley had no brothers or sisters, and experts had been warning teachers for decades that children with no siblings were peculiar: they tended to social awkwardness and they played with imaginary companions. As one psychologist put it, being an only child was a "disease in itself." And Shirley was mollycoddled by her parents, the teachers thought. Her mother held her hand and walked her to school every day, even though school was just across the street from home. Leave it to the Masons, the teachers huffed, to aggravate Shirley's "disease" of only childhood.[17]

Her parents did dote on her. Walter was a man who rarely talked, but like his daughter, he was gentle and artistic. Shirley loved how he taught her to use hammers and saws, and how in the dead of Minnesota winter, he dressed her in little boys' overalls for warmth and called her Mike. When Mattie didn't have the blues she and Shirley often played games. Mattie had not outgrown her own childhood love for dolls, and she often compared her daughter to them. "Oh you're so cute, Peggy Ann," she would say to Shirley, laughingly referring to a very popular fourteen-inch girl with a winsome face and molded Dutch-boy hair topped with a bow. Delighted, Shirley would laugh back.

During her periods of "nervous" energy, Mattie loved to mimic people in town. She could do a perfect rendition of distant cousin Grace Sorenson, who attended the Adventist church. She could parrot the squawks of demanding customers on Main Street and the long-suffering sighs of the salesclerks. Shirley imitated her mother's imitations. "That's not very nice!" Walter would protest. But he laughed anyway. Copycatting people's voices was great fun, and Shirley had picked up her mother's gift for it.

Then Mattie would get the blues. In the living room she would obsessively polish her cut glass and Haviland dishware, turning the pieces over and over, murmuring about their beauty. When Shirley interrupted to play the Peggy game, Mattie kept talking about dishes.

"Look at the cat!" Shirley would implore, and Mattie would snap. "I can't look at the cat. I've got work to do. Who do you think would get things done and meals ready on time if I stood around looking at the cat?" Shirley would feel enraged, with an overwhelming urge to smash her mother's glassware. But she stayed quiet and docile. For Adventists it was a sin to be angry.[18]

Shirley had few friends, but there was one boy she adored—Bobby Moulton. Skinny and snaggletoothed, Bobby was pitied by other children because his mother was ill and he had to push his baby sister's stroller through the neighborhood. But he and Shirley were kindred spirits in creativity. At age eight Bobby was tap dancing professionally. He loved dolls and doll clothes, and could sew costumes for Shirley's Peggys and Peggy Anns. He made little playhouses out of wood and cardboard, and recruited Shirley's dolls to stage Shakespearean dramas in the sunroom.

And there was a pretty little girl named Anita Weeks, who was almost three years younger than Shirley. She was the only other Adventist in public school besides Shirley, and the two girls saw each other in church.[19]

———————

The Second Coming seemed nigh to the congregation after the stock market crashed in October 1929. Walter lost his contracting business then and felt lucky to have an $18.50-a-week job as a hardware store clerk on Main Street. Not long after, the Dust Bowl blew out of the Dakotas, blackening the Minnesota sky even by day. Soon the countryside was withered with drought.

Desperate to make ends meet, Mattie took in a $12-a-week boarder, an elderly man from church who was so sick that he needed her help eating and using the toilet. He died in 1935. So did Walter's father, Neill, who had spent his final years rejoicing in international financial collapse and its prophetic relationship to the End Time. After his death Mattie accepted more boarders. The Masons, once one of Dodge Center's "best" families, were financially strapped and practically running a hotel.

Things had gotten so bad that Walter stopped tithing to his church—a major travesty for Adventists. And Shirley was still kept from Adventist schooling. After local Adventist children completed their grade-school studies in town, they graduated to a boarding academy over a hundred miles away and only came back to Dodge Center on weekends. Shirley's parents did not want her to join them. The plan was for her to receive twelve years of secular education in Dodge Center.[20] That decision was hard on Shirley, and as the years went by she developed severe problems at school and at home.

She moped about how Adventism was separating her from her classmates. Her faith absented her from the Sunday schools that everyone talked about, and it kept her from birthday parties on Friday nights or Saturdays. Even at festivities held on other days, she couldn't dance or play checkers or cards. Because Adventism banned pork, she had to skip after-school wienie roasts—important social occasions for the town's young people. The other kids knew about her strict diet and the fake, vegetarian "meat." "Cow food," they taunted, and called Shirley the "White Jew."

She was angry with her religion but fearful about her ire and worried that her hostility was Satan's work. She tried to broach her concerns to her father. But Walter, a man of few words and a workaholic, never wanted to talk about anything, much less religion.

Her mother made things worse. If Shirley came home from school looking sad, Mattie would quiz her insistently until Shirley confessed about an invitation she'd had to turn down because of Adventist Saturday. Mattie would blow up. "They could have had the party another day!" she would rage. "They knew you couldn't do this. So why did they even ask you?" Then her tone would grow softer, tender. "We'll do something nice," she would tell Shirley. "Just you and Mamma. Mamma loves you. You and Mamma don't care what the kids do. They don't count, anyhow." And she would take Shirley to Main Street to buy a new doll for her ever expanding collection. Shirley craved Mattie's affection. But accepting it meant separating herself even further from her classmates.

At some point, Shirley decided it was her own bad character, not her faith, that distanced her from her peers. "I don't care," she told herself. "I don't want to belong, anyway." She turned to Adventism for solace and strived to be "letter perfect." She spent additional time studying religious literature, looking for reasons to believe. She entered reveries, memorizing page upon page of Bible verses, trying to please God with sacred labors.[21]

But what she really loved was drawing, painting, and stitching clothes for her dolls. She had more than fifty of them by the time she finished grade school, perched on shelves in her bedroom and on the window ledges of the sunroom. As she played with them she made up stories, with herself as heroine. She would imagine that one of her relatives secretly entered her artwork into a contest at the Dodge County fair, and that she had swept the competition, winning first, second, and third place, as well as honorable mention! She dreamed of being asked to come to the fair and accept her ribbons, and declining because pride was sinful. Often she became so absorbed in these gorgeous imaginings that she forgot what was happening around her.[22]

Things had long been difficult for Shirley, but they started going very wrong in sixth grade. Perhaps influenced by increasing Adventist anxiety about the Depression and the approaching end of the world, she began feeling odd anxieties about time. Often when she sat down to play with her dolls or to draw, she got nervous, thinking she wouldn't be finished when Mother ordered her out for a walk. On Main Street she fretted over and over that the Masons' house, a block away, would burn down or blow away, destroying her playthings. She told Mattie about her fears. Mattie said they were silly because toys were just toys and could be replaced. Besides, when Shirley grew up, she would really have things to worry about.

Then her body stopped working. She got colds all the time and felt congested, listless, and weak. Worse, she began squinting uncontrollably. She started staying home from school, and her report cards were flecked with marks tallying her absences. Her parents bought her glasses, but the tic got so bad that Walter threatened to take Shirley out of school entirely. Desperate to stop the squinting, she discovered that it got better if she used her hands to trace in the air pictures she was seeing in her head.

And another, stranger problem developed—intense phobia about certain types of print. Whenever she picked up a newspaper, Shirley would become so frightened that she almost passed out. Worried about seeing her "scared stiff" and "acting funny," Mattie and Walter canceled their subscription to the *Minneapolis Journal*. For good measure, they also stopped the *Ladies' Home Journal* and Walter's subscription to *Fortune*. No matter. Shirley began picking up magazines in other people's trash and hiding them in the back of her closet. Alone in the house, she took magazines out, counted them and secretly read them, then hid them before Mattie returned.

She probably read as many magazines in secret as she ever had when they were allowed—including, possibly, the April 1935 issue of *Fortune*. It devoted twenty-four densely printed pages to an article titled "The Nervous Breakdown." The piece included an explanation of Sigmund Freud's theories of hysteria, along with a description of what happened to the typical person with the disorder: "He may seem to lose his sight or his hearing. He may make endless quick repetitive movements with one set of facial muscles. . . . His arm or leg may be functionally paralyzed or it may lose all sensation." [23]

After reading, Shirley always scrubbed her hands with hot water, then with the Lava soap Dad used to remove paint and grease from his skin. Then twice again with hot water. Then a final, cold rinse. Despite her furious scrubbing, she still worried that she was infected with venereal disease or cancer from handling the magazine pages. She would show the tiniest spot to Mattie and ask if it was serious. "Of course not," Mattie would answer brusquely, but Shirley started peering at her hands every few minutes. The looking made her more anxious. The anxiety led to more looking. "For Heaven's sake girl," her mother would snap, and threaten that if Shirley didn't stop this disturbing habit, "I'll do something so you won't have any hands to look at."

Shirley started sneaking looks, with a lightning quick, palms-up gesture she hoped no one would notice. Sometimes, when the urge overwhelmed her, she would leave the room her parents were in so she could "look and look and look." Mattie and Walter knew what she was doing. She started experiencing the trance-like feelings again, a sense of "going blank." She would come to with the sound of her parents' worried scolding.

She began to get creeping, tingling feelings in an arm and a leg. They radiated to one side of her face, affecting her vision. She would look at someone and not see them unless she swiveled her face around. And she would twitch and lurch crazily, heading for a door but ending up at a window. She was terrified by these "spells," as she called them. When she got one she would lie in bed and fall into a leaden, hours-long sleep.[24]

Mattie took Shirley to see Dodge Center's family physician, Dr. Otoniel Flores. A stocky man with a cigar constantly hanging from his mouth, he was a Central American immigrant who had a kindly manner and was beloved in the community. Dr. Flores determined that Shirley was anemic, and he gave her injections of extract of hogs' liver, a newly developed medication for treating the problem. By summer after the sixth grade, the tingling, blindness, lurching, and headaches were gone. But the hand-looking and finger tracing persisted.[25]

Shirley was so ashamed that she became reclusive. Mattie would drag her to classmates' birthday parties and she would enter a daze, failing to answer when talked to. Back home she sat alone on the porch steps, leaning her head on her knees, pretending she was Vicky, her imaginary friend from London with the big, Catholic family. Or she lay in bed inventing complicated, heroic scenarios with herself as a doctor who specialized in hearing problems, and as a teacher of children at a school for the deaf. She was the best teacher the school had ever had, and she performed brilliant feats of instruction, silently miming painting lessons to the children and mounting their art in prize-winning exhibits.

Shirley spun detail after detail, remaining awake all night, not sure what was true and what was invented. As morning dawned and she emerged from her reverie, she wondered why she felt so terribly blue, so unlike other kids. She prayed to God for relief, promising to be a good girl if He would only cure her.[26]

He didn't, and she became angry, not just at God but at her mother. She began bickering and fighting with Mattie, though she knew Adventist children were supposed to love their parents and never disobey them. As a result of this sinful behavior, it seemed that God exacted revenge. Her mother never found out about Shirley's fiction secret, but she discovered something far worse. When Shirley was in her senior year in high school, Mattie caught her in bed, under the sheets, with a hairbrush, masturbating. She marched her daughter to Dr. Flores's office for diagnosis and treatment.

Though no records of the visit survive, Dr. Flores probably did the same tests on Shirley's blood that he had in the past, to see if the cause of her strange behavior might be a recurrence of anemia. In all likelihood the studies came out negative. According to Flores's daughter, Virginia Cravens, who was interviewed almost sixty years later, Flores ultimately decided that Shirley's problem was loneliness. So he asked Virginia, who was sixteen years old at the time, to help out. She was already assisting her father on weekends, taking temperatures and giving injections, and now Flores assigned Virginia to make therapeutic house calls to the Mason home once a week. Her task was to play cards with Shirley, make chitchat, and try to be her confidant.

When Virginia visited the Masons, Mattie puttered around, desperately plying the two girls with fresh-baked cookies to create a semblance of sociability. Shirley would not touch the food; Virginia gobbled it. Shirley was remote and sluggish, perking up only when the conversation turned to her art work. She conversed a little then, but she never asked her visitor about her own life. She would not let Virginia touch her dolls.

After a few weeks Virginia decided she could not stand this sullen and self-absorbed girl. Still, she had a job to do. She knew perfectly well why she was feigning friendship with Shirley—her father had explained everything in medical terms, and she told herself she was performing valuable work with her house calls. She pasted a smile on her face, and when she visited Shirley she never ever mentioned the solitary, secret vice.[27]

CHAPTER 2

CONNIE

SHIRLEY MASON FIRST EXHIBITED HER puzzling physical and mental problems in 1935, the same year that a young medical student a few hundred miles away, in Michigan, also came down with mysterious ailments. Twenty-seven-year-old Cornelia Wilbur was diagnosed with a thyroid condition, most likely Graves' disease. It affects mainly women, and causes them to feel anxious, moody, and sad, with a heart that beats too fast and hands that shake. In the 1930s, Graves' disease sufferers frequently were diagnosed as mentally ill. Often they were packed off to psychiatrists.[1]

Cornelia Wilbur may well have had this experience, but we cannot know for sure; after her death in 1992, virtually all of her papers were disposed of by the executor of her estate. Still, we know at least one important thing about her early days. In an interview she gave in her old age, she was asked about influences during youth that made her—and this was her word—a "maverick" psychiatrist. "I was raised in a family of pure scientists," she said proudly, then heaped praise on her chemist-inventor father, Arthur Warner Burwell. But Cornelia Wilbur seldom talked about how her father had tried to keep her out of medical school. It was all right for girls to study a little, he thought, but not too much. Besides, he told his daughter, she was too stupid to be a doctor—and her mother did not argue. Cornelia never discussed the desperate measures she took to overcome her parents' lack of encouragement, even as she tried all her life to be an encourager herself and a famous and rich "pure scientist."[2]

Arthur Burwell never achieved the renown of Alexander Graham Bell or Thomas Edison. Even so, during the late nineteenth and early twentieth centuries he was one of America's most respected scientists. He made the electric battery that powered early streetcars. He figured out how to purify oil in Texas, launching the Gulf Oil Company and becoming well-to-do in the process. He came up with a way to use salt water and electricity to extract valuable metal, like zinc, from rock pulled out of mines in the West. The last invention made him think he would get even richer, and it earned him a spot in the *World Almanac* in 1909—a year after his daughter, Connie, was born.[3]

Ten years before that, Arthur had married Connie's mother, Bertie. She was an unusual person: college educated when very few women went to high school, and a secretary when women working in offices were considered practically as disreputable as prostitutes. The Burwells were from Cleveland, but they were living in Montana when Connie was born so that Arthur could do his mining work. As she spoke her first words, the little girl was surrounded by adults talking excitedly about chemicals, fortune, and fame.

Connie spent her early childhood on a parcel of land in northwestern Montana near the majestic Purcell Mountains, by the Kootenai River. It was one of the most gorgeous parts of the United States, and one of the most remote. Arthur moved his family there so he could go big game hunting, and for Connie and her brothers, Richard and Oliver, the new home was a nonstop playground. In warm weather they found wild baby rabbits and tried to tame them. They scrambled over cliffs. Nature was everywhere, and so was their father. He home schooled the children, and his method of teaching them "pure science" was unsentimental, even brutal.

Once Arthur went hunting with Connie and Oliver, who couldn't have been more than nine and ten years old, respectively. The trio spotted a deer behind a bush. "There's a buck," Arthur whispered. He fired and killed it. But he had erred—it was a doe, a pregnant one. Arthur decided to dump the carcass because he didn't want to eat meat contaminated with what he distastefully called "pregnancy hormones." But first, he thought, it would be good to instruct his children about "what reproduction is like" by performing an impromptu abortion. As Oliver and Connie watched, he sliced the doe open, revealing two fetal fawns covered with spotted fur and still moving. "Daddy, why can't we keep them?" the children begged. Because the babies, Arthur explained, would very soon be dead. He dumped them along with the doe.[4]

The Burwells' Montana adventure ended when Connie was nine years old, after other inventors fashioned cheaper methods than Arthur's to extract metals from rock, and Arthur's company went bankrupt. The Burwells went back to Cleveland, then drifted through various cities. By 1921 they were in Poughkeepsie, New York. In some respects their life there was ordinary. Connie and Oliver attended junior high school and spent their spare time at Girl Scout and Boy Scout meetings, earning merit badges. But the family didn't have a home of its own. Their permanent residence was a hotel.[5]

Connie was tall and gangly by then. Like her father she had a ruddy face that freckled and burned easily in the sun. She felt ugly. In her imagination she fashioned an alter ego, slender and sinuous, with raven hair and clear white skin. But, though she suffered from insecurities about her body, she did not lack confidence or ambition when it came to the idea of a profession. At age fourteen she told her mother she wanted to be a doctor. Bertie demurred. "Women are not doctors," she sternly advised her daughter. Women get married and have children, Arthur added. A husband might run off and leave a betrayed wife to earn her children's keep, Bertie corrected her husband. Girls needed college as a safety net. But they did not need to be doctors.[6]

To drive the message home, the Burwell parents did something drastic. Bertie had recently taken up with the First Church of Christ, Scientist— better known as Christian Science. Founded in the late nineteenth century, it was a religion whose members were overwhelmingly women, and despite its name, it was extremely hostile to science and scientists. Arthur remained staunchly irreligious. But he went along with his wife's plan to send their daughter someplace where, they hoped, the desire to be a doctor would be knocked out of her. Connie was packed off to Winnwood, a boarding school in the farmlands of rural Long Island.

Winnwood was a Christian Science school,[7] dedicated to the teachings of Mary Baker Eddy. She had grown up in the early nineteenth century in Maine, not far from the earliest home of Ellen G. White, the leader of

Seventh Day Adventism. Like Ellen, Mary was fervently devout as a girl; she was also frail and sick, with symptoms that nineteenth century doctors deemed typical of girls and women. At age eight she heard voices calling her name, and she turned to the Bible for guidance. As she grew to adulthood her health worsened: to her long list of childhood maladies were added gastric attacks, melancholia, and episodes of incoherent babbling and foaming at the mouth.

She was finally cured in the 1860s, by a professional hypnotist, or "mesmerist," as they were called back then. He treated Mary by discussing her problems with her, rubbing her head, and preaching the power of positive thinking. Mary felt grateful and inspired. Like Ellen G. White, she fell into trances, had visions, and developed a religion. Hers had a special appeal for women like Bertie Burwell because its tenets rescued them from all those nineteenth century medical men who dismissed the female body as a walking, talking disease.

Mary Baker Eddy called her treatment "mind cure." She believed bodies were illusions, nothing more or less than the thoughts of God. Illness came from lack of faith, and the only cure was Godly thought in the company of other Christian Scientists. People who thought they were coming down with something serious, like tuberculosis or smallpox, were told they could get well by simply "disagreeing" with the symptoms. As soon as they felt fever or pain they were to "shut out these unhealthy thoughts and fears," since "mind is not sick and matter cannot be." [8]

Connie was plied with Mary Baker Eddy's anti-doctor views at a school in the middle of nowhere, far from her family and friends. We do not know how this banishment affected her. Did it make her furious? Did she attempt to rebel? All we know is that she would later reject Baker Eddy's hostility toward materialism and sternly describe herself as a "pure scientist." Yet, not long after that, she would begin to embrace perhaps the biggest "mind cure" of all—American psychoanalysis.

When Connie graduated from Christian Science high school in 1926, her parents were living in Niagara Falls, New York. The banks of the Niagara River were jammed with factories all the way south to Buffalo in those days. They churned out tons of industrial chemicals, including lubricants for axles, gears, and metal grinding machines, which Arthur invented and manufactured in his own company. He oversaw the firm's research activities, and Bertie was his secretary.

They sent Connie to a nearby women's college, William Smith, where she studied mostly liberal arts subjects, including English. But after her sophomore year she decided to transfer. She told her parents she wanted to be a chemist, like Arthur. The chemistry courses at William Smith college were too easy, she said, so she applied to the University of Michigan. In 1928 she matriculated there as a junior.

Connie threw herself into things traditionally considered masculine and heroic. There was chemistry, as she had planned, but she also discovered flying. The university's Aeronautical Society was a pioneering new club with a women-only section, but Connie ignored it and joined about a dozen young men who flew a glider. Their sport was ridiculously daredevil. One club member would play the role of pilot, and others launched the fragile machine by tying rubber ropes to it, grabbing them, then sprinting down a hill and quickly releasing the ropes. Crashes were common, and one male pilot was killed. In literature about the club, the other members listed themselves as engineering students. One would have expected Connie to announce chemistry as her specialty. Instead she called herself an English major. She seemed conflicted about what she wanted to do with her life.[9]

When it came to sexist work environments, chemistry was one of the worst fields Connie could have chosen. Four percent of American chemists had been women at the end of World War I, but a decade later that ratio had plummeted. Employment ads asked for "Christian males only," and chemical plant managers blithely rationalized their refusal to hire the second sex. Women doing laboratory experiments were "inferior to men in interpretation of results," pontificated an editorial in the *New York Times*. Besides, women were too delicate to gather samples in the plant.

Connie graduated in 1930 with a bachelor of science degree. She went back to Niagara Falls and joined her parents at the hotel. She got work, but she didn't do experiments. Instead, she was hired as a librarian—a position that must have disappointed and humiliated her. Chemical librarian jobs in the 1930s were dead end, low paying, and reserved strictly for females.

But many young women accepted librarian work because their women professors told them such jobs might eventually lead to something better. In the meantime, they were told, women who accepted the work should act pleasant so as not to discredit themselves and their sisters in chemistry.[10]

Connie did try to be pleasant. She volunteered with the Northwestern New York section of the ACS—the American Chemical Society, the nation's most prestigious association for professionals in the field. ACS membership was so overwhelmingly male that some meetings in the 1930s were still called "smokers"—a word implying cigars, beer, half-naked girls, and pornographic movies. Few women chemists attended these meetings, but few women were ACS members anyhow. Even fewer took an active role in the organization.[11]

Connie attempted to be the exception. At her father's company, which was just down the block from where she worked, Arthur Burwell was running oxygen through petroleum and coming up with soap. This was something new, because soap traditionally had been made with animal fat, not industrial chemicals. Connie started spending free time at Arthur's lab, and soon she came up with an idea.

"Discover new soap to cure skin disease," the *Syracuse Herald* trumpeted in a headline in June 1932. The American Association for the Advancement of Science was meeting in upstate New York, and "woman chemist" Cornelia Burwell—as the *Herald* dubbed her—used the occasion to announce that her sticky substance was "one of the most important cures yet devised" for athlete's foot.

For decades people had treated their itchy feet by soaking them in herbal tinctures and mild chemicals that painlessly removed the topmost level of the dermis, taking the pesky fungus with it. But now, Connie declared, she could attack the very root of the problem—the fungus itself.

As a roomful of overwhelmingly male scientists gazed at her flaming red hair, Connie described her invention in ways that recalled a predatory animal or a femme fatale: "The penetration power of the soap is so great," the *Herald* reported, "that when an oily broth of it is deposited in a test tube, the small active molecules creep up the glass and render cotton plugs completely useless." The substance in the tube attracted fungi and bacteria "just as a spider fascinates a fly." After this seduction, it took only ten minutes for the miracle goo to wreak destruction on microbes.

Months later Connie did an encore presentation in Washington, D.C., before the big-city press and the American Chemical Society's most prominent members. Her name and news of her invention made it into *Time Magazine*. She was poised for fame and fortune: Her new substance was easy to make, and she was using chemicals to improve people's health. So much for Christian Science. And so much for Arthur and Bertie Burwell, who had not wanted their daughter to dream. Her parents be damned, she was dreaming anyway.[12]

Then everything fell apart. Connie's first patent application for the athlete's foot soap was filed by her father. It was lengthy, filled with instructions for running oxygen through petroleum, and with tables outlining the death rates of various strains of bacteria when exposed to the product in test tubes. But a year after this optimistic material was so confidently submitted, Connie filed a bleak, spare addendum—just a half page. It noted that, unless it was greatly diluted with an oil or salve such as Vaseline, the substance she had invented could not be applied "to mammals, including man, without irritation or detrimental effects."[13]

It appears Connie had jumped the gun on her soap's miracle properties. In the lab she'd proved it quickly killed fungus inside a test tube. But she hadn't tried it on people. It was a strong acid, and when applied to skin, it burned. Adding Vaseline may have made the soap too expensive to sell profitably, or rendered it no more effective than athlete's foot medicines already on the market. Either way Connie's invention turned out to be a dud.

She was twenty-five years old and she must have felt exhausted and humiliated. Of this period of her life, the only thing she ever said publicly was, "I became very bored with chemistry." "Bored" seemed to be a euphemism for darker emotions. "I felt that if I had to deal with any more test tubes," she elaborated, "I would deal with them by dropping them on the floor and breaking them."[14]

Well then, Arthur said. Now it was time to do what women do—get married, have children. Her mother, Bertie, did not disagree.

Connie wanted to go back to school and finally fulfill her dream of becoming a doctor. But tuition was expensive and Arthur refused to foot the bill. It was money down the drain, he said. Connie was not smart enough for medical school. Enraged, she defied him, returning to the University of Michigan in fall 1934. But to bankroll this endeavor, she got married.

At twenty-three, Henry Marsh Wilbur was two and a half years Connie's junior. He had just finished a degree in dentistry, and despite his youth he already had a steady income that would pay for Connie's studies. They were married in 1934. Much later in life, she reminisced to her brother and her nieces and nephews that she had married for money and never loved her husband.[15] She did not say whether Henry knew about her true motives and feelings. Did she try to muster feelings of romance for her new husband?

Shortly after the wedding, Connie developed Graves' disease, the thyroid condition with the mood swings, heart palpitations, hand shaking, and other disturbing symptoms. She had to drop out of medical school for almost a year before her doctors arrived at the correct diagnosis. Even then, they may have continued to blame her emotions for her illness. In the 1920s, psychiatrists had attributed high thyroid levels in women to "incestuous fixation upon the father." As late as 1934, the same year Connie got sick, Graves' disease was being blamed on "extreme dependence on the mother" and on fear of "assuming the maternal role."[16]

When she returned to school Connie chose psychiatry as her specialty, and she became fascinated by patients with hysteria: girls and young women who twitched, grimaced, lost their sight, fainted, forgot how to walk, and had pains for no reason that doctors could detect. Connie, too, had suffered from symptoms that her male doctors could neither see nor measure. Maybe that is why she was drawn to these patients, and why, by the time she finished medical school, she was concentrating on their treatment.

She did not know Shirley Mason yet. But in the late 1930s, she began rehearsing for what would happen when they met.

CHAPTER 3

FLORA

FLORA SCHREIBER NEVER STRUGGLED WITH God when she was a child, or with chemistry, school, or the devil. She was an atheist, with atheist parents who would have been loathe to keep her from following her passions. Her mother and father encouraged Flora to experience everything, then to pick up a pen and write about it. By the time she was a teenager she was bold at seeking out novelty and keen at putting her observations on paper. She was a budding author.

But she was also wounded, a young girl made ashamed and confused by parts of her family life which would haunt her into adulthood and influence what she wrote about in magazines and books.

Flora's parents, William and Esther Schreiber, were Jewish immigrants to America. William—or Willy, as everyone called him—was five years old in 1891, the year his parents arrived in New York City. They settled on the Lower East Side, a vast Jewish ghetto. Ignatz Schreiber, Flora's paternal grandfather, found work as an insurance salesman. He immediately applied to have his family naturalized.

Willy learned English effortlessly and excelled as a student. After finishing high school he won a scholarship to Columbia University, where he got a masters degree in classics in 1908. He loved intellectualism and high culture—German literature over Russian, Wagner more than Bach.

Flora's mother, Esther Aronson, arrived with her family in New York in 1889. Her father could read but not write; her mother was completely illiterate. But Esther finished high school, and by 1910 she was working as a clerk at the Astor Library. Founded decades earlier by multimillionaire John Jacob Astor, the namesake institution had just become part of the New York Public Library but still had its own elegant building, attended by doormen in uniform. It was a grand job for Esther, a dark-haired twenty-four-year-old with thick brows and deep-set eyes.

Willy worked in the Astor's cavernous back rooms, in the cataloguing section. Quiet and bespectacled, he took to the the intricate, meditative Dewey Decimal System. Later, in 1921, he would move to the city's recently built main library, a grand beaux-arts building on Fifth Avenue, graced by paired statues of lions. Appointed chief classifier and subject header there, he would take his place at one of the largest, most prestigious libraries in the world.

He and Esther wed in 1913 and moved into a small apartment in Brooklyn's Crown Heights section. The area was a haven for Jews escaping from the slums and overcrowding of Manhattan. Brooklyn had slums and poor people, but it also had residents who were upwardly mobile, and the Schreibers belonged to that group. They lived in a noisy tenement building, but their apartment was orderly and boasted glass bookcases containing Willy's collection of phonograph records—particularly the symphonies of Gustav Mahler.[1]

Flora was born at home in 1916. She was a strapping baby, weighing in at eight pounds. Esther quit her job, and her widowed father moved in, along with Esther's unmarried sister, who had little education and could not support herself. Willy and Esther put their money into taking care of these kin, and they decided they could not afford more babies. Flora grew up as an only child.

She was lavished with attention. Her father conversed with her constantly, even before she first talked at eight months. She spoke her first sentence while cheerfully throwing pillows from her go-cart. "Now stop it, Flora," Willy ordered. She kept throwing them. He warned her again. "But Daddy!" she explained, "I'm happy." Willy thought that was brilliant. He was equally impressed when two-year-old Flora said she wanted to write letters to various people. She didn't know the alphabet but she dictated her correspondence. Willy was awestruck by his toddler's literary abilities and predicted Flora would be a writer when she grew up.

Willy Schreiber wished that he, too, could be a writer. His job gave him access to virtually every fact in the world, but his writing was never done under his own name. Instead he contributed anonymously to other people's work. He did behind-the-scenes research for a son-in-law of John D. Rockefeller who authored books about farming and dairy cows. And he compiled the index for Emily Post's first edition of *Etiquette*, published in 1922. (Some of his entries: *Asparagus, how to eat; Bones, management of, at table; Ex-President of the United States, how to introduce; Vulgar woman, the*.)[2]

He fantasized about seeing his name in print and felt that the isolation of the library was stifling his dreams. To be a writer, Willy thought, one must be out in the world, not cloistered in a catalogue room. But he saw no escape: he had a young wife at home, needy in-laws, and a child. To give them good, secure lives he needed good, secure employment. As the years passed he got quieter and quieter, and by late middle age he seldom smiled. Instead he walked. After work beginning at 5:00 p.m., he made a habit of silently strolling New York's streets for miles and miles. It was his escape from the stasis of his life.

But his daughter didn't feel stuck. He and Esther had big dreams for her, and from early on they instilled in her an appreciation for high culture, intellectual and professional aspiration, and plenty of derring-do.[3] Willy put his 78 rpm records on the Victrola and played classical music for Flora. He told her about Mahler and Wagner and poetry and Shakespeare. Her piano lessons were arranged to make her not just cultured but courageous; there were countless piano teachers in Brooklyn, but the Schreibers got Flora an instructor in the Bronx. Once a week she rode the subway more than thirty stops north. She went by herself. She was nine years old.

The bravado Flora was developing in the outside world did not help her in her own home. Years later, she would confide to a good friend that as a child she was sexually molested by a family member. She did not give details, and she took to her grave the name of her victimizer. From various facts about her family, though, and from memories of an elderly relative, we can surmise what happened.

Dr. Stanley Aronson was eighty-eight years old and living in Providence, Rhode Island, when he was interviewed for this book about his first cousin Flora. Born six years after her, he grew up a few blocks away from the Schreibers and often visited them. His and Flora's Uncle David lived in the same tenement building as the Schreibers. David had a son named Irving who was twenty-two by the time Flora was eleven.

Irving was a ham radio hobbyist. He tinkered at home, building short-wave sets and using Morse code to communicate with other ham enthusiasts worldwide. Irving was fanatical about his pastime. He spent days and nights cooped up in the tenement, listening to signals and tapping out his own.

His parents encouraged his obsession, because when Irving wasn't absorbed with his radio he was acting out-and-out crazy. He was a schizophrenic, and eventually he would become too ill for his aging parents to deal with. But he was still at home when Flora was entering adolescence in the same apartment building. According to Stanley Aronson, various oddities about her behavior that he recalled from boyhood later led him to believe she was sexually abused around this time.

For one, she started dressing so modestly that she looked "as if she was going to a parochial school." She almost always wore middy blouses with long, sailor's flaps over the chest that completely hid the shape of her developing breasts. She seemed strangely silent and shy. When five-year-old Stanley would come over to visit she would chase him and beat him on the head. Stanley was frightened, and he learned to run when Flora came after him.

Her quiet, angry behavior lasted a year or two. Then, suddenly, she was a different person. She started using vulgar language, sexual words. And she began striking dramatic poses, with her back arched and arms akimbo as though she were on the stage of a Greek tragedy or a play by Shakespeare. She became extravagantly verbose. A nice night would start out as, "Oh! This is a lovely evening." It would turn into "A magnificent evening!" Then, "A celestial evening!" "A stirring evening!"[4]

By the time Flora was fourteen, she was writing as dramatically as she was speaking and moving. Her literary work began earning ribbons in citywide student essay contests; her name appeared on winners' lists in the *New York Times*. These accomplishments gained her acceptance into Brooklyn's world-famous Girls High School. It was a female meritocracy filled with the smart daughters of the city's salt-of-the-earth neighborhoods: Jewish girls, Italian girls, Irish girls, black girls.

The Depression was raging when Flora started Girls High in 1930. Like the rest of the country, New York was plagued by joblessness and bread lines, and Flora's Brooklyn neighborhood roiled with left-wing politics. By 1932, brigades of Communist organizers and housewives with children were surrounding the apartment buildings of unemployed people who could not pay their rent, defending them against eviction by city marshals. Voters were electing Socialists to the State Assembly. People stood on soapboxes, calling for the downfall of capitalism, or at least for the rise of the New Deal. Even the revolutionaries liked FDR.

Willy Schreiber was the neighborhood's political oddball. As a civil service employee with the library, he had a steady if modest income, and he was not a member of a union—no civil servants were. He worried that the New Deal would redistribute public funds, including his salary, to the unemployed. He despised Roosevelt, to the great annoyance and even anger of the rest of the family, including his wife. At birthday parties there were heated arguments between Willy and the other adults. Flora listened and felt divided. In her world, being as politically conservative as her beloved father was like being from Mars.

In school, Flora lacked friends despite trying hard to fit in with the rest of the girls. Her face was not pretty; her jaw was square and her nose too long. She compensated by carefully styling her hair, and shaping her face with powder and bright red lipstick. On a good day of primping she was handsome—a handsome young Jewish woman who looked like her peers. Still, she stuck out when she began broadening her vowels and dropping even more "r's" than everyone else did in her community. She affected a British accent, speaking the way she fantasized Shakespeare had spoken— mixed with 1930s Brooklynese. Her voice irritated some people at school. It intimidated others.

But she still had two friends: her parents. After she was accepted to Columbia University's Teachers College in 1934, her mother and father moved to upper Manhattan so Esther could visit Flora's dormitory room once a week, gather her dirty laundry, drag it to the Schreiber apartment, wash and dry it, then carry it back to the dorm.

Columbia in the 1930s was full of political ferment. In 1934, Flora's freshman year, Teachers College was launching an innovative program called New College. Its aim was to push young people into the world. Its curriculum dealt with topics related to poverty, economic inequality, and racism. New College was hardly conservative, and Flora found herself in a unique environment.

New College had a rural branch, in a part of the nation almost beyond the imagination of people in New York City. "The Community," it was called. It spanned 1,800 acres of Appalachia in North Carolina, and all New College students were required to spend time there. They studied social sciences and psychology, as well as home economics and agriculture. They also spent hours every day harvesting vegetables and tending barn-yard animals, and they tutored impoverished rural children. These activities put them in contact with some of the poorest people in 1930s America.

Flora wrote extensively to her parents during her time at The Community. Often she described life in Appalachia, as in a letter she sent about a church service she'd just attended in a mountain church. The congregants, she told Willy and Esther, "have drooping shoulders. Their features are set. They are stern. . . . The preacher worked himself into a frenzy. . . . 'God,' he cried, 'Help this people that is good. We are all good, God. We want to go to Heaven. Hear us—I've been larnin' all these good souls here that you'll make them welcome when they come. God, do you hear us?'" [5]

Flora was nineteen years old and already a natural nonfiction writer.

But she fantasized about an acting career, and in 1937, as part of the study-abroad program at Teachers College, she won a fellowship to study in London, at the Central School of Speech Training and Dramatic Art, one of the most famous schools in the world for would-be actors. It was run by Elsie Fogerty, a commanding eccentric. She was in her seventies when Flora arrived, and always wore a hat and a severe black dress on which, as one student recalled years later, "we could see the remnants of her breakfast." [6]

Besides acting, Fogerty taught speech, using turn-of-the-century methods that emphasized what was then called "the voice beautiful." That meant speaking imposingly and forcefully, using pronunciation that mimicked the elites in Oxford and London. Hollywood and Broadway stars talked this way in the 1930s. So did announcers on the radio and rich people such as President Franklin Roosevelt and his wife, Eleanor.

In a booming voice, Fogerty would order students to chant, "Around the rugged rock the ragged rascal ran." She exhorted them to "Roll those r's! Roll them 'til they roar like lions!"[7] Flora developed her own "voice beautiful." A pricey automobile turned into "ahhhn exxxpennnnsive nyoo cawwww." If something was difficult to put up with, it was "jusssst toooo hahhhd to beahhhh." This became her ordinary conversational style, even though she never did take up acting and instead decided to be a writer.

Cracking the literary world was slow going, however. At age twenty-three, Flora was still living with her parents and could not afford to move since she was giving her writing away practically for nothing. For obscure poetry magazines and fusty journals of belles lettres, she wrote about the poet Emily Dickinson's fear of going outdoors, and about what nineteenth-century philosopher Henri Bergson would have thought of twentieth-century comedian Charlie Chaplin. She was paid for this work in copies of the magazines. She reviewed Broadway productions for a magazine read by college drama teachers and their students.[8] The job got her free tickets to plays, but it did not pay the rent.

"Money is God and controls the puppets in the Greek tragedy," she wrote a friend in frustration. "But one does hope for some *deus ex machina*—out of the relentless machine, a saving god."[9]

Her god would turn out to be Madison Avenue.

PART II

DIAGNOSIS

CHAPTER 4

DR. WILBUR

WHEN SHE STARTED MEDICAL SCHOOL during the height of the Great Depression, Connie Wilbur still felt humiliated by her failed athlete's-foot soap, angry at being stifled as a chemist because of her gender, and weak from her long bout with thyroid disease. Barely a decade later, at the height of World War II, she was healthy, brash, and very busy. She had left chemistry for psychiatry, and she was a rising star. She had earned her medical degree by then and was working at a large hospital in Omaha that treated the mentally ill. There she specialized in helping patients who suffered from hysteria. She was considered so effective at this effort that her boss, a prominent neuropsychiatrist, once called in a camera team to produce a training film of young Dr. Wilbur in action.

Connie developed her ideas about how to treat hysteria during the 1930s, when she studied under a psychiatrist named Dr. Robert Dieterle, a professor at the University of Michigan medical school and a man of many talents. He had an operatic voice, fine taste in cars, and a penchant for hypnotizing people. Dieterle got his M.D. in 1923, and at first he practiced pathology; his specialty was cutting open the skulls of people who had gone mad before dying from syphilis.[1] He saw many syphilis sufferers in the hospitals—and other kinds of patients who exhibited extreme behaviors. Schizophrenics talked jumbles of nonsense, heard voices, and claimed to be Jesus Christ. Manics, who stayed awake for weeks on end

37

and dropped dead from exhaustion. Depressives, who sobbed and starved themselves.

In the early twentieth century, mentally ill people from rich families were kept in back rooms at home or sent to one of a handful of private, luxurious sanatoriums. The less affluent mentally ill—about a half million of them by the 1930s—were packed off to public mental hospitals, bedlams that housed thousands of patients apiece. Patients were often confined for years before becoming well enough to be discharged, and many never showed improvement. For psychiatrists, working in mental hospitals was a thankless job. They were poorly paid and looked down upon by other doctors. The patients they cared for, year in and year out, were a grey, disheartening lot.

One group, the hysterics, were different. For one thing, they didn't spend all day, every day, doing nothing but scream, sob, stare, or rub their feces on walls. Certainly hysterics had disturbing conditions: blindness, legs that wouldn't move, and numbness to pain, for instance. But they often exhibited what doctors called *la belle indifférence*, a blithe unawareness that anything was the matter. Their cheeriness made them more pleasant to be around. Even better, most were young women—in a time when almost all psychiatrists were men. These patients were considered interesting to spend time with and fascinating to treat.

They were also considered neurotic, as opposed to psychotic. The difference, according to Sigmund Freud, was related to how the mind balanced the ego and the id. The id was the seat of the unconscious, where infantile, antisocial impulses roiled, especially those related to sex. The ego and superego were partly conscious, one sensible and pragmatic, the other constantly warning about evil, sin, and God. The anarchic id pushed against these higher structures. They usually pushed back smoothly, creating a balanced individual.

But if the ego was weak and the id broke through—or if the superego was too harshly tormenting—then psychosis developed, or its milder variant, neurosis. Neurotics were like overworked sentries who spent night after night guarding a palace without enough sleep. They were exhausted, anxious, and sad. Still, they managed to make a living—or their husbands did. Most neurotics shambled through life without ending up in public mental hospitals.

But hysterics' behavior was at the extreme end of the neurotic spectrum, and they were often institutionalized. Freud's earliest fame had come from working with hysterics during the 1880s; all of them were women. He had first learned about hysterics a decade earlier, while studying with Jean-Martin Charcot, a French neurologist and the most celebrated medical man of the nineteenth century.

Charcot worked at La Salpetriere, an enormous hospital for indigent women in Paris. The ancient Egyptians and Greeks had developed their "wandering uterus" explanations for hysteria. Later the Vatican had taught that the disorder was caused by Devil possession. Charcot believed it was set off by brain lesions that some people were born with and which were activated when they suffered shocking experiences. No matter that he could not find the lesions when he performed autopsies on patients who died. Once a week he opened the Salpetriere to public shows of his doctoring. It was said that on the days of these exhibitions, traffic jammed the entire Left Bank as people—virtually all men—streamed to the hospital for a look.

Charcot led his hypnotized patients, most of them women, into a big amphitheater. Attempting to activate "psychophysiological pathways," he pressed his fingers into their pelvises and under their breasts, and he screwed a leather and metal contraption above their ovaries. The women thrust their bellies upward, grabbed their throats, and swooned. Some even did a back bend, which Charcot named the "arc-en-cercle," or circle arch. He photographed these artsy, libidinous movements, then bound the pictures into coffee-table-style books that he said illustrated the "laws" of hysteria. The books sold worldwide.[2]

After a while suspicions developed that hysteria at the Salpetriere was mere theater, unconsciously acted out by suggestible women, and unconsciously created by Charcot himself. People started wondering why there was so much more of the disease in Paris than anywhere else in the world.

Despite this bit of skepticism, the late nineteenth century remained a golden age for hysteria. Doctors throughout the West latched onto the disorder, labeling it, as always, a women's illness caused by the weak female system. It's probably no coincidence that a modest rash of "double consciousness" or "multiple personality" cases—perhaps a dozen of them—emerged in Europe and America at this time, often among women already diagnosed as hysterics.

Many in the medical profession believed these women were defective, just as hysterics were weak. But a neurologist named Pierre Janet disagreed. Working in France alongside Charcot, he came to believe that some children had a hard time dealing with traumatic events in their lives. Seeing something frightening, being sexually abused—such experiences could cause a little girl's or boy's mind to dissociate impressions of the terrible event. The dissociated memory would lie outside of consciousness but push against it, causing hysteria. In particularly stressful situations, the dissociated recollection might even erupt as a fully formed alternate self— a second personality.

The cure was to hypnotize patients and push them to remember the trauma which caused the splitting. People thus hypnotized often moaned, screamed, and shook as though they were reliving something horrible. This response was called "abreaction" and "catharsis." Janet thought it was the only thing that could heal hysterics.

Freud was impressed with Janet's theory of childhood trauma as the cause of hysteria. It made much more sense to him than Charcot's idea of inherited brain lesions, and Freud suspected that the problem was usually sexual abuse. He began hypnotizing his hysteria patients and asking them over and over to verify his suspicions. Many denied being molested, but Freud refused to take no for an answer. Eventually, virtually all his patients "abreacted" memories of childhood sexual assaults by older relatives and nannies.

But some patients described impossibly bizarre scenarios during their relivings, including mass, Satanic rapes straight out of the medieval witch hunts. Freud was stunned by these phantasmagoric stories and did not believe they were true. Eventually he concluded that his patients were fantasizing. He stopped using hypnosis because he worried it was too easy for doctors to inadvertently encourage people to "remember" events that had not in fact happened.

Freud's theory about the cause of hysteria began to evolve. No longer did he believe it was provoked solely by sexual abuse. Instead, he now said, the normal child had sexual impulses beginning in infancy, including Oedipus and Electra complexes—desires to possess their fathers and mothers. Children before adolescence successfully suppressed these fantasies, but during the sexual storms of puberty they could reactivate, creating conflicts and guilt feelings that were powerful but remained unconscious. Neurosis could result, including hysteria. The trick during therapy was to dredge up repressed sexual memories and fantasies, using a technique Freud called "free association," with the patient saying whatever came to mind. Often their utterances were not overtly sexual. But when Freud interpreted them, he always found sexual meanings.

Thus was born psychoanalysis, a theory about repressed childhood wanting, not forgotten childhood trauma. In this new context, patients with multiple personalities were nothing special, and neither were hysterics. They were simply people—mostly women—who badly needed to uncover their repressed childhood desires. Bring on the couch, and the talk.

With the rise of psychoanalysis, multiple personality theory died out as a mainstream psychiatric diagnosis. So did Charcot's hysterical seizures and postures. For middle-class, urban women, fits, paralyses, deafness, and blindness became bemusing things of the past. It was as though hysteria were a fashion of clothing: first worn in Paris, then exported to citified Americans who eventually tired of it, and finally remaindered as a behavioral style for women in small towns and the countryside.

In the summer of 1933, Dr. Robert Dieterle—the Michigan psychoanalyst with the beautiful voice and the penchant for hypnotism—was working at the State Psychopathic Institute, a charity hospital in Ann Arbor. One day a dark-haired, fair-skinned sixteen-year-old girl was admitted. Her left arm was paralyzed for no physical reason, she couldn't walk, and sometimes she went blind and lost her sense of taste and smell. She could be hypnotized very easily, and while in a trance she walked with no problem. But once on her feet she went deaf.

When Dieterle talked about his new hysteric to people outside the hospital, he called her by her initials, L.M., to conceal her identity. Just as Charcot had done fifty years earlier with his women patients in France, Dieterle started using L.M. as a teaching subject at the University of Michigan. He would hypnotize her and place her on display in front of the (mostly male) medical students. He was preparing L.M. for a demonstration one day in late October when she offhandedly remarked that she was only two years old. Dieterle was intrigued.

Several weeks after L.M.'s hypnotic declaration of toddlerhood, another teenaged hysteric, L.R., was admitted onto the ward. She was nineteen years old. L.R.'s main problem, Dieterle decided, was "convulsive attacks in which her body arched."[3] He looked at Charcot's old book of photographs from Paris, the one that showed the "circle arch," and it looked a lot like L.R.'s posture. She also licked her lips, something else Dieterle had noticed in Charcot's work (he called it "tongue eroticism"). Dieterle thought tongue eroticism looked babyish.

Once he noticed that L.R. was hypnotizing herself by staring at a light. He got the idea to put a baby bottle filled with milk into her mouth while she was in her trance. He did this several times, and on each repetition L.R. acted younger. It was as though she was changing from an adolescent into a newborn.

One day, while he was showing his students how L.R. liked to drink from baby bottles, Dieterle brought L.M. to the room and put her in bed with L.R. Until then, L.R. had been the only patient to get a bottle. But this time, Dieterle gave it to newcomer L.M. instead. Old-timer L.R. then went into convulsions until she got a bottle for herself. But when L.M. started whimpering that Dr. Dieterle—she called him "Dada"—"had a new girl," L.R. responded by making strange, primitive sounds that the hospital staff swore were the cries of a newborn. Throughout the afternoon they plied L.R. with additional baby bottles. L.M. responded by sucking her thumb. L.R. sucked *her* thumb. L.M. wailed. Not to be outdone, L.R. peed in her pants, drenching herself from head to foot.

The doctors and nurses were in a tizzy at seeing adolescents acting like infants. Nurses clapped their hands to the chant of "patty cake." Young male psychiatrists blew into the faces of attractive young female patients and yelled, "booh!" Someone came and took photographs, including at least one of L.R. in the throes of a trance. In the photograph, L.R. is wearing nothing but panties, her breasts completely exposed.

Dieterle also made a movie of L.M. and L.R. together. It features the young women on their backs with their bottles, kicking, stretching, and cooing when Dieterle's colleague, a thirty-something, mustachioed psychiatrist named Edward Koch, walks by. Koch rocks the young women's shared hospital bed up and down like a horsy ride. He jingles his keychain. And he sneakily tweaks L.R.'s right breast.

The four-minute film was shown in 1935 in Washington, D.C., at the annual convention of the American Psychiatric Association. Hundreds of psychiatrists attended, nine out of ten of them men. No doubt they were a rapt audience. In an article the two doctors published in 1937 to accompany the film, they assured readers they had done nothing to cue abnormal behavior in their patients. They were merely trying to determine some "laws" of hysteria, the doctors said.[4]

While the doctors seemed to be enjoying themselves, it is far less clear that they were helping these very troubled young women. Not long after she awoke from her "babyhood" trance, which had lasted almost three weeks, L.M. tried to commit suicide. Her life after that is a mystery, and so is L.R.'s. Dieterle and Koch declined to say publicly what happened to the young women after they left the Psychopathic Institute.

It was Dieterle who ignited Connie Wilbur's passion for treating hysterics. In 1937, the same time he was publishing his paper and touting his film about women regressing to infancy, he was teaching at the University of Michigan medical school. Connie was a junior then, with middling grades: mostly B's and C's. Early in her studies, however, she made an A in psychiatry,[5] and Dieterle may have noticed. He recommended her for a summer job at a state mental hospital.

Of more than one hundred students in Connie's class, only eight were women,[6] but Michigan was gender-equality heaven compared to even worse ratios at other schools. Still, it had long been recognized—for reasons of modesty and perhaps to avoid accusations about male physicians tweaking their patients' breasts—that female doctors were needed to treat female patients. That is the reasoning that sent Connie, in summer 1937, to Kalamazoo, a small city one hundred miles east of Ann Arbor.

Kalamazoo State Hospital was top-notch compared to most public facilities for the mentally ill—at least in the "hopeful wards." Separated from the back wards, they were dedicated to patients who weren't very ill and who were expected to stay only a short time before being discharged. They were concentrated in an area of the grounds called Fair Oaks. It looked like a country club.

Fair Oaks was a collection of elegant Victorian cottages. As their nineteenth-century architects put it, they were meant to be so beautiful that people "sitting upon the capacious porches" would look just like "summer resorters, rather than patients suffering from mental disease."[7] Fair Oaks' gauzy idyll was reserved for Kalamazoo's "hopefuls." Young women diagnosed as hysterics usually qualified, and during the summer of Connie's externship, one of the most appealing of this group was a seventeen-year-old who refused to come out of her room.

The girl's mother had unexpectedly died not long before, and she had suddenly developed agoraphobia—the fear of going outdoors. She could not even get near windows: She was terrified of the vastness of the sky and afraid she would die.

Connie was twenty-eight that summer, barely a decade older than the troubled girl, and Kalamazoo's director asked her to help treat the patient. Connie entered the girl's room and coaxed her to venture out. "I'm with you," she soothed, and as she spoke her normally hard-edged, clipped voice slowed and softened. She clasped the girl's hand in hers, and the two exited the cottage and inched through ranks of tall trees, in a slow-motion walk that turned transcendent for Connie. Never before had she felt so free of physical boundaries. Guiding the girl, she would later remember, was like "dissolving the walls the souls [were] looking at."[8]

The medical director later told Connie that the patient's problem was a severe Oedipus complex, involving unresolved childhood sexual desires for her father which had flared up after her mother died. Hence her hysteria, expressed as fear of going outside. Connie was impressed by this explanation and even more struck by the girl's rapid recovery after they started taking walks. She was completely well by late August and never suffered a relapse. Her case convinced Connie of two things. First, it was easy to cure hysteria. And second, Connie herself was—as she would boast to interviewers years later—"a genius," at treating hysteria, "a magician."[9] What she had accomplished at the hospital was not just science but poetry—another subject in school she had always loved. She committed herself to becoming a psychiatrist.

She started an internship in neuropsychiatry in 1939, and very quickly found herself involved in a controversial procedure: shock treatment.

For most people today, that phrase conjures images of patients with electrodes wired to their skulls. In fact, electricity was not the first modern method for shocking the brains of the mentally ill. In 1933, at a Viennese clinic for drug addicts, a doctor, Manfred Sakel, was treating a diabetic morphine addict and accidentally gave her an overdose of insulin that put her into a coma. To Sakel's surprise, the woman had no more craving for morphine when she regained consciousness.

Later, Sakel accidentally overdosed a second diabetic who happened to be psychotic. He, too, seemed better, and Sakel started deliberately putting schizophrenics into insulin comas. He claimed stupendous results, though by today's research standards, his claims of improvement are completely unscientific. For one thing, a certain, large percentage of schizophrenics always got better no matter what treatment they got (or even if they got no treatment at all). For another, judgments about which patients were "cured" and "improved" were very subjective in Sakel's time, made by the very people who were promoting the treatment. It would be years before psychiatrists began using control subjects, double-blind procedures, and other scientific techniques now mandatory for medical research.

But by the end of the 1930s, mental institutions worldwide were using "insulin-coma therapy" on patients. It may not have helped them, but it definitely was a boon for the psychiatrists, for many wanted to use chemicals in their work. They were university trained and tired of merely warehousing their patients. They wanted to cure them with medicines and operations, just as other physicians cured their patients.

Three years after Sakel introduced this risky therapy, Hungarian psychiatrist Ladislas von Meduna came up with another shock treatment, using Metrazol, a poison related to camphor. Meduna's shots of Metrazol produced immediate, strong convulsions. And though his "science" was as primitive as Sakel's with insulin, Meduna claimed that Metrazol shock cured many psychotics. The practice spread like wildfire through the asylums. Doctors preferred it because it didn't kill people as frequently as insulin did. But Metrazol convulsions caused the body to arch and twist with great force. Patients often woke up with fractured spines and broken limbs. If these injuries weren't bad enough, in the few seconds between the injection and the convulsion, many patients experienced a horrible sense of dread, or, as one doctor put it, "agonizing fears of dying and crumbling away." The feeling was so devastating that it was hard to do second treatments. Patients fought their doctors and ran away from the nurses. The wards shook with their screams.[10]

By 1938 at the University of Michigan's Psychopathic Hospital, where Connie was studying at the time, patients as young as fourteen years old were being put into Metrazol convulsions.[11] Two years later, the university introduced into its mental wards yet another assault on the brain: electroconvulsive treatment (ECT), popularly known as electroshock. Invented in fascist Italy in 1938, ECT was not as frightening to patients as Metrazol. But many doctors worried about how it caused short-term side effects including massive memory loss and inability to learn new things. Medical consensus was that if ECT knocked out psychosis, it did so by damaging the brain. Many psychiatrists found that revolting.[12]

Dr. Dieterle agreed. He stopped teaching to register his disapproval of convulsive therapies, and thereafter he raised a family on a farm near Ann Arbor and set up a private psychiatry practice on the property. Patients, mostly women, came from all over Michigan for treatment. He diagnosed many as hysterics and developed idiosyncratic theories (he believed, for instance, that blondes had a higher propensity for developing hysteria than brunettes did).

It was at this time that Dieterle diagnosed one of his patients as suffering from multiple personality disorder. The young woman drove hours each week to see him, and even when she got better she stayed in touch for years, keeping him apprised of her ability, thanks to him, to marry and raise a family. Dieterle never published any articles or books about this patient, but he often mentioned her case to Connie.[13] Connie became intrigued by multiple personality disorder and started reading up on it. Although interest in the subject had waned, especially among psychiatrists, she was fascinated with her mentor's work. But she was too ambitious to get stuck in psychiatric backwaters. She strove to forge ahead. By 1941 she was in Pontiac, Michigan—a General Motors factory town with a giant, crisis-ridden asylum, and plenty of work for the bold.

Upon her arrival some two thousand patients were jammed into Pontiac, virtually all very sick and very poor. In the early 1940s the press began publishing revelations about patients being beaten to death by staff. A state legislator sent in a young investigator disguised as an attendant. She worked for a month and constantly witnessed hospital workers assaulting and abusing patients. Even if they didn't get hit, they slept with no bedding, on cold, tile floors covered with urine and feces. No one got enough to eat. The only therapy available was heavy drugging with sedatives, and patients were never examined by doctors, though a few psychiatrists did "walk through the halls, at times noting to this one and that one as they go along." The investigator was unnerved.[14]

It certainly was not clear what a person who was mentally ill might get from such a place except for warehousing and mind-numbing drugs. But there were definite benefits for an ambitious psychiatrist like Dr. Cornelia Wilbur. Through no fault of their own, she and the other doctors found it impossible to give quality care to patients. There were just too many of them and far too few staff. But their sheer numbers created a vast human Petri dish for experimentation. For anyone wanting to research heroic, cutting-edge interventions into psychosis, a colossal asylum like Pontiac was the place to be. Soon Dr. Wilbur was injecting and shocking patients in ways that had never been done before, then writing up her "scientific" experiments for publication.

Pontiac only had Metrazol convulsive therapy while Dr. Wilbur was there, but she made do.[15] Ever since Metrazol and the other shock treatments had been launched in the 1930s, doctors had argued about which diseases responded best to these radical new treatments: Schizophrenics? Manic depressives? Psychoneurotics?

Dr. Wilbur decided to find out once and for all, using a group of chemicals called barbiturates. These are powerful drugs that cause long-lasting unconsciousness in large doses, and in smaller ones a trance state popularly known as "twilight sleep." In the 1920s and 1930s, police departments were trying all kinds of coercive (and today illegal) techniques to get suspected criminals to confess their alleged wrongdoings. The "third degree" included sleep deprivation, beatings with rubber hoses—and injections with barbiturates. Detectives had noticed that people shot up with these drugs became woozy and talkative, chattering away and not remembering what they said after the drug wore off. Barbiturates, the police thought, lowered inhibitions so that telling lies would be impossible. Hence Pentothal's nickname "truth serum." For years, it was used it during interrogations.

Psychiatrists had for decades also used barbiturates, to relax agitated psychotics and put them to sleep for days in hopes that when they awoke they would feel better. Then, in the late 1930s, a British doctor, J. Stephen Horsley, began wondering if the drugs could help patients do more than just sleep. Researchers had noticed that injections of small amounts of barbiturates made mental patients and even normal people seem like criminals under "truth serum": they began prattling, confiding embarrassingly personal details about themselves to people they hardly knew. Horsley did an experiment, gathering twenty nurses who agreed to be injected with barbiturates. They laughed and swore they would never tell him any secrets, but once injected, most started spewing revelations. One "chatted gaily" and described so many "indiscretions," as Horsley later wrote with obvious embarrassment, that he quickly ordered her to wake up.[16] She did and recalled nothing, but other nurses remembered talking. They said they'd felt powerless to keep quiet.

Without drugs it usually took months to coax this kind of honesty from patients, and Horsley believed barbiturates could dramatically speed up psychotherapy. He started putting his emotionally disturbed patients into "twilight sleep" and listening to them talk about their lives. Then he woke them and discussed what they had said. He wrote about his treatment in medical journals.[17]

Inspired by Horsley, Dr. Wilbur picked out forty patients at Pontiac and injected them with barbiturates like thiopental (the generic name for Pentothal). Most were psychotic, including an eighteen-year-old schizophrenic whose usual speech was so garbled that Dr. Wilbur called it "word salad." After barbiturates were pumped into the patient's vein he got so groggy he could hardly talk. But the little he said made sense, at least to Dr. Wilbur. Another of her patients, a seventeen-year-old girl, was expressionless and mute. With Pentothal she spoke lucidly about her problems. It didn't work on everyone, though: One sixteen-year-old girl never communicated anything clearly, no matter how much Pentothal she got. Dr. Wilbur predicted that Metrozol shock therapy would do this patient no good. But she believed it would help those who spoke rationally during their chemical trances.

After making her predictions for each patient, Dr. Wilbur led them to the shock room. She injected each with Metrazol, and their bodies crashed and writhed. After they came to, she decided she had been right: the people she thought would get better did get better, and the ones she had little hope for stayed just as sick. She wrote up her findings without specifying how many of her guinea pigs had fractured bones during their Metrazol convulsions. Dr. Wilbur sent her work to the prestigious journal *Diseases of the Nervous System.* She signed it "C.B. Wilbur," making it impossible to tell she was a woman. Her article was accepted for publication.[18]

In late 1942, Dr. Wilbur got a job at a leading research institute in Omaha. She moved there just before Christmas and hit the ground running—not just by injecting people or shocking them. Now she was also drilling holes in their skulls and turning their brains into pulp.

The pioneer of American lobotomies was neurologist Walter Freeman, whose first patient, in 1936, was a woman suffering from depression, sleeplessness, and obsessive thoughts. Freeman drilled holes into her skull and extracted cores of brain tissue. He thought that she emerged much calmer, and during the next few years he operated on hundreds more patients. Freeman boasted of good results but talked very little about complications. Patients often permanently lost the ability to control their bladders and bowels, and many gained up to one hundred pounds. Worst of all, as one psychiatrist observed, they became "dull, apathetic, listless, without drive or initiative, flat, lethargic, placid and unconcerned, childlike, docile, needing pushing, passive, lacking in spontaneity, without aim or purpose."[19]

In Omaha, Dr. Wilbur's new boss was Dr. Abram Bennett, head of the neuropsychiatry department at Clarkson Memorial Hospital. Bennett had recently become famous for figuring out how to keep mental patients from breaking bones during Metrazol therapy.[20] He had been approached by lobotomist Walter Freeman, who happened to know an American adventurer who had befriended indigenous tribes in the Amazon jungle.[21] The Indians hunted with darts dipped in a paste made of curare, a plant which paralyzes animals when it enters their blood. The recipe for the paste was a secret until the adventurer convinced some Indians he was a witch doctor. In 1938 he brought several pounds of the product to the United States.

He gave the curare to Bennett, who injected his Omaha patients with it before he gave them Metrazol. They went into convulsions, but the curare paralyzed their muscles, preventing the arching and snapping that broke spines, limbs, and jaws.[22]

Soon Clarkson hospital was renowned for its dramatic interventions into the brains of the mentally ill. Bennett usually worked with Paul Cash, a young colleague from Iowa. But Cash went into the military during World War II, leaving Bennett shorthanded. He hired Connie to take up the slack. A sort of Rosie the Riveter for mental illness, she helped him do some of the first few hundred lobotomies performed in America. As a result, for the first time since her miracle soap days, Connie was back in the national press as a science pioneer.[23] And she gained fame for other work which was as groundbreaking as lobotomies—and almost as dicey.

To treat hysterics, she began using new a technique that at first looked miraculous. It involved injecting patients with a fat hypodermic syringe loaded with barbiturates such as sodium Pentothal. Connie had gotten this idea not just from her earlier work at the troubled mental hospital in Michigan, but also from brand new developments in military medicine. By 1944, with World War II in full swing, "twilight-sleep"-inducing barbiturates were central to the treatment of hundreds of thousands of soldiers who were leaving the battlefronts mentally ill. Many had symptoms—uncontrollable shaking, paralysis, crying, and an inability to speak or walk—that in previous decades were noticed mainly in "hysterical" women. Now, large numbers of men had these debilitating problems, and they seemed to be caused by traumatic experiences on the battlefield. Earlier experiments on civilians had shown that an injection of barbiturates could get almost anyone tranced out and talking about painful memories. Now, military psychiatrists embraced the technique and called it "narcosynthesis."[24]

But what if soldiers' traumatic memories weren't literally true? What if they were fantasies—or lies? Quietly, many military psychiatrists recognized that some soldiers were imagining events, just as Freud's "abreacting" woman patients had once imagined Satanic sex rituals that couldn't possibly have occurred.

Sometimes it was clear that the memory was false. But it might also sound perfectly believable, though it was later disproved by checking the soldier's combat record. It was obvious, the doctors warned, that narcosynthesis did not always produce a true account of events. Further, patients should receive Pentothal injections only once or twice. If they got more than that, they risked becoming addicted to barbiturates.

These sobering revelations were not discussed publicly until years after World War II. In the meantime, most psychiatrists compared the mind to a movie camera. Memory was like a strip of film, they said. After it recorded an event, the film could be rewound with a dose of chemicals. Memories would return with cinematic precision, even if what was being recalled had happened many years earlier.[25]

In Omaha, Dr. Cornelia B. Wilbur knew very little about the potential problems of narcosynthesis. She was interested in using barbiturates and abreactions to help civilian hysterics. She began injecting her patients with Pentothal, and she did her work with such aplomb that in 1944, her boss, Dr. Bennett, had her filmed so that other psychiatrists could learn her techniques. The black-and-white movie can still be viewed in the archives of the federal government's National Library of Medicine, in Bethesda, Maryland.[26]

In the film, the young Dr. Wilbur plays to the camera as though she's in a blockbuster out of Hollywood instead of a grainy instructional film from Nebraska. Her hair is swept loosely back, then rolled and pinned in a coil. She wears a dark suit with a form-fitting jacket, and a ruffled jabot. She exudes an elegant mannishness, à la Katharine Hepburn. You half expect to peer over her shoulder and spot a winking Spencer Tracy.

Instead, Dr. Wilbur's co-stars are harried, real-life psychiatric nurses and their charges: people who are glassy-eyed and stony, or crawling and quaking with madness. A thin, balding man with big lips jerks uncontrollably. A young woman lies in bed with eyes closed and her hair cut off, as though she hacked it in a fit before lapsing into waxy immobility. Another woman moves but can't stand, and her hospital gown hangs half on her and half off, in lunatic immodesty. A fourth patient, an eleven-year-old girl, wears a cute pinafore dress. A normal child in these clothes would be ready to skip off to school. But this one is far from normal. As the camera follows, she jackknifes her body, straightens up, and hobbles next to a wall. She suffers from astasia abasia, a subtitle printed across the screen explains: She cannot walk, though there is nothing wrong with her legs. She is a child hysteric.

Dr. Wilbur handles these patients with supreme calmness and ease.

"You don't have to shake," she tells the trembling man. She pats the catatonic woman's head. She starts to pick up the little girl, but the patient resists, twisting her hands into claw shapes, contorting her face, crashing to the floor.

Dr. Wilbur is unfazed. She smiles for the camera as she overpowers the struggling child, preparing to push a thick needle into her forearm, full of Pentothal. In the next scene the girl swoons, her head and body lolling like a rag doll's. Smiling, Dr. Wilbur shakes her, tickles her stomach, and tries to keep her from falling. The girl's lips move. She is abreacting. Her dissociated secrets are beginning to emerge.

Across the silent screen a subtitle flashes: "My father says my mother hates me." A second subtitle announces more abreaction: the girl remembers how her father "beat her and said she was going to die."

Then, a happy resolution: The final scenes show the child cheerfully playing hopscotch as Dr. Wilbur looks on. Her patient has been cured. End of movie, though several questions remain unasked and unanswered. What happened to the child after she finished therapy? Was she returned to a mother who hated her, and to an abusive father? Did the mental hospital report her barbiturate-induced statements to child welfare authorities? If so, what did investigators find? Were the little girl's stories of mistreatment true?

The movie was sent to medical schools. Its star, Dr. Cornelia B. Wilbur, was a scientist, making miracles through chemistry. And because of her connection with Dr. Bennett at the hospital, she got to teach at the medical school of the University of Nebraska. She had staff privileges at the university hospital and at the county charity hospital.[27] She even had her own small, private practice on the sixth floor of the Medical Arts Building, an art-deco structure downtown that was Omaha's tallest piece of architecture. She was a doctor and she was going places. Finally, being a woman didn't matter.

Until it mattered again. After World War II ended, the soldiers came home and displaced the working women. Dr. Bennett wanted Dr. Paul Cash back, and that meant Dr. Wilbur would have to go. Without her tie to Bennett, she would lose everything: the hospital affiliations, the secretarial help, the office downtown, the private practice—even her prestigious position as president of the Omaha branch of the American Women's

Medical Association. Once again she was furious, this time at Bennett's lack of appreciation for all the innovative research she'd done for him. Once again, she had no idea what to do with her life.

Her husband offered a suggestion. Henry Wilbur had spent the war teaching dentistry at the University of Nebraska's medical school. Now, he had a job offer from the University of Louisville, in Kentucky. Connie could go with him and be a dentist's wife. They could start a family—after all, she was already thirty-seven years old. Time was running out to begin.

Yet Connie knew that being a mother would be impossible. It's uncertain when she found this out, since she only told people many years later. But at some point when she was of childbearing age, she learned she was infertile. There would be no babies; the only thing she would have in Louisville would be the life of a childless woman in a small city south of the Mason-Dixon line—a woman with too much time on her hands and a spouse whose life's work was drilling molars. She did not know what to do. Between the job she was losing and the empty future she faced with her husband, she felt sad, anxious, and enraged. During the summer of 1945, still at the hospital in Omaha, her stormy moods had even the secretaries noticing and gossiping.

While Connie mulled things over, she continued treating hysterics and was immensely proud of her cures of young women. Two patients had come to her because they'd lost the ability to talk. With Dr. Wilbur's help, one realized she was conflicted about a love affair she'd had with her uncle. The other, a new mother, unearthed and acknowledged negative feelings toward her baby. Both quickly recovered their voices while working with Dr. Wilbur. A third patient, a soldier's wife, came to the office unable to walk. After a few sessions on the couch and some injections of Pentothal, she was dancing.[28]

In late July, Dr. Wilbur's secretary took a call from yet another hysteric requesting treatment, a young woman currently living in Omaha but originally from rural Minnesota. An appointment was made, and on the first day of August the patient walked in to Dr. Wilbur's office.

Her name was Shirley Mason.

CHAPTER 5

MISS MASON

S HIRLEY WAS NEATLY DRESSED, POLITE, and well-spoken at her first therapy session in Connie's office. She was also a basket case. Eight years had gone by since she'd closed herself in her room with a hairbrush. Since then, she had received many assessments of her behavior. Mattie called her a girl with "the blues." Her father, Walter, said she was "funny" and "nervous." The town doctor sometimes thought she was anemic, and other times merely lonely. No one knew what to make of her numbness, twitching, and compulsive hand inspections, not to mention the masturbatory acts she'd performed in front of her four dozen baby dolls.

For a while she'd shown some improvement. As Shirley advanced through her final months of high school, Walter picked up construction work and recovered somewhat from the Great Crash. One of his new jobs was building Dodge Center's first movie theater, in 1940, and he'd paid Shirley to act as his assistant. She'd ordered all the building materials, "down to the seats," as she recalled years later.[1] She kept track of expenditures with the bookkeeping skills she'd learned in school. She collected the workers' time cards, added up their hours, and climbed the scaffolding every Friday to give out their paychecks.

Shirley had also begun private painting and drawing classes; her parents had accepted that the only thing that made her happy was art, whether the abstractions in her style were acceptable to Adventists or not. Her instructor was Wylene Frederickson, a young woman who had just arrived in town to teach at the public school. Frederickson gave private lessons, and she came to the Masons' with paints, chalks, and pencils. She soon announced that her new student had talent, and Shirley basked in the praise. She thought she might like to be an artist.[2]

She still felt angry with her mother, and shut off from her classmates. She continued to spin scenes in her head, knitting real events with fantasy. In the summer before senior year started, John Greenwald, a junior-high-school-aged boy, was accidentally shot to death while playing in a barn with a loaded .22 rifle. The barn was not in Dodge Center; it was a few miles away, in another small town, and the witnesses were some other boys who were playing with him when the accident occurred.[3] Nonetheless, Shirley imagined watching the shooting, cringing at the sight of John's blood, and trying desperately to save his life.

She wanted to get away from home and pursue higher education. Though her religion had for years pushed marriage, motherhood, and homemaking on women, academic ambitions became more common among Seventh-Day Adventist girls during World War II. The church acknowledged the country's labor shortage as men left to fight, and female church members were encouraged to work outside the house for wages. It also became more acceptable for young Adventist women to go to college as long as they attended Adventist institutions. Shirley still dreamed of being a doctor, but Mattie and Walter thought she was too sickly to go into medicine. It would be better for her to be a teacher. Maybe even an art teacher. For that they would send her to college.

Shirley ordered a catalogue from the Adventist institution that Walter had attended before dropping out to wait for the Apocalypse. But Frederickson, who had studied at Mankato State Teachers College in Minnesota, sixty miles west of Dodge Center, raved to Shirley about an art professor at her alma mater, Effie Conkling. She also raved to Professor Conkling about Shirley. Walter and Mattie drove Shirley to Mankato for a visit in the summer of 1941.

"Oh! You are the one Wylene Frederickson has told me so much about!" Effie Conkling boomed the first time Shirley walked into her art room. She was middle-aged and elfin, with a domed forehead, furrowed cheeks, and a bemused little smile. Her voice was ten times bigger than the rest of her, and Shirley was so thrilled by the attention that she "almost had a heart attack," she would later recall. She couldn't wait to start college, though she was stricken with dread that she might not measure up to Miss Conkling's expectations.

She measured up and more. As soon as classes began Shirley realized the other students were even more scared of their professor than she was. Her art background was based on what Wylene Frederickson had imparted to her, and as a Mankato graduate herself, Frederickson taught just like Miss Conkling did. Shirley was already used to mulling over cheap reproductions of the works of Michaelangelo and Gauguin, and discussing their technical features. When she did a drawing or painting she knew how to fill the canvas and give it energy. And after she finished the piece, she was accustomed to standing calmly as her teacher peered at the work and launched into a critique.

But all this was new to Shirley's classmates, and soon they were begging her to explain Miss Conkling's lessons—and even to do their homework. They told Shirley not to try too hard: any painting or drawing she did in someone else's name must be just good enough so Miss Conkling wouldn't "holler at it." But "not so good," as one student added, "that she will know I didn't do it myself, Mason!" Shirley's newfound social success was dizzying. "I had never in my life had any sense of being looked up to or accepted," she remembered later. "It soon became a perfectly wonderful life to be in college."[4] She entered a modest whirl of extracurricular activities: working as art editor of the yearbook, writing columns for the campus newspaper about topics such as how Samuel Clemens got the nom de plume Mark Twain.[5]

Only about 16,000 people lived in the city of Mankato, but as the region's biggest industrial and market town, it was a sparkling metropolis compared to shabby Dodge Center. Shirley marveled at the porticoed, multistoried buildings; the limestone public library; the tree-lined main boulevard; and Sibley Park, with lush flower beds, a lake, and a zoo.

The teachers college was a new world, too, especially when it came to sex roles. Virtually all the women back in Dodge Center were married by their twenties. But at Mankato State, most of the female staff members were single—and apparently happy and fulfilled without husbands or children. Miss Harriet Beale, as the school yearbook called her, taught French during the academic year and spent her summers far away, on Cape Cod. Effie Conkling motored around the countryside in her car, which was so much a part of her life that she'd given it a nickname: Hermes. Another art professor, Julia Schwartz, never cooked on Friday evenings. Instead she read *Time*, *Newsweek*, and eight other magazines until her eyes started to water.[6]

For Seventh-Day Adventists, these independent, secular women were straight out of Sodom and Gomorrah. But no one blinked at them in Mankato. People could do what they wanted there, including not attending any of the town's many churches if they didn't want to. Even Jews in Mankato were modern: The town's big, Jewish-owned department store, Salet's, was always open on Saturdays, with the Salet family matter-of-factly toiling behind the counters.[7] So much for the Israelite day of rest. Or Shirley's day of rest, for that matter. In Mankato Adventism was just a curiosity.

During social science classes and in bull sessions at Cooper Hall, the women's dorm, students argued about religion and other controversies. Miss Conkling introduced her art students to the work of Wanda Gág, from the tiny town of New Ulm, thirty miles from Mankato. Born in 1893, Gág had started life as a country girl, then moved to New York City during the flapper era and become a prominent printmaker and illustrator. Her art work was curvy-edged and frenetic, with houses, telephone polls, and curtains looking as though they'd been squeezed from a toothpaste tube then shaken to the beat of a rhumba. Gág sent her work to socialist magazines and was a self-styled feminist. She cut her hair short, avoided marriage in her youth, and touted free love. She was practically the only female artist that students in Mankato's art department had ever heard of. The women there worshipped her.[8]

Jean Lane was one such student. When interviewed for this book, in 2008 and 2009, she was in her late eighties and one of the last people alive who had been a good friend of Shirley's during her youth. In her old age Jean is a tall, hefty woman, and in her college photos she was just as imposing. She reminisced about being born in a farmhouse, to a mother who was raised Seventh-Day Adventist and later renounced the faith. She vividly recalled the first time she met Shirley Mason, when Shirley was a freshman at Mankato and Jean was a sophomore. Jean was also majoring in art, and she made the rounds of the dorm to check out the department's new students.

She was not impressed. Shirley was "very tiny," with a "sort of long" hairstyle that Jean found dull and old fashioned. In the coming weeks, as the two young women socialized along with the rest of the students, Shirley's devotion to religion also put Jean to sleep. "She did a lot of Bible study," and while everyone else partied on campus on weekends, Shirley left to attend church with her parents. Jean sought livelier friends and at first dismissed Shirley. But eventually they became close.

One topic that fascinated both young women was psychoanalysis. It was a fashionable topic among bright students just off the farm, Jean remembered, and she and Shirley soaked Freud up, talking constantly about his theories and trying to psychoanalyze their own childhoods. The U.S. edition of *The Basic Writings of Sigmund Freud* had just come out in the early 1940s in a cheap, mass-market edition. Readers could learn about "The employment of the mouth as a sexual organ," "The Activity of the Anal Zone," "Castration and Penis Envy."

Another recently available book was *Studies in Hysteria*, co-authored by Freud and his colleague Joseph Breuer. *Studies* introduced readers to Miss Anna O., a daydreamy twenty-one-year-old from a "puritanical family."

Anna O. suffered grievously from hysteria. For no organic reason, one of her arms would not move, and a leg was paralyzed, too. Anna was cross-eyed. Sometimes she went deaf and sometimes partially blind. Once, in the kitchen, she meant to walk to the door but instead headed for the oven. She frequently went into trances and acted like someone else. This happened, according to *Studies in Hysteria*, because she had "two entirely separate states of consciousness."

In other words, Anna O. had two personalities. One was "sad and anxious but relatively normal." The other was "naughty." It scolded people, threw pillows, ripped buttons from bedclothes and underwear, and even smashed windows. Anna didn't remember wreaking this mischief. It happened, she said, during "absences" of time—time lost to the consciousness of her normal self.[9]

For Shirley, Freud's case histories must have had the drama and dirt of those novels, plays, and soap operas which Adventist girls were supposed to avoid because they were not true. But Freud *was* true! Further, he and his colleagues helped troubled people, including young women who got sick and acted in frightening ways.

Shirley complained to Jean about her mother's overprotection and erratic moods. But, Shirley added, she could make Mattie do anything she wanted. In grade school she had often wondered what her teachers thought of her. Instead of asking, though, she sent Mattie to inquire. This sort of impromptu parent-teacher conference might be normal today. But according to Jean, it was completely over the top in the small-town Midwest of the 1920s. She tactfully pointed out to Shirley her tendency to be manipulative. Both girls decided that "most of our problems were related to our parents."

Jean was so inspired by Freud that she decided to study psychiatric social work in Chicago after finishing her undergraduate degree. Shirley wanted to do graduate work in psychology, then teach art in a mental hospital. The intellectual ferment pulsing through Mankato was pushing each girl to novel ambitions, though both had come from rural, fundamentalist girlhoods.

While Jean adjusted easily, Shirley felt overwhelmed at Mankato with "too much emotion," as she later put it. By the second semester of freshman year, in early 1942, she was tossing and turning at night, wracked with insomnia, her mind swirling with vague and fearful thoughts. She developed more physical problems. "She didn't look well," according to Jean. "She was always sick—she got colds, she got this, she got that." Her joints throbbed. Her throat felt scratchy. Her sinuses ached. Her groin hurt badly every month when she got her period. Once again, she got a tentative diagnosis of anemia from the campus doctor, and some liver shots. The anemia disappeared.[10]

Even so, she relapsed into her old "spells." When she set off walking in one direction, she would suddenly change to another. She would head for the door and end up running into the window.[11] She started acting dramatically out of character.

On most Friday afternoons she went home to Dodge Center or she met her mother, who often came to Mankato to celebrate the Adventist Sabbath with her daughter and bring her money, which Walter was always forgetting to send. During her visits Mattie would sometimes wander into other girls' rooms, asking who Shirley's friends were and what she did in her spare time. Shirley hated these intrusions, but she tried not to complain to her mother.[12] Usually quiet, demure, and eager to follow the rules, she took to visiting the dorm's living room late at night, where she would sit at the piano and bang out classical music at ear-splitting volume.[13]

And she occasionally talked strangely. Jean remembered Shirley saying a few times that "she'd spent the day downtown in bars, drinking with men." Jean thought this was very odd behavior for a devout Adventist girl, and she didn't know whether her friend was "telling the truth, lying, or fantasizing." Stranger still was the time Jean was in Shirley's room and Shirley began talking in a high, childish voice. Demonstrating the small-town, Midwestern reticence shared by everyone at Mankato, Jean politely said nothing, and she left the room. She never heard the high voice again.

But these problems seemed trivial compared to Shirley's blackouts.

"She could be doing anything," remembered Jean. "And suddenly she would become comatose. It usually happened in class. She would be just sitting there, then pass out, slump over. Like a faint."

The blackouts turned into a weird drill. Shirley would go limp in her chair. The professor would stop lecturing, students would leap to carry their classmate to the infirmary, and the college nurse would arrive, sometimes followed by the doctor. Within a few minutes Shirley's eyes would flutter open and she would regain consciousness, remembering nothing. At that point she was often injected with luminal, a barbiturate used in the early twentieth century as a sedative for anxious, agitated patients. Once she overdosed and was hospitalized, frightening the school administration. The campus physician thought she was a hysteric, but he felt his diagnosis should be checked by a specialist. He referred Shirley to the Mayo Clinic.[14] Walter drove her.

There Shirley had a brief consultation with Dr. Henry Woltman, a prominent neurologist who specialized in studying the relationship between psychiatric conditions and certain organic illnesses. His research had revealed that when patients suffered from symptoms such as fatigue, depression, inability to tell fantasy from reality, and confusion about their identity, sometimes these problems were due to metabolic and blood disorders. Woltman asked Shirley what was wrong and she replied that she was "discouraged, nervous, and everything bothers me." When she felt "bothered," she added, she lost her breath and her muscles twitched. Woltman told her to come back the next day for a physical exam and tests. But Shirley refused, and sent Walter in her place.

Woltman found himself in the awkward position of trying to make a diagnosis by interviewing the patient's father instead of the patient herself, and without doing any tests. With little to go on, he recommended that Shirley spend more time outdoors in the fresh air, and he wrote to the school doctor in Mankato, agreeing with his assessment that Shirley was a hysteric.[15]

Back at Mankato, Shirley took to her bed and asked other students to run errands and bring her food and medicine. Some Cooper Hall girls complied, trying to keep their friend under the radar of the school doctor and the dean of women.[16] But in 1943 Shirley got kicked out of school after overdosing while being treated with phenobarbital for her "spells." After spending several months at home, she returned to college but again had to leave. The Masons by then had moved to Nebraska, four hundred miles from Mankato, to follow an Adventist minister who was starting a church there. Arriving in Nebraska in 1944, Shirley was put on bed rest—on a regimen so strict that she was not allowed to draw or to write any more than her signature on Christmas cards.[17]

Her behavior grew bizarre. Once, when her father took her for a ride and went into a store to buy something, he came back to the car to discover Shirley gone. He found her at a nearby playground; she said she couldn't remember how she got there. At home, she got so manic that she started walking on the furniture. Her parents locked her in the house.[18] In a few months she felt better. But she continued to muddle between Mankato and Nebraska, returning to school for a term, then relapsing and dropping out.

The minister tried to help her by getting her an English and art instructor position at an Adventist school in Nebraska. She didn't yet have her bachelors degree, but World War II had created a teacher shortage. Women like her, with partial academic credits, could get provisional teaching certificates.[19] As she got busy with her coreligionists, Shirley's worst hysteria symptoms faded, but she was still skinny, achy, moody, and chronically angry with Mattie and quick to torment her. Her college friend Jean once paid a visit to the Masons and remembered that "Shirley was keeping cages of pet rats in her bedroom. Why? To irritate her mother, I think."

In 1945 Mattie developed stomach problems and began seeing a general practitioner in Omaha. In late July Shirley accompanied her mother to a medical appointment, and the doctor noticed that Shirley herself looked ill. He suggested she see psychiatrist Cornelia Wilbur, who reputedly was working miracles with young women hysterics. An introductory appointment was made for August 1.[20]

There was instant mutual attraction. Dr. Wilbur came to therapy sessions in her Katharine Hepburn suits, a cigarette poised in her manicured hand. From late summer to December, Shirley had only five sessions with her new doctor: just one fifty-minute hour per month. Those smidgens of time helped her immensely, though. And they gave both women the chance to become fascinated with each other.

Connie took one look at shaky, anorexic Shirley—she was five-foot-three and weighed perhaps eighty-five pounds—and felt there was "something about her," she would recall years later. She was a vision of Connie's fantasied teenaged self, with the dark hair, the pallid skin and weed-like slenderness. And the ambition of this young, small-town Midwesterner! Most of Connie's patients were unschooled girls who thought of little but marriage and having babies. But Shirley was passably schooled despite all her problems, and she was desperate for more education. Unhappily dependent on backward parents. Ever ready to deprecate herself even as she boasted constantly about her artistic talent.[21]

There but for fortune, Connie thought. What if she herself had followed her mother's Christian Science dicta that doctors were useless and evil? What if she'd bowed her head after her miracle soap fell through and accepted her father's pronouncement that she was too stupid for medical school? She might easily have ended up like this poor, struggling girl. Connie felt a pull toward Shirley. She wanted to help her fulfill her dreams.

And Shirley was taken with Connie. Lying on the office couch for an hour each month, she poured her heart out about abstract art, fiction, and Freud, without the slightest fear of shocking or annoying Dr. Wilbur. She could curse life and pity herself without being told she was a sinner. She could talk about her daydreams and fantasies, telling stories that weren't true—about how she'd won an art contest at the Dodge County fair, for instance, even though in reality the fair didn't have an art contest during the years she said she'd entered. She could be congratulated, consoled, even coddled by an older woman who wasn't her mother. Shirley felt like a happy child. She worshipped Dr. Wilbur as a little girl worships a parent. She decided she wanted to be a psychiatrist, just like Dr. Wilbur. She ruminated constantly about her new career plan.

As a diagnosed hysteric, Shirley was a prime candidate for Pentothal, Connie's favorite treatment. But her Adventism prohibited such drugs. Connie gave Shirley mild sleeping pills for home use, but there would be no "truth serum" injections. Instead, she got pep talks similar to the "mind cure" techniques of the Christian Scientists.

Question the authority of your parents and your religion, Connie told Shirley over and over. Be your own person. Follow your dreams but learn to control your emotions. Shirley complained that she had trouble typing because she had a habit of constantly looking at her hands on the keyboard—possibly a remnant of her earlier obsession with germs. Connie told her to fix her gaze on the page rather than the typewriter. Shirley complied, and soon she no longer felt like checking her hands. She was tremendously grateful for Connie's help.[22]

When Connie announced she would soon be leaving Omaha to become a psychoanalyst—perhaps in Detroit, not far from where she'd attended medical school—Shirley was distraught.

Connie had no option but to reconfigure her life, because the soldiers were coming home. For her part, she was not only losing her job—she was also fighting with her husband, whose career looked as promising at the war's end as Connie's was becoming shaky.

The summer Connie met Shirley, Henry Wilbur had just been offered the dentistry professorship at University of Louisville's medical school, in Kentucky. Connie's pink slip in Omaha must have seemed like a blessing to him.

Connie felt torn. Not only were her husband and boss telling her to stop working, but American psychoanalysts whom Connie highly respected had begun stressing—in popular magazines and professional literature—that childless women with careers were emasculating, unfeminine, and neurotic. Even so, as she recalled years later, she began to explore the possibility of getting a divorce.

Meanwhile, Shirley thought about Connie all the time. It seems likely that she had developed a relationship with her doctor that Freudians call "transference"—an unconscious projection onto the therapist of deep-seated feelings which the patient harbors for important people from her past. During therapy with Connie and at home later, Shirley began yearning for the unlimited attention from Dr. Wilbur that she got from Mattie, her classmates, and the school nurse. She daydreamed about Dr. Wilbur. She wondered whether Dr. Wilbur really cared for her. How could she make her see what she felt? How could she get Dr. Wilbur to stay in Omaha?

Then, as Shirley would remember decades later, she was gripped by an idea for impressing Dr. Wilbur that was half conscious, half unconscious. One day in late 1945, before going to her psychotherapy appointment, she busied herself making block prints, holding a sharp knife to etch the lineoleum tiles used in the process. While cutting she found herself "dwelling morbidly" on Dr. Wilbur's imminent departure. Suddenly the knife slipped. It cut Shirley's hand so deeply that it hit an artery, and a geyser of blood shot out. She pressed hard on her hand, improvising a tourniquet as she ran to her mother's doctor's office, which was a few blocks from her house. He stanched the wound and wrapped it with gauze. It started to throb something fierce. Looking and feeling like a war casualty, Shirley proceeded to Dr. Wilbur's office, in the same building.

There she had what doctors today would call a panic attack, and a rather theatrical one at that. She flew off her chair, rushed blindly to the office window, and pounded on the unbreakable glass with her bloody, bandaged hand. Amazed, Connie grabbed Shirley and sat her down. She thought her patient had just suffered a seizure, though in this case it didn't have an organic cause, the way epilepsy did. Connie believed it was psychogenic—brought on by emotional disturbance, and that Shirley needed psychiatric hospitalization. Connie worked on the locked mental ward of Clarkson Hospital, and she suggested Shirley check herself in for several weeks. That way, the doctor and the patient could do therapy daily.

Shirley was delighted. As though preparing for a stay at an art colony instead of Omaha's equivalent of an insane asylum, she started planning which sort of colored pencils and paper to take with her.

Her parents were aghast. Walter worried about mind-bending drugs and lobotomies. The Masons told Shirley they would send her to an Adventist psychiatric facility instead. But Shirley wanted only Dr. Wilbur, and they hit an impasse as summer turned to fall and winter. The Masons argued and argued. Shirley did not go to the hospital.[23]

Instead, she continued seeing Connie once a month. Connie made useful suggestions: get out of the house more, do some teaching—maybe not full time, because too many hours might be overly tiring, but at least part time. Shirley followed her advice, teaching high school at the local Adventist academy, and doing a fine job of it.

But, just as she had developed a transference toward Connie, Connie apparently developed a countertransference—unconsciously projecting onto Shirley the deep-seated feelings *she* had for key people in *her* life.

Psychiatrists nowadays constantly warn each other about the dangers of unexamined, uncontrolled countertransference. A married male doctor develops erotic feelings toward a female patient who seems to worship him. Her behavior reflects the babyish way she acted toward her father to get attention from him when she was a child in a family of many siblings who competed for his time. As for the therapist, his patient reminds him of his younger sister, who worshipped him when he was sickly little boy and made him feel strong. As a psychiatrist, he ought to be helping the patient analyze her transference so she can stop feeling compelled to act like a baby. But the doctor's need to keep a baby girl in his psychic life impedes his therapeutic work.

Connie seems to have been swamped by the transference/countertransference dynamic between herself and Shirley. Instead of recognizing the patient's feelings toward her and staying emotionally neutral, she encouraged what Shirley later called her "crush" on Dr. Wilbur. Years after their first meeting, Connie would admit that she felt as though Shirley was her daughter.[24] To sustain that feeling, she apparently set out to depose Mattie Mason from Shirley's affections.

Connie started giving Shirley reading assignments, and much of the material was about nasty, devouring mothers. One recommendation was the popular play *The Silver Cord*, about a young woman scientist and her new husband, who is dominated by an absurdly smothering mother. Connie also began confiding in Shirley about her life, stretching back to years long preceding the start of Shirley's therapy. She talked about her mentor from medical school days, Robert Dieterle—the doctor who made the film of the teenaged hysterics acting like babies.[25]

Connie probably also discussed Dieterle's young woman patient with the dual selves, because she told Shirley to read psychologist Morton Prince's *Dissociation of a Personality*. First published in 1905, it described a prim, quiet young Boston woman whose pseudonym was Miss Christine Beauchamp. She had a childlike, troublemaker alter self, Sally, who loved to wander to other cities without Miss Beauchamp's knowledge. Shirley also read about Miss Beauchamp's memories being altered, and the way that she "lost time."

Shirley hadn't gotten far in the 569 pages of *Dissociation of a Personality* when the book started to trouble her. Dr. Prince always did his therapy with Miss Beauchamp by hypnotizing her, and hypnosis was strongly forbidden among Seventh-Day Adventists. Ellen G. White had outlawed it years ago, back when critics were dismissing her as a charlatan who was going into trances due to hypnosis rather than because she was receiving inspired messages from God. Shirley was repulsed. For her, allowing oneself to be hypnotized was as sinful as masturbating. At the same time she may have felt titillated, especially when she read about the undivided attention Dr. Prince paid his patient's multiple personalities.

Shirley never went to the hospital's psychiatric ward. In November 1945, she came down with a bronchial infection and was too sick to keep her therapy appointment. Mattie picked up the phone and pretended to call Connie's office to reschedule, but in fact she was furtively pressing the disconnect button at the same time she was dialing. As a result, Shirley missed her appointment without canceling in advance, though she thought she had canceled.

But the faux pas barely registered with Connie, who was manically trying to keep her position in Omaha. She was also talking to divorce lawyers. And she was strategizing about how to send her things—and herself—out of Nebraska. By Christmas it was clear she would be laid off, and when Shirley and her mother visited the office on December 26 to refill Shirley's sleeping pill prescription, Connie brushed past with barely a hello.[26]

Shirley understood then that her beloved doctor really was leaving. She would have to carry on in life by herself. And she did, with great success. Nine years would pass before she went into therapy again. The second time around would also involve Connie's treatment. It would prove to be disastrous.

CHAPTER 6

PROFESSOR SCHREIBER

FOR FLORA AND HER CONTEMPORARIES in the 1940s, Madison Avenue was the Wall Street of advertising, material plenty, and the hot media, radio. A generation earlier, back when radio had been a brand new technology, the government had vowed to turn it into a public utility to inform and educate the nation. Instead, within the next two decades the air waves were almost wholly privatized and commercialized, by NBC, CBS, and other networks. Radio had saturated American homes by the time Flora was in college, Connie Wilbur was in medical school, and a teenage Shirley Mason was moping around in Dodge Center. Audiences heard newscasts, roundtable political discussions, and the president's fireside chats. But they were also inundated with pop music, comedians, quiz shows, and soap operas.

The importance of the role that advertising agencies played in these programs is hard to imagine today. Not only did Madison Avenue buy air time for clients' commercials, it created and produced the programs that hosted those commercials, including torrents of theatrical dramas. One big ad agency, BBDO—short for Batten, Barton, Durstine & Osborn—produced the hugely popular *Cavalcade Theater*. It was sponsored by the politically right-wing Dupont Corporation, and the show featured patriotic plays about American heroes such as Benjamin Franklin and Abraham Lincoln. Another large firm created most of America's radio soap operas. By the late 1930s half the women in America were listening to them and their nonstop advertisements for laundry detergent. Everything and everyone was drowning in ads. More people in the United States had a radio in their home than a telephone.[1]

Not everyone was happy with this commercialism. Here and there could be found a surviving university or municipal station. One of the latter was WNYC, named for its owner, New York City.

In the late 1930s and early 1940s, WNYC broadcast plays performed by college students, poetry read by high school pupils, and free science and liberal arts courses on the air. WNYC's annual American Music Festival highlighted new works by American composers. There was even an hour hosted by the black folk musician Leadbelly, wailing songs such as "The Boll Weevil."

WNYC's avant garde sheen was burnished by the government. The Works Progress Administration—WPA, as the New Deal agency was known—created the Federal Theatre Project, which hired out-of-work writers and actors to put on plays nationwide. The theater project's director in New York City, a former Broadway producer named George Kondolf, brought his WPA plays to WNYC.

Flora, in her early twenties at the time, volunteered there, writing scripts for music education programs. That's probably where she met Kondolf. After the government shut down the Federal Theatre Project, he accepted a job as "story editor" for *The Cavalcade Theater* at the prestigious ad agency BBDO. He took Flora with him.[2]

Once at BBDO, Kondolf hired all kinds of people to produce stories. Many of his writers were avowed leftists. They included Carl Sandburg, Orson Welles, Sinclair Lewis, Arthur Miller, and folksinger Woodie Guthrie, who had once written for the newspaper of the American Communist Party. Kondolf didn't care about these people's politics. If they were talented, famous, and willing to help the right-wing Dupont Corporation promote "better things for better living through chemistry," they were welcome to work at the ad agency.[3]

For Flora, a young woman raised partly conservative in a leftist world, *Cavalcade* must have been heaven. She loved walking into BBDO's offices in a tailored suit, swinging a purse in one hand and a briefcase in the other. She was thrilled to hobnob with writers like Arthur Miller, and with the show's superstar actors and actresses: Edward G. Robinson, Helen Hayes, Basil Rathbone, Humphrey Bogart, and others.

Flora may have done some editing at BBDO, and she probably showed George Kondolf some of her own radio scripts. She'd written one about Haym Solomon, a Jewish resident of colonial Philadelphia who helped finance the American Revolution. *Cavalcade* didn't want it, and in fact, no one seemed interested in her dramas. Were they not good enough? Or was it that the author was a woman? She shopped around an adaptation of Franz Kafka's novella *The Metamorphosis*, about a man who wakes up one morning to find he's turned into a giant cockroach. Instead of revealing her gender with a full name, Flora bylined herself "F. R. Scheiber." She still couldn't sell it.[4]

There was one kind of job in commercial media that was easy to get, however: audience research. Flora did some work at NBC, the network that aired *Cavalcade*. NBC wanted to know more about the people who listened to its soap operas, and Flora was assigned to review the mail. Millions of letters poured in each year, and researchers sorted them by the sex, age, geographical location, marital status, and education of the writers, as well as by their opinions about the shows. The data was tabulated for advertisers, and comments about program content were forwarded to higher-ups. A well-crafted letter might convince a producer to tweak a plot and change a story. Flora learned that radio theater was not art for art's sake. It was art for the sake of selling things, to millions of people.

By the end of World War II, Flora had spent several years, as she worded it on her resume, "in direct contact with the key men in the advertising agencies and [radio] networks."[5] From these men she'd learned that radio was the new *machina* of national life. But its *deus* wasn't God. It was Money.

Flora worried about this, and as the 1940s wore on she struggled to do serious writing about the mass media, in tiny publications specializing in analysis of the theater, radio, and the revolutionary new technology, television. For *Film and Radio Discussion Guide*, she likened the melodramatic plots of soap operas to the great plays of Shakespeare. For the scholarly *Hollywood Quarterly* she described how old plays such as *Macbeth* changed when they were produced for television instead of Broadway.[6]

But her passion became teaching. Toward the end of World War II she was hired to substitute in the Speech and Theater Department of Brooklyn College for a male professor who had gone to war.[7] The school was a branch of New York City's public university system, and the Speech and Theater Department was run by gentile men from the Midwest. They seemed anti-Semitic to Flora, and she was sure they looked down on women. She responded by acting proud, witty, and outrageous. She wore lipstick so thick and red that it almost seemed purple, and she delighted in shocking her superiors with clever retorts.

At an event in front of an audience, a Brooklyn College colleague once jokingly introduced Flora and her department chairman with: "This is Professor O'Neill, the front of the organization. And this is Miss Schreiber, the brains."

"Professor Maloney," retorted the large-breasted Flora, "that's unfair to Professor O'Neill's brains and my front."[8]

After the war ended and she was laid off from Brooklyn College, she went on to teach at nearby Adelphi College, where her students wrote and broadcast radio plays. Flora's taste in the genre was rarified. She favored what she called "poetic documentary," with wispy recitations of work by Emily Dickinson and Goethe. Such fare was a far cry from *Cavalcade Theater*. It established Flora as an intellectual—as her father's daughter.[9]

She was starting to feel like an aging, anonymous scholar. Her squarish face was getting squarer. Her hooked nose hooked lower. Her cigarette habit had evolved to the chain-smoker level. Her tendency to walk around with food stains on her dress—and now, ashes—was growing more pronounced. The 1940s ended and she'd never in her life had a boyfriend, much less a famous one.

When she was thirty-four, she got one. His very name evoked stardom— Eugene O'Neill, Jr. His father was the author of *Long Day's Journey Into Night*, whose work won him Pulitzer prizes and a Nobel. But Eugene Sr. suffered all his life with crippling depression and alcoholism. Other O'Neill family members did, too, and some drank themselves to death or committed suicide.

It was 1950 when Flora first took up with Eugene Jr.—whom everyone called Gene. He was forty years old and a man of the world, six-feet-three inches tall, broad shouldered, and handsome. A Yale University–trained scholar of Greek and classical literature who did book reviews for the *New York Times,* Gene did radio broadcasting work as well, and his on-air voice was often compared to Orson Welles'.

Gene also lectured at small colleges, and in early 1950 he gave a talk he called "Shakespeare and Soap Operas," in which he favorably compared potboiler radio dramas to the works of The Bard.[10] This was one of Flora's pet topics, and she probably met Gene because of their shared interests. In the summer he invited her to visit him in Woodstock, an artists and writers colony two hours north of New York City, where Gene had a cottage. Flora planned to stay at a local inn but ended up spending the night with Gene. Almost immediately he asked her to marry him.

She spent the rest of the summer in an erotic haze. Gene didn't seem to mind that she spilled food and cigarette ash on her clothes. Nor was he bothered that she was overweight. He told her he adored big, floppy breasts. "My fat wench," he called her, and she was overwhelmed by the strength of her emotions.

By September, however, she was worried. Gene had a terribly conflicted relationship with his father, and by the time Flora met him he had been married and divorced three times. He had a stormy relationship with his past lovers, and rumor had it that he sometimes beat them. He was also a longtime alcoholic who suffered from bouts of depression. By the time Flora entered the picture he was in grave decline.

Completely inexperienced with men, she had little idea of how to take Gene's measure. He noticed her ignorance and didn't like it. Too "girl-ish," he called Flora, particularly when it came to sex. In a sheaf of notes she later wrote to herself, she described feeling pain at having his finger inside her, let alone his penis. "Be an animal," Gene would urge her, and he blamed her reticence on the fact that she had a profession. "You bring Adelphi College into the bedroom. It is not that career women don't want to go to bed—it is that they don't know how," he scolded Flora.[11]

Flora blamed herself for their incompatibility. She concluded that she could not say "I love you" in bed because she had spent her entire life as a person or a daughter, and not, as she ruefully wrote, "a woman." Gene accused her of rejecting him.[12]

In mid-September, after Flora's customary weekend visit, Gene drove her to the train station so she could return to New York City. They planned to skip the next weekend rendezvous, but Gene promised to travel on the Monday after that to see her.

As soon as Flora was gone, Gene looked up an old lover and spent days begging her to marry him. At the end of the week she agreed, but Gene was acting so strangely that on Saturday she broke off the engagement. Gene spent all day and night on Sunday drinking, and on Monday morning a neighbor found him dead—he had slashed himself with a straight razor. Papers nationwide reported that the great playwright Eugene O'Neill's son had killed himself because a woman refused to marry him. That woman was not Flora Schreiber. Not a word was published about her.[13]

She went into deep mourning and took to calling Gene "My almost husband." She thought about all the other almosts: being a daughter-in-law of the greatest dramatist in America, and sister-in-law to Charlie Chaplin, husband of Gene's half sister, Oona. "I hate to mention his name," she wrote a friend about the suicide, "because it is a famous one." But she could not restrain herself: "Eugene O'Neill, Jr." she added a few lines later, and bragged about her "brief membership in that tragic family."[14]

A year later Flora was still brooding over Gene's indictment of her as a "career woman" divorced from her feminine nature. She had lost her taste for full-time college teaching and cast about for a more exciting way to make her mark on the world. Soon she found it. She took what she'd learned about salesmanship at the advertising agency. She reinvented herself as a writer for women's magazines.

PART III

TREATMENT

CHAPTER 7

MANHATTAN

WHEN SHIRLEY AND CONNIE MET again, it was a new decade and a new world for both. Shirley was a graduate student at Teachers College of the world-famous Columbia University, in New York City—the same school Flora Schreiber had attended years earlier. Connie had become a psychoanalyst, and she now saw patients, some of them Broadway stars, in her posh home-office complex on Park Avenue. When she and Shirley reunited there, nine years had passed since Nebraska, and in many ways each had changed dramatically. But when it came to their relationship, things picked up exactly where they had left off. On the Upper East Side of Manhattan in 1954, the two women were as smitten with each other as they had been in 1945.

How, they asked, had they ended up a second time in the same city? What had brought each of them to Manhattan? Seated at a small table in Connie's office, Shirley poured out her story.

She had gotten no more psychotherapy after Connie left Omaha. But thanks to their work in that city, she had done fairly well in the years that followed. Thinking positive, peaceful thoughts when she was nervous, and popping an occasional sleeping pill at night, Shirley generally controlled herself so well that she was able to teach part time.[1]

Her Adventism seemed like less of a problem, too. She had started to openly read novels after her father bought her a subscription to the Book of the Month Club and she ordered *Jane Eyre* and other classic novels. Adventism was changing: fiction reading was no longer the automatic sin it

75

had once been. Shirley basked nervously but excitedly in the new freedom. She decided to finish her degree with a double major in English and art.[2] Deep down, though, she still wanted to be a psychiatrist. Her secret vice was no longer literature. Now it was Freud.

Amid days filled with lesson plans and classes full of noisy teenagers, Shirley studied at the University of Omaha, taking several psychology courses and making good grades. In the fall of 1946 she returned to Mankato, only a few courses short of earning a bachelors degree. But she dropped out of school again—this time because Mattie, who was only sixty-three, was sick with stomach cancer, an unusual disease in a woman that young. Doctors had diagnosed her cancer as terminal, and Mattie begged Shirley to stay home and nurse her.[3]

During her final days Mattie made some deathbed confessions, including about the time she'd pretended to cancel Shirley's appointment with Dr. Wilbur. And she apologized for being "so cross" and "so nervous" when Shirley was young. Shirley forgave her mother's transgressions.[4]

Mattie died in 1948. Shirley was devastated—her contempt and irritation with her mother was hopelessly tangled with love—but she returned to Mankato to finish her final courses. Her old friend Jean Lane was there, a teacher now, too, and the women ended up in the same rooming house. Shirley tried again to latch onto Jean as a surrogate mother, but again Jean backed off.

Mattie's corpse was hardly cold before Walter got a girlfriend, whom he would marry a decade later. Florence Eichman was a widow whose first husband had been a prominent Adventist leader before he died in middle age.[5] Florence curled her hair, wore low-cut blouses, and exuded a churchy sensuality. She had a grown son and no interest in mothering Walter's adult daughter. She could not understand why Shirley needed so much attention. Walter kept silent about Shirley's psychiatric past, but Florence felt something was odd. Shirley was too thin and she never dressed up. Worse, she still needed Walter to support her even though she was twenty-six years old.

Influenced by Florence, Walter stopped sending Shirley money, and there were times at Mankato when she was reduced to eating nothing but oranges for every meal. She complained bitterly to Jean. But not to Walter, and she had nothing but smiles for him when he came to her graduation. She was proud of her senior project: an exhibit of three dozen of her paintings and drawings, hung in the college's art studio and lounge.[6] While in school she had held exhibits in small-town galleries, but she seldom sold anything. She knew she would have to find another way to make a living besides marketing her paintings.

The first job Shirley got after graduating was as an art therapist for the mentally ill. Porter Hospital and Sanitarium, in Denver, was an Adventist institution, and in 1949 Walter Mason moved to Colorado to build an addition to the facility. Florence's son worked there, too, and Shirley was probably hired because of these connections.[7] Soon she was teaching painting, drawing, and ceramics to mental patients. Immersed in real-life abnormal psychology, she had ample time to observe how schizophrenics, melancholics, and hysterics acted. Sometimes her own behavior mirrored the pathological doings of her patients. She started to feel ill again, with aches, pains, extreme weight loss—she wasted to seventy-six pounds—and "nerves." Still she tried to be a good art therapist, and she loved the work.

Then Walter moved to Michigan to build more churches. Shirley followed, but within weeks Florence showed up and decamped in the house next door. Shirley was now a third wheel. She moved on her own to Memphis, a tiny town north of Detroit. She became a teacher again.[8]

Her new school was not Adventist. For the first time in her life, she was cut loose from family connections and propelled into the secular world. Her workload was daunting: each week she taught four hundred grade-schoolers—and not just art courses, but English and public speaking as well. Even so, in Michigan she was able to stay calm and energetic enough to juggle lesson plans, grade mountains of student work, and hang that work on walls or send it to contests. She could even grab the disruptive students—the backtalkers and spit wadders—and give them a shake or kick them out of class. The thickest-skinned teacher might have been unnerved by these challenges. Shirley wasn't. Heretofore a timid person, she learned to help children stand before a crowd and voice an opinion.[9]

But she remained physically and mentally fragile. Her nose often got stopped up, her throat hurt, every month she suffered from excruciating menstrual cramps, and she remained seriously underweight. She sometimes got nervous and did the old, odd things in private—lying on the bed at home and moving her hands, for instance, in what she called "tracing" patterns.[10]

She was thirty years old and her life was taken up with piety, construction paper, and pinch-pot ash trays. At home by herself, she felt lost in a black hole of loneliness. To soothe herself she fell into her lifelong fantasies. What would it be like to win a big art contest? To be a famous psychiatrist? To spy on Nazis and other bad people? For hours she spun scenarios as she sat in a chair or lay down, her eyes rolled upward like those of a saint or a prophetess. Ruminating and talking with people later, she sometimes had difficulty telling which of her thoughts were true and which were fantasy. She once told a news reporter in Memphis that she had taken all the ribbons for art at a county fair in southern Minnesota when she was a young child. The paper printed the false claim.[11] Shirley may have been consciously lying about it, but more likely, she believed she was telling the truth.

In 1953 she applied to graduate school. It was an ambitious but somewhat rote plan; for unmarried women who taught art in the 1950s, the next step to advance one's career after college was to earn a masters or doctorate degree in art education. The brightest people in Shirley's world were doing this. Jean Lane was still single, and she was going for her Ph.D. So was Julia Schwartz, the professor at Mankato whose spinsterhood allowed her to garden in the summer and read eight magazines on Friday night.

The very best program was in New York City, at Columbia Teachers College, where Jean and Professor Schwartz were studying.[12] Shirley was accepted and excitedly made plans to matriculate in September 1954. Not only did she pack her belongings, she attended to some of her health problems, particularly the menstrual cramps. A few months before classes started, she flew to the West Coast to be treated at an Adventist hospital where a family friend worked as a physician. Doctors there operated on her and discovered an enlarged, malfunctioning ovary. In addition, she was suffering from endometriosis, a common condition in which, for reasons unknown, tissue from the uterus migrates outside of that organ and causes pain and bleeding. Shirley got hormone pills for the ovary, and her surgeons removed much of the endometrial tissue. When she started Teachers College her pelvic pains and menstrual problems were gone.

So were many of her other maladies, to her amazement and delight.

New York City seemed a tonic for whatever had bothered her for so many years. Within four weeks of arriving, she wrote her father that "I have not had a bit of sinus trouble nor any cold nor any sore throat" and "I eat and sleep well and really feel tops." She was gaining weight, so much that she worried she would have to buy larger clothes. "It is perfectly wonderful to me to be able to feel good day in and day out," she wrote happily.[13]

And she was making friends. One, Willie Price, was a tall, square-shaped woman in her late thirties who had come to New York from Arkansas to study early childhood education. Another, Maureen Maxwell, was a fellow Adventist. Shirley explored the city with these two and basked in their company. "Sunday night," she wrote, "Willie and Maureen and I went to a Chinese restaurant and had vegetable chow mein—was it ever good—never had any like that before and really enjoyed it. And we had the best time." She added that she could "really relax and laugh."

The new friends rode subways and buses through the city. They rubbernecked and window-shopped. ("We stood in front of the Empire State Building the other day and looked up—did it ever sway!") They savored grand art museums, shopped at famous department stores, and laughed at the New York accents of the clerks at "Lawd and Tayla (they just don't pronounce the R's around here)."

While walking around the moneyed Upper East Side one day, Shirley noticed the area's parade of "black Cadillacs, with chauffer and one lone occupant in the back seat."

Bemused, she bet Willie that the passengers "were rich ladies on their way to keep an appointment with a Fifth Avenue psychiatrist to find out why they were so unhappy!"[14]

Just two blocks east of where Shirley spied the traffic parade, black Cadillacs were rolling up to a luxury apartment building at the corner of Seventy-seventh Street and Park Avenue. In its spacious lobby a liveried doorman directed patients toward the elevator. They pressed the button for the fourth floor, then proceeded to 4D. Entering a stylishly decorated foyer, they were greeted by their psychoanalyst, Dr. Cornelia Wilbur.

Arriving in Manhattan in early 1946, Connie had first rented a modest apartment and was not sure how she would achieve fame and fortune in

New York. It turned out she had little to worry about—the city offered a wealth of opportunity for mind healers like her.

Less than a year had passed since the war ended, and damaged soldiers were still streaming into Veterans Administration treatment centers. Pilgrim Hospital, out on Long Island, housed thousands of the wounded and shell-shocked, so many that a documentary movie about their sufferings was being filmed on site, by famed director John Huston. Halloran, on Staten Island, was also filled to capacity. Connie was hired for part-time work at Halloran and at a handful of VA outpatient clinics.

Her experience with narcosynthesis and electricity was a plus at these facilities, where most of the patients were psychiatric cases. They often walked into the VA clinics, got shock treatment, and walked out without having to be hospitalized. Others received Pentothal injections for their shell-shock symptoms, then went right back out on the street. These quick fixes were unorthodox and innovative—traditionally, patients back home from war had been hospitalized for days, weeks, or months after these treatments. Now the VA psychiatrists prided themselves on keeping veterans in the community, where they could work and care for their families even if they were mentally ill. Connie's first years in New York were spent in this treatment milieu.[15]

But what she really wanted was to learn psychoanalysis. Throughout America after the war, creative people fluttered around therapy like moths to light, and the buzz had nothing to do with grim, biological treatments like pills and shock. What beckoned now was the talking cure: the fifty-minute hour and the patient on the couch spinning dense threads of free association and dreams, digging deep into childhood, down to the dank taproot of conflict, dragging it to the light of consciousness and comprehension. When practiced critically and compassionately—when therapists treated patients as individuals and helped them express themselves as such—talk treatment was often felt extremely helpful, even liberating. Good therapy inspired the whole society.

And for those who had enough money and lived in big cities, there were plenty of doctors to provide the treatment. Los Angeles, Boston, Chicago, Washington, and New York were stocked with practitioners, in a country that had long considered itself the world capital of optimistic self-improvement—including, now, via psychoanalysis. It became particularly fashionable after it was proudly embraced by the nation's most glamorous. Lee Strasberg, master of "method acting" at the Actors Studio in Manhattan, told his students to enter therapy: getting psychoanalyzed, he advised stars like Marlon Brando and Marilyn Monroe, would bring them success in Hollywood and on Broadway.[16]

Freud had always despised this sunny Yankee attitude. To him, psychoanalysis was a scientific and subversive theory. It dealt with bodies and their desires being driven underground by social demands. Civilized people needed repression to survive. Life was cruel and could not be otherwise unless the whole world became kinder. Freud was a stoic. He believed his ideas could illuminate the deep meaning of literature and "life in general." But those ideas could not wreak miracle transformations in individuals.

So what was therapy good for? Hypnosis or drugs could quickly make a shell-shocked soldier feel better. People with the most florid neurotic behaviors, such as compulsive hand washing or hysterically paralyzed limbs, might improve on the couch. But no one should expect joy or fulfillment. For most patients, "ordinary unhappiness," as Freud dubbed it, was the most that treatment could offer. The difference "between a person who has not been analyzed and the behavior of a person after he has been analyzed," Freud suspected, was "not so thoroughgoing as we aim at making it and as we expect and maintain it to be."[17] With their extreme pragmatism, Horatio Algerism, and lust for a buck, Freud opined, Americans were the nationality most likely to misunderstand and degrade psychoanalysis.

The going rate in New York City for a psychoanalytic treatment hour on Park Avenue in the late 1940s was $50[18]—about $550 in today's money. Lillian Hellman's therapist, a Russian immigrant named Gregory Zilboorg, charged twice that.[19] People like him were grossing the contemporary equivalent of over a million dollars annually. Not surprisingly, more and more psychiatrists flocked to the city's new psychoanalytic training programs.

Each new insitute had a different theory, but most called themselves neo-Freudians, meaning that they departed radically from many of the master's basic teachings. In an orthodox psychoanalytic session, the therapist is a blank slate. He or she stays silent except to occasionally interpret a patient's free associations. Eye contact rarely happens and touching is strictly forbidden.

All this standoffishness is said to encourage transference neurosis, during which the patient, imagining the therapist as a parent or other influential grownup, generates painful recollections of childhood. These recollections might describe events that really did happen. Or they could be what Freudians call "screen memories"—fantasies overlaid onto infantile imaginings too primitive to be expressed in words. Sorting real memories from screen memories is not necessary for Freudian therapists, however. What is important are the emotions accompanying both productions. Analyzing those emotions is thought to lead to deeper truths.

Many neo-Freudians got rid of the couch and replaced it with two chairs, set face to face. They stopped acting like blank slates, sometimes even talking to patients about their own lives. They offered verbal praise—and even touch. It became acceptable to give encouraging pats on the back. Hugs still raised eyebrows, but they were at least thinkable.

These changes flowed from neo-Freudians' changing ideas about the source of painful childhood recollections. No longer were they thought to be based upon infantile conflicts with one's parents—from the Oedipus complex, for instance. Instead, they came from actual injuries committed by these caretakers, and to heal, it was not necessary to develop a transference neurosis. Instead, patients needed to dredge up memories of the hurtful things done to them so long ago.

Most of those bad things, the new thinking went, had been perpetrated by mothers, some of whom were so cruel that they were even creating psychosis in their children. Psychoanalyst Frieda Fromm-Reichman, who worked at a private mental hospital in Maryland, invented a term to describe such mothers: "schizophrenogenic." Medical journals echoed Fromm-Reichman. Psychiatrists who treated schizophrenic children began interviewing their mothers. Inevitably, the doctors found these women to be "guileful," "self-indulgent," "irritible," "sarcastic," "ostentatious," "exhibitionistic," and prone to "manipulate," "exploit," and "ignore" their offspring—which was precisely the reason these children were psychotic.[20]

At least one psychoanalyst even believed that when children were constipated, mothers could cause lifelong trauma by giving them enemas. In his book *Childhood Experience and Personal Destiny,* Dr. William V. Silverberg spared no details. He used eight pages to discuss nozzles, anal sphincters, abdominal cramps, and gas—not to mention the noxious effect enemas produced in boys and girls: "a permanent state of low self-esteem and rage."[21]

For her psychoanalytic training Connie chose the New York Medical College, in the suburbs just north of New York City.[22] It offered a program tied to Flower and Fifth Avenue Hospital, a public facility bordering the city's poverty-stricken Spanish Harlem. At the hospital Connie continued working as a neuropsychiatrist. At the college, she lay on a couch several days a week for months, getting psychoanalyzed by one of her professors. This "training analysis" was required for her certification. Today no records survive indicating who psychoanalyzed Connie. But clues she dropped in letters and conversations suggest that it was William V. Silverberg, the doctor who believed that enemas could ruin children's lives.

Though she now had psychoanalytic credentials Connie continued to work as a hospital psychiatrist.[23] One case she treated was a twenty-two-year-old psychotic male. For four days he had been so agitated that he could not sleep a wink, and his mania had given him a 105 degree fever. His doctors feared he would die if he didn't calm down. Connie was called in because of her expertise in administering Pentothal. "You are going to go to sleep," Connie murmured as she injected the patient. "You're going to let go of all the responsibility, you are simply going to turn over to us." The patient went to sleep and his fever dropped. Connie boasted that her treatment had saved his life.[24]

She was now able to supplement her hospital work with a private practice in psychoanalysis, and she started the work in a lackluster building not far from the hospital.[25] One of her early patients was Frederick Keith Brown, a shy, obese lawyer from the rural Midwest who was five years Connie's junior. Brown—known to all as Keith—sought therapy to get through a divorce. Connie learned he was a former federal prosecutor who now worked in a corporate law firm and spent most of his time representing the insurance company Lloyds of London. He was also a fellow alumnus of the University of Michigan. And he was rich. Very rich.[26]

As soon as his divorce came through Connie married him. In 1953 the newlyweds moved to Park Avenue,[27] to a grand apartment with soaring ceilings, a marble fireplace, two living rooms, a dining room, three bedrooms, and a maid's quarters. There was more than enough space for an office. Connie furnished hers with fresh-cut flowers, photographs she had taken of tropical beach scapes, an overstuffed chair for herself, and a long, leather couch for her patients.[28]

The practice grew, and soon she was seeing not just neurotics, but schizophrenics. In New York in the early 1950s, very few psychoanalysts did office work with psychotics—they recommended committing them to mental hospitals. A handful of doctors were willing to see such patients, however, and Connie allied herself with these exceptionally nurturing colleagues.[29] One of her office patients was a twenty-eight-year-old woman who, when she first came for treatment, hadn't spoken for months and was a "filthy slob," Connie said years later. She was "pulpy fat," she wore no makeup, and her clothes were torn and dirty. For the first four weeks of her therapy, she sat wordlessly pulling her hair. Finally Connie intervened. "You sit there and pull your hair and I know it's because you're absolutely furious. Now I want to know what in the hell are you so damn mad about?"[30]

"I want to scream," the patient answered.

"Go ahead and scream," Connie replied. The young woman screamed, then started talking again. Eventually she lost weight, began dressing nicely, and looked "just stunning," according to Connie.

Connie also saw what were then called "psychoneurotics," and her treatment seemed to help many of them. Yet she appeared eager to engage her patients in a hunt for someone to blame for their troubles. Manhattan psychiatrist Arthur Zitrin, a contemporary of Connie's, recalls seeing a woman patient who had previously gone to Connie for therapy and came out hating her family. Zitrin was disheartened that Connie seemed to have made no effort to help the woman understand her relationship to her parents, and instead simply urged her to blame and reject them.[31]

In 1953, the same year Connie set up her practice on Park Avenue, thousands of psychiatrists and psychoanalysts traveled to Los Angeles for the annual convention of the American Psychiatric Association. There, two doctors from Georgia read a gripping paper and showed a stunning film. The presentation concerned a patient of theirs, an achingly beautiful woman in her twenties who could split on command into three completely different personalities. The doctors gave one of these personalities the pseudonym Eve White, whom they described as demure, retiring, quiet, and rigidly conventional. A second personality, named Jane, seemed better adjusted. She was mature and "capable."

But it was the third personality who fascinated not just the psychiatrists, but eventually, all of America. Her pseudonym was Eve Black. Her primary doctor, a burly blond man named Corbett Thigpen, who practiced psychiatry as a profession and stage magic as a hobby, described Eve as "childishly daredevil" and "erotically mischievous," with "a touch of appealing sexiness."[32] Thigpen quoted Eve Black's recollections of taking over Eve White's body to enjoy a wild night on the town: "I go out and get a little polluted, [and Eve White] wakes up with the hangover and timidly wonders what in hell's made her so damned sick."[33]

Thigpen and Eve's secondary psychiatrist, Hervey Cleckley, used their work with Eve to challenge traditional psychological concepts. "The developmental integration of what we call personality," they told their audience, "appears to be a complex process of growth or evolution, a not-too-well comprehended unfolding of germinal potentialities." Eve's experience raised the question: "What is the real referent of this familiar term *personality?*"[34]

The mass media was bewitched. Rennie Taylor, a male science writer for the Associated Press, wrote an article after the APA convention which featured details about Eve Black, and it ended up in dozens of newspapers nationwide. "A demure, pretty brunette . . . turned into a dare-devilish, irresponsible creature in front of her doctor and later into a bright, agreeable, conscientious girl," Taylor wrote. "Eve Black went out with men casually, got a job as a night club entertainer, bought and charged expensive clothes. The third personality, called Jane, took the clothes back to the stores. Later Eve Black bought more clothes and had them altered so Jane couldn't take them back."[35] *Time* magazine covered Eve's case, too, with similar information about her wild misdeeds.[36] News spread that Thigpen and Cleckley had a book in press which would appeal to lay readers.

It would come out four years later, titled *The Three Faces of Eve*, and quickly become a bestseller, for good reason. Those multiple faces, after all, symbolized the biggest dilemma faced by American women in the 1950s.

Expelled from the workplace after World War II ended, they'd been pressured to settle in at home as docile housewives and mothers. Passively accepting this new domesticity recalled the joylessness of Eve White, while feeling dissatisfied and rebellious suggested the immaturity and immorality of Eve Black. Psychotherapy could integrate these conflicts, the new book suggested. It could turn a distressed woman—a split-personality woman—into a contented, responsible Jane.

Even if Connie missed the APA convention in 1953, she surely heard about Eve that year. Eve's multiple personality disorder was said to be the only case psychiatrists had heard of for decades. Connie knew that to be untrue. Her medical school mentor in Michigan, Dr. Robert Dieterle, was still in touch about the woman he had diagnosed with multiple personalities back in the 1930s. In this climate, and with this inside knowledge in her back pocket, Connie must have been alert to every possibility—particularly after the paper Thigpen and Cleckley presented at the convention was published in 1954 in a prestigious mental health journal.

In October of that year Connie's office buzzer rang. It was Shirley.

CHAPTER 8

THE COUCH

SHIRLEY DOUBTED THAT CONNIE WOULD remember her when she made her first visit to Park Avenue, but Connie knew her immediately and "was genuinely pleased to see me," Shirley wrote to Walter. As the two women sat and chatted, Shirley recapped her life since Omaha. "I think it is just wonderful all you have done—I always knew you had brains," Connie exclaimed. Shirley was ecstatic.[1]

She remembered how just a handful of psychotherapy sessions nine years ago had enabled her to keep going ever since. Of course, she'd suffered relapses of her longtime symptoms of hysteria: constipation, colds, sore throats, sinus trouble, headaches, nausea, weight loss, aching joints, painful menstrual periods, fatigue, depression, anemia, and times when she felt confused and unable to remember things. But now her former doctor was in New York! A half dozen more sessions might keep her nerves from ever acting up again. She booked a few weekly appointments and didn't tell Walter she was back in therapy. She had run into Dr. Wilbur by chance, she lied to her father.

Her sessions with Connie immediately veered in odd directions. Lying on the couch, Shirley talked about her teaching in the Midwest, her work at the Colorado mental hospital, and her current graduate studies. But Connie also talked about *her* life, and she offered to help Shirley fulfill her own professional aspirations. According to Shirley's letters to her father, Dr. Wilbur described her work with the Veterans Administration and talked of lecturing throughout the city and the world. She said she knew psychiatrists in charge of local mental hospitals for children, and she could give references if Shirley wanted to work in art therapy. Or if she wished to study psychology she could take classes at the New York College of Medicine. That would be easy, Dr. Wilbur said. She had studied psychoanalysis there and was working at a college-run hospital. She had connections.

Further, Shirley wrote, Dr. Wilbur was "doing some kind of research in the use of certain drugs and their effects on certain types of mental illnesses."[2]

Shirley's old crush on Connie came roaring back, along with her buried ambitions to be a doctor—a psychiatrist, she said, just like Dr. Wilbur. She was still finishing her masters degree in art education, and she'd been planning to get a Ph.D. Now she made a mental shift to medicine. Long ago her parents had told her she was too weak to go that route, too nervous. Dr. Wilbur disagreed. Shirley was strong and brilliant. More therapy would enable her to become a psychoanalyst.

Shirley nursed her new plan, turning inward and losing interest in Teachers College. By day she went to classes as usual, but by night she became nervous again for the first time in years. She lay in bed fantasizing, yearning, worrying, tossing with insomnia, exhausted when the sun came up.

She had started therapy thinking she needed only a few sessions.[3] But soon she wanted more. And more. On the couch she talked about her old feelings of loneliness, her simultaneous feelings of superiority and abject worthlessness, her puzzling body aches. To pay for the treatment, which cost $15 per hour, she wrote to her father and lied, telling him she needed more money for school. But after several sessions with Connie, the insomnia got worse and the clogging of her sinuses returned. So did the old menstrual pain.

To treat these problems, Connie wrote prescriptions for powerful, habit-forming drugs, many of which had just been patented in the 1950s and were being aggressively marketed by pharmaceutical companies.[4] To help her sleep, Shirley got tablets of Seconal, a highly addictive barbiturate. Taking it regularly and then trying to withdraw can cause anxiety, vivid dreams, and even hallucinations. Connie treated Shirley's menstrual pains with Demerol, an opiate related to heroin. It is extremely habit forming, with side effects that include light-headedness, confusion, and blacking out. Shirley also got Edrisal and Daprisal for her monthly pain. Both combined aspirin with amphetamines—now commonly known as speed, which if taken excessively can cause hallucinations and paranoia. Edrisal and Daprisal eventually proved so addictive that they were yanked from the market. But they were readily available in the 1950s, along with the narcotics and barbiturates Connie prescribed.[5] Soon Shirley was in her second semester at Teachers College, still managing to attend classes and complete her school work. But she spent her free time half zonked on mind-bending medications.

Weekends were especially difficult. Shirley was alone then, mulling over her problems, hating her dead mother and simultaneously pining for her. She wished she could see more of Dr. Wilbur, but Dr. Wilbur was too successful and important for a garden-variety neurotic like Shirley. Soon the therapy would come to an end. Dr. Wilbur had provided several hours of talk and a veritable medicine chest of pharmaceuticals. That was all she could do to help.

One day in late winter, during a therapy session that had begun routinely, Shirley surprised Connie by telling her about some bizarre "jams" she'd gotten into over the years. Sometimes, she said, she would "come to" in antiques shops, her mind a blank, facing dishes or figurines that were smashed into pieces. She could not remember breaking them, but to avoid trouble she would politely apologize and pay for the damaged merchandise. She told Connie she'd had $2,000 worth of these jams. Equally disturbing, she added, was that she sometimes found herself in strange hotels with no idea what city she was in. She would struggle to figure out her location, then catch a train or bus home.[6]

Astounded, Connie decided that Shirley was experiencing fugue states, and she told her about having treated that very condition in the first patient she'd had after getting her medical degree in Michigan. The patient back then had been a soldier who wandered off for long periods of time, then came to with no memory of disappearing.[7] Fugue states were no garden variety condition, Connie realized, and as she talked with Shirley she went back in her mind to wartime Omaha. She recalled the day Shirley walked into her office, charged to the window and pounded her hand on the glass. Back then Connie had thought this strange behavior was a hysterical seizure. Now she believed it was a fugue state. A person suffering from the condition would leave home for hours, days, or even weeks, acting like a completely different person. None of this behavior was intentional, for fugue states were caused by dissociation—the splitting of consciousness. They were a very rare form of hysteria. And from Connie's point of view, they were spectacular.

Ten days after receiving her fugue-state diagnosis, Shirley had a Tuesday morning appointment with Connie. Answering the doorbell, Connie found her patient looking different than usual and acting oddly. Shirley always came dressed in modest little suits with color-coordinated hats, gloves, and shoes. Today she wore only a skirt and blouse—no jacket, no accessories. Usually, she settled herself primly on the couch, and spoke softly and timidly. Now her movements were energetic, her voice loud and childish. Connie was confused.

"How are you today?" she asked her patient.

"I'm fine but Shirley isn't," was the answer. "She was so sick she couldn't come. So I came instead."

Connie did not miss a beat. "Tell me about yourself," she said.

"I'm Peggy!" the patient chirped.

She gave details. Peggy was a little girl with dark hair and a Dutch-boy haircut. Shirley couldn't stand up for herself, so Peggy took over her body to stand up for her. Shirley couldn't get angry, so Peggy got angry. Shirley was always scared and Peggy liked to have fun. When she gained control she went anywhere she felt like. Including to Philadelphia.

Peggy did not tell Connie about the game Shirley and her mother had played when Mattie would call her daughter Peggy, Peggy Ann, or Peggy Lou. When Mattie playfully used these names Shirley would act saucy and mischievous. Mattie would laugh and tell the "Peggys" how cute they were.

Peggy talked all during her therapy hour. Connie acted as though speaking with her were the most natural thing in the world, and she invited Peggy to come back three days later. Privately she hoped Shirley would emerge then for at least part of the time. Connie planned to gently break it to her then that she had a condition even stranger than fugue states.

The woman at the door on Friday had on a suit with all the accessories. It was Shirley, and she apologized for missing her last appointment. Connie told her she hadn't missed it—she had actually been in the office as someone else. But before Connie could introduce the subject of multiple personality disorder, Shirley changed the subject to something mundane. She kept it there until the end of the session.

Next week, the patient showed up with no hat or gloves. Still, she seemed poised and well mannered rather than loud and childish, like Peggy. "I'm Vicky," she announced to Connie—short for Victoria Antoinette Charleau. She did not mention that Vicky had been Shirley's imaginary playmate when she was a child. Her teachers had known about her, and as a child, Shirley herself had recognized Vicky as a daydream. But Vicky merely explained she'd been raised in Minnesota but her real family lived in Europe. Soon they would be coming to America.

Connie asked Vicky if there were any other people inside Shirley besides herself and Peggy.

"Oh yes!" Vicky answered. As a matter of fact, there were two Peggys. The real name of the one Connie already knew was Peggy Lou, but there was also Peggy Ann. Both were outgoing, though Peggy Ann was more aggressive.

Connie told Vicky that she and the Peggys were welcome to come see her on Park Avenue anytime. Anyone who happened to be using Shirley's body should feel free to drop by, she said.[8]

Vicky left, and Connie, flabbergasted, did the math. She'd known about multiple personality disorder for years, of course. Shirley Mason's case was stunning. She had a least four personalities, more than Connie had ever heard of. "This is one of the most outstanding cases of all time," she told herself. "It exposes what Freud called 'the unconscious.'" Curing a patient of multiple personalities would be the ultimate test of Connie's capabilities. As she recalled years later, she believed Shirley would make an excellent research project.[9]

Connie decided that she would have to psychoanalyze not just Shirley but Peggy Ann, Peggy Lou, and Vicky—yet no one had ever used psychoanalysis to dig into the mind of a multiple. No one had trawled for the dark traumas that must have caused such an extreme dissociation of memories and identity. Even Eve's doctor had touched only lightly on his patient's childhood history. The worst experiences he'd found were a time when Eve saw a man whose body had been cut into pieces in an accident, and a funeral she attended in which she had to touch her dead grandmother's face. Much worse things must have happened to Shirley, Connie surmised. Things as awful as the horrors of war that shattered soldiers. Things so bad that they fractured a child's mind into many pieces, many personalities.

Connie vowed to cure her patient no matter how much time it took. She would do it in her office, because Shirley deserved personalized, loving care, not warehousing in a crowded mental hospital.[10] She decided to see Shirley for three therapy sessions a week. Money was irrelevant. If need be, the treatment would be given on credit.[11]

At Shirley's next appointment she showed up as Shirley, and Connie broke the news that she had multiple personalities. Connie expected her patient to be horrified and frightened; instead, Shirley seemed curious, and even relieved to have "a bona fide condition." She rushed out to the library to read Morton Prince's 1905 book on multiple personality again.[12]

Within weeks of receiving her new diagnosis, Shirley was regularly presenting herself at Connie's office as Vicky or one of the Peggys. Then, one day, she appeared as a fifth person: a young boy named Mike. He talked about using carpentry tools to make things with his dad, Walter Mason.[13]

By now, Connie had noticed the difference between Shirley's multiple personalities and those of notables Miss Christine Beauchamp and Eve. Those women's alters had also been women—adults. But Shirley's were all children. Even Vicky, with her beautiful manners, told Connie she was only thirteen years old. Talking about her family, Vicky described having brothers and sisters in England, and loving parents there who one day would cross the Atlantic to rescue her from Minnesota. When Connie asked why she lived there, Vicky described herself as a caretaker for Shirley and the children, and she hinted at terrible secrets in the Mason family. She would not elaborate.[14]

Connie decided to use World War II–era narcosynthesis therapy to extract details. But before she went back to Shirley's childhood, she wanted to know what happened during the "fugues"—particularly a recent trip to

Philadelphia. She asked Shirley's permission to inject her with Pentothal. As an Adventist, Shirley was frightened of mind-bending drugs, but by the end of 1955 she reluctantly agreed to the treatment.

The first Pentothal session occurred in her apartment. As Shirley lay in her bed, Connie tied Shirley's upper arm with a tourniquet to make her veins pop out. Then she filled a large syringe with the chemical and plunged the needle into one of the veins. Shirley groggily became Peggy. In a little girl's voice, she talked of traveling to Philadelphia, checking into a hotel near Center City, and getting a yen for some new pajamas. She found a children's clothing store and bought a brightly colored pair. She put them on in the hotel, curled up in bed, slept well, and later awoke and did some sight-seeing. Then she turned back into Shirley and didn't know where she was.[15]

Connie turned on a tape recorder to capture the story. For years thereafter, she would inject Shirley, then push the "on" button of her reel-to-reel machine.

Almost all the tapes have since been destroyed. But some transcripts remain, together with the transcriptionists' accounts of how Shirley sounded while she was talking. One record of an early Pentothal therapy session suggests that Shirley produced torrents of what the old military psychiatrists had recognized as dreamlike, false-memory garble.

The transcript, from a recording made in 1955, indicates that Shirley had received prior Pentothal injections. Earlier, Peggy had told Connie she first appeared to Shirley at the age of seven, when Shirley was playing in a hayloft with a boy named John Greenwald. He had jumped onto an old cash register with a gun in it, Peggy added. The gun went off, shooting John and killing him. The horror of witnessing his death caused Shirley to dissociate. She disappeared mentally, and Peggy took over her body.[16]

Peggy's story was chilling, but it was fantasy. Dodge Center newspapers from the early 1940s and state death records in Minnesota indicate that John died when Shirley was seventeen years old, not a young child, and that she was not present at the gun accident which killed him. But Connie didn't know about these records. She assumed that Shirley's Pentothal-induced story was a real memory.[17]

Now, in the session memorialized in the transcript, Shirley trembled and screamed. "The people, the people!" she wailed.[18]

Who were "the people"? Had they abused her when she was a child? In earlier Pentothal sessions Connie had pressed for details but gotten none. Now she hoped Vicky would talk. She called for her, and Vicky's well-bred voice responded from the couch.

"Tell me about Peggy," Connie asked.

"She's always mad," answered Vicky. "She's mad at her dog because he won't listen to her, and he doesn't love her."

Unaffectionate terriers revealed nothing about mind-shattering trauma. Connie pushed on. Vicky offered another angle.

"Peggy thinks that she's a boy. She gets mad because she knows she isn't. She wants to get married when she grows up and she wants to be the boy . . . the man."

Connie changed the subject, still looking for abuse. During previous Penthothal sessions Shirley had said she was afraid of music. She said she hated her childhood piano recitals because when she made a mistake the audience laughed, humiliating her. Connie wondered if something much worse was involved. She asked Vicky why Shirley had such animus toward music.

"Because music is beautiful . . . and it's sad and nobody cares."

"Why should something beautiful hurt?" Connie asked.

Inadvertently or not, she had cued her patient she was looking for trauma.

"It's like love and love hurts," Vicki answered. "When people love you they hit you this way and this way with the knuckles and they slap you."

Trauma. Finally. But Vicky had more. Her voice began chugging like a locomotive, clacking faster and faster down a track of terrible injury.

"And they put flashlights in you and bottles out of little silver boxes and they put a blanket over your face and hold a light over. You can't breathe and it hurts and you kick and you can't move."

Connie was unaware that when Shirley was seven years old she had been terribly frightened by a tonsillectomy. She'd gotten the surgery in the home office of family doctor Otoniel Flores, and she'd been tricked into it. Walter and Mattie had lured her into the surgery room by telling her she was going to the Floreses' to visit their daughter Virginia. When Shirley arrived, Mrs. Flores, who was a registered nurse, beckoned her upstairs and told her to put on what she called "Dr. Flores's white shirt" so she could play. This strange demand made Shirley uneasy. Before she had time to think, she was grabbed and forced onto a table. She screamed.

Bottles of liquids lay nearby, and an old man, the town pharmacist, loomed over her. Other people held her down and looked in her throat with a light. The pharmacist slapped a cloth over her nose and mouth. She kicked and flailed, then she couldn't breathe—the cloth was soaked in ether. She thought she was dying. When she awoke her throat ached and she was still terrified, as well as enraged. She never forgot the experience.[19]

It would take years after the Pentothal session before Shirley, in her right mind and not dosed with mind-bending drugs, would tell Connie about her tonsillectomy. Now, when Connie heard about the flashlight, the silver bottles, the overpowering people, and the suffocating cloth, she assumed her patient had been raped as a child.

Who had done it? Probably Mattie Mason—after all, people with emotional problems had almost always been hurt by their mothers. But why would this mother commit such extreme horrors? Connie began to suspect that Mattie Mason was a paranoid schizophrenic.[20]

Connie tried to get more information from Vicky. But suddenly Vicky was gone and Peggy was lying on the couch with the Pentothal coursing through her veins. She screamed so loudly that Connie could not understand what she was saying, except for some repetitive phrases:

"The people! The people! The people! The door! The door right here!"

Peggy sprang up and lurched through the office, crashing into furniture and walls. She ran to the window and pounded. The glass broke. Her hand trickled blood.

"Wake up!" yelled Connie. "Wake up! Wake up! Wake up!"

Peggy kept screaming.

"Come on . . . wake up. Wake up."

She finally did. "Oh, oh, oh, what did I do?" she whimpered. "I was over by your window, wasn't I? Oh, I'm sorry. Did I do that?" Still high from the Pentothal, Shirley had bizarre sensations. The walls were laughing and moving. She sobbed hysterically.

Connie reassured her. Then she probed for additional crimes committed by the lunatic Mattie Mason. She told Shirley she wanted to speak with Vicky.

"Hi," Vicky said. Connie asked what Mattie had done to little Shirley. Vicky tried to help but was incoherent. "First it's one thing, then another. All the old feelings she used to crow about before."

And that garble was the end of the Pentothal session, at least as recorded in the transcript.

Connie was not discouraged. To get to the bottom of the atrocities committed against her patient, she would just have to do more work.

By summer 1955 Shirley had earned her masters degree despite being heavily drugged most of the year. Now, feeling both very sick and very ambitious, she dropped her earlier plans to get an art education doctorate and decided to work on becoming a psychoanalyst. She moved from her dormitory to a rooming house. To gain a foundation for medical school, she enrolled in a chemistry class at Teachers College. She was unemployed but picked up odd jobs painting posters for university events.[21] Otherwise she was a full-time "analysand," as patients in psychoanalysis are called by their doctors.

She confided to her friend Willie Price that she was in therapy, and Willie didn't laugh when she learned Shirley had multiple personality disorder. Not only did she accept the claim, but she asked if she, too, could see Dr. Wilbur as a patient. Soon she was in therapy, and she and Connie often discussed Shirley's amazing case. Willie moved into Shirley's rooming house and volunteered to observe Shirley and report on her alter personalities. She encouraged Shirley to eat, take her medicines, and dress warmly in cold weather.[22] When the Peggys appeared, Willie took notes.[23]

"*Oh, the noise and the pain*," read one of Willie's transcriptions of a day when "Peggy" lay on Shirley's bed, quaking and screaming for hours.

Take the pain away . . . the pain in my head and the music and the hands . . . Can't tell anyone about the music just remember and remember and remember . . . The people—all the people. I'm afraid . . . Take the knife and put it away! . . . All the people are dancing in the hall—all white—and the music . . . all the black boxes and all the white boxes—Take them away . . . my head hurts, it hurts, it hurts . . . I'll read what I want to read, I'll paint the way I want to paint . . . Got to find Dr. Wilbur. Mother won't let me . . . Don't want to get shot . . . the guns . . . I'm afraid of white—I'm afraid of nurses . . . All the nurses, all in white, stood around the table.

Amid the raving, "Peggy" jumped out of bed and crawled under the furniture. Once she cowered under a dresser for two days. Willie tried to coax her out but couldn't. She called Connie, who came to the apartment and got Peggy to come out.[24]

Shirley never acted like Peggy or the other alter personalities in front of anyone but her analyst and her roommate. Both doted on her. She loved only one, though: Connie.

Connie loved her back, without reservation. Besides the office therapy, she made regular house calls, even during evenings and weekends. Her colleagues probably did not know about her unorthodox visits. And they almost certainly were unaware she was injecting Shirley with Pentothal. She continued to give the shots in Shirley's own bedroom, with no medical backup if Shirley were to suffer a reaction from this potent barbiturate—if she stopped breathing, for instance.[25]

As rogue as all this treatment was, Connie felt justified. Shirley's disorder was so serious, and so little studied, that radical approaches were called for. The alternate personalities each required therapy, so Shirley needed many more hours on the couch than other patients did. And she needed to remember the horrors inflicted on her by her terrible mother. Pentothal and other barbiturates would relax her, softening the resistance. Benzadrine and amphetamines would also lift her spirits, bucking her up to recall Mattie's crimes.

Shirley did not argue with this regimen. Connie spent hours every week listening raptly to her problems, doling out encouragement, and offering to pay Shirley's tuition for pre-med courses. She asked Shirley for childhood photographs, and when she looked at them she saw Peggy's face in some and Mike's in others.[26] She read Shirley's teenage diaries, and she suggested that Shirley write daily, even hourly accounts of her feelings between therapy sessions.

Shirley had other reasons for doing as Connie said. For one, she burned with desire for her doctor to pat and hug her, and every time Connie did so, Shirley happily reported on it in her diary. "[C]ame up behind me and put hands on my shoulders with a little shake, and drew me close," she reported on November 4. And on November 18: "Reached over. 'Let me have your hand.'"[27]

Connie was also encouraging Shirley's artistic endeavors by acting as a dealer for her work. The walls in her Park Avenue home were hung with her patient's paintings. A visiting friend liked one and wondered if Shirley could do another. Connie negotiated the price: $85. She relayed the order to Shirley.[28]

Shirley was terribly grateful, and within a few days after the painting deal was executed, she walked into therapy as yet another alter personality. This one said she was tall and had brown eyes. Her name was Helen.[29] Connie recorded Helen on reel-to-reel tape. The next day, when Shirley showed up, Connie had a proposition:

"Would you like to earn some money?"

"That's a question?" Shirley joked rhetorically.

"I would like to have you collaborate with me on something," Connie answered. "I want to write a book about your difficulties and I would like you to help with it."[30]

Shirley was skittish at first. But Connie encouraged her by telling her she was talking to other psychoanalysts about her special patient.

One of these other doctors, Dr. Sandor Lorand, was an international leader in psychoanalysis and ran the psychoanalysis program at the State University of New York's medical school in Brooklyn. Connie had told him she was treating a brilliant young woman with multiple personalities who wanted to be a psychoanalyst. Dr. Lorand said the patient could attend his medical school. Connie told Shirley, adding that after she got her MD degree, Dr. William V. Silverberg—Connie's probable former analyst—would do Shirley's training analysis.[31]

In exchange for agreeing to do a book about her case, Connie said, she would pay for Shirley's medical school tuition and living expenses.[32] Shirley agreed to the deal; now she was a professional multiple personality patient. Later, she figured, she would get well and have new work, as a medical student, then a psychoanalyst. She was ecstatic.

She lay on her back and Connie pushed a needle into a glass vial of Pentathol. She pulled the plunger up. Shirley held out her arm.

By late winter 1956 Shirley had been in therapy for a year and a half. But instead of getting better, she was as sick as she'd ever been. She felt so depressed that she often couldn't finish her chemistry homework or make it to class. She told Connie about more fugue states. Once, after taking Willie to the bus station to go back to Arkansas for Christmas, she walked all night in the cold. Other times she traveled by herself to Altoona, Pennsylvania; White Plains, New York; and again to Philadelphia.[33]

It is hard to know how much these disturbing feelings and behaviors were Shirley's way of seeking more attention from Connie, and how much they resulted from the confusion she must have been suffering from being dosed with an ever burgeoning variety of medicines—apparently as part of Connie's research into the effects of new drugs on mental illness. Connie had recently added Dexamyl, another barbiturate-amphetamine combination, to Shirley's pharmacopeia.[34] As well, she gave her Equanil, an anti-anxiety pill more popularly known as Miltown. It had been put on the market in 1955, accompanied by great fanfare from pop media like *Newsweek, Time,* and even *Cosmopolitan,* which suggested that the decade's new crop of psychotropic pills could even cure female "frigidity," and help career women who were nervous about matrimony to make the decision to marry.[35]

When Shirley felt particularly depressed or anxious, she frequently doubled, even quintupled, her prescribed dosages of Daprisal, Demerol, Dexamyl, Edrisal, Equanil, and Seconal. And Connie added Serpatilin, a combination of a tranquilizer and the stimulant Ritalin, as well as Thorazine, a medicine originally prescribed to relieve nausea and the kind of pain Shirley experienced with her periods. Thorazine would later be recognized as a potent antipsychotic whose side effects, particularly at high doses, include restlessness, confusion, blackouts, and unusual thoughts and behavior.[36] With this powerful drug and all the uppers and downers, Connie also gave Shirley phenobarbital, another barbiturate, on top of her regular, intravenous doses of Pentothal.[37]

Connie's colleagues probably never learned of her extravagant medicating. Nor did they hear about another irregular treatment she gave Shirley. For house calls she carried a machine of the kind that many psychiatrists had used back in the 1940s. It came in a sturdy box the shape and size of a briefcase, with snaps and a handle. On the front were dials, meters, and on-off buttons, and one side had a hole for attaching a wire connected to two paddles. Connie would carry her apparatus to Shirley's apartment and climb in bed with her. She would clamp the paddles to Shirley's temples, twirl the dials, and press the buttons. Shirley's body would arch and crash with convulsions. Connie's gadget was an old electro-convulsive therapy machine she had retired years earlier. But she felt Shirley was becoming suicidally depressed, and Connie thought electroshock would help.[38]

It is quite likely that all the drugs and electricity addled Shirley, erasing her short-term memory, generating frightening phantasms, and causing blackouts. They also may have provoked new alter personalities.

Even so, Connie was relentless, administering Pentothal round the clock. Shirley complained she was getting these injections when she didn't need them. During a confrontation about this issue one morning in Connie's office, she went into a rage, ran to the window, and started pounding it—behavior typical of Peggy. Next thing she knew, she was sitting on the couch with Connie's arms around her. She wept as Connie held tight and told her, "You're just marvelous."[39] She felt better.

Her diary records one impromptu Pentothal treatment. She had taken a chemistry class in the early evening, and she described what happened afterward:[40]

"Checked out of lab, 7 to 7:30. Worked with Willie at Teachers College. Home by 9:45. Then Doctor called."

The diary described how Connie said she had "been thinking it over" and decided to do narcosynthesis on Shirley that very night. "But it's late," Shirley protested. "Germs and disease don't wait," Connie answered, adding that she would be at Shirley's home in seven minutes. She arrived at 10:15 and injected Shirley with Pentothal. The session lasted until midnight.

Shirley remembered nothing except falling asleep, then trying hard to wake up. "Who is Mary?" Connie asked when she was conscious again.

"My grandmother," Shirley answered. But according to Connie, another personality had appeared, named Mary. Besides Mary there were five others now: Peggy Ann, Peggy Lou, Vicky, Mike, and Helen.

Connie talked more about Mary, then about Peggy. She finally left at a quarter to one in the morning. Shirley lay in bed, dizzy from the barbiturates, half in and half out of her mind. She heard Willie walking outside her room. She thought it was her dead mother. She screamed.

A few days later, according to the diary, on a Saturday in February,

Connie and Shirley began a week-long marathon of daily Pentothal injections and shock treatment. Shirley reported it made her terribly sick and nauseated. According to Connie, Shirley's urge to vomit came not from the drugs and shock but from Shirley's traumatic past. "What are you trying to throw up?" she asked. "Mother?"

Shirley didn't answer.

On Sunday, Connie gave her more Pentothal, Shirley's arm became sore from the injection, and she spent Monday crying. Toward evening she had a "Peggy episode." Connie made a nighttime house call, bringing her syringes with her. On Tuesday Shirley went to Connie's for a therapy session and Willie came to the office to pick her up. Shirley got sick on the bus and later remembered nothing about the office visit or the ride home.

On Wednesday Connie administered phenobarbital. Shirley slept for two hours until Connie roused her and took her home. Again, she did not recall the trip. Next day Connie again injected Pentothal, as well as another barbiturate. Shirley got so nauseated and woozy that she couldn't walk to the bathroom; Willie had to carry her. Connie left Shirley's apartment, came back, left, came back, left, and came back. At the end of several hours Shirley began talking about her mother.

On Friday—again according to Shirley's diary—Connie came to the apartment three times. She "[g]ave Pentothal and shock, sustained release spansules of Phenobarbital," Shirley later wrote, using technical language which suggested she was already thinking of herself as a doctor. "Began to menstruate," she wrote about herself.

Saturday, Connie left town for a weekend trip to Michigan. She called Shirley as soon as she got home on Sunday, and next day she came to the apartment.

Peggy appeared during that visit, then disappeared. Shirley returned, and Connie informed her she had dissociated into her other personalities and "lost over a week" of her life. Connie put her arms around her amazing patient. She held her tight.

CHAPTER 9

ADDICTION

WITHIN TWO YEARS OF STARTING therapy with Connie in New York, Shirley had turned into a drug addict. Pentothal was her fix. She experienced pain and terrible forebodings when the needle first went in, along with strange, sickening smells and tastes. But as the potent barbiturate coursed through her veins she grew woozy and joyful. She opened wide up to Connie then, talking and talking—even about shameful things, such as masturbation, that she would otherwise never dare mention.[1]

Connie would keep the thick needle in place in Shirley's arm for hours, intermittently pushing the plunger to release more Pentothal. As she manipulated the syringe, she asked about Shirley's childhood and recorded the answers. Afterward, she would cover her with a blanket and let her sleep off the drug. Shirley would awaken hours later with no memory of what she'd done or said on the Pentothal.

At her next therapy session Connie would tell her how she'd acted, assigning proper names to each behavior. When Shirley had run around pounding her fists and cursing her mother for not letting her paint green chickens, Connie identified the complainer as Peggy. When she'd sat and chatted demurely, she was Vicky. Praying, reciting poetry, and warning about the Adventist end of the world earned her the identity Mary Lucinda—Shirley's dead grandmother's name.

While high on Pentothal, Shirley herself started to feel that she was remembering having recently spent time as different selves. "There were two people: Mary, and the one Willie previously referred to as the quiet one who doesn't know her name," she wrote in her treatment diary after recovering from a session with the needle. "Each knew what the other was saying and doing. They took turns talking, planning, buying, etc." One of the alter personalities, Shirley recalled, had even taken her old paper doll collection from childhood out of a cupboard and spread it on her bed.[2]

For two or three days after these injections Shirley often would feel peaceful and relaxed. She could take a chemistry test without shaking and hyperventilating, and instead of tossing and turning at night she slept like a rock. But she started to crave Pentothal. Even when she wasn't high she could taste it. Sometimes after receiving a dose, she wandered on foot through Manhattan talking to herself, and the next day she would feel so depressed that she would pop fistfuls of pills, then get jittery hands and diarrhea. She couldn't remember what she read in her chemistry books or heard in her lectures. Once she left a laboratory class in Manhattan and ended up in the Bronx without knowing how she'd gotten there.[3]

Despite Shirley's increasingly troublesome dependence on Pentothal, Connie was still convinced that narcosynthesis would return her to her early childhood and unearth the secret traumas that had split her mind. She pressed her patient relentlessly for more "memories." She sat on Shirley's bed, chuckling, as Shirley's cat batted its paws at the Pentothal injection equipment.[4] During this time she discussed other patients: the woman, for instance, who suffered an emotional crisis in the wee hours and kept Connie up all night. When Shirley asked if it was OK for one patient to hear about another patient, Connie said yes, if the patient doing the hearing was special, as Shirley was. "I don't deal with you like I do the others," Connie said.[5]

Still, Shirley could not remember trauma—nothing beyond her earlier talk of what probably was her tonsillectomy, and the "vaginal assaults" that could well have been a childish misinterpretation—a screen memory—of what Adventist enemas felt like. But this was old material, from the first months of therapy in the mid-1950s. Now years had passed, and Shirley's new "trauma" memories were pathetically trivial. Mattie Mason had been opinionated, Shirley told Connie. Mattie was pushy. She yelled when Shirley made a mistake practicing the piano. The therapy stalled.

Pentothal had seemed so promising at first, but now she was constantly depressed and anxious again—and begging for another injection. The veins in her arm often swelled with clots that threatened to cause a stroke or even death. It eventually dawned on Connie that Shirley was getting addicted. Connie decided Pentothal was dangerous and tried to stop administering it. A tug of war began around the addiction. As Connie tried to withhold Pentothal, Shirley frantically demanded more. She spent hours scolding, cajoling, and groveling, on the phone and in single-spaced letters.

"*[T]his morning I felt so depressed,*" one such letter to Connie began. It continued in a gush of entreaties and subtle suicide threats:[6]

You didn't explain why I could not have Pentothal today . . . I felt so confused . . . you said to take the Dexamyl . . . I said I had been taking more and more per day since Thursday and still I had dissociated and was so much more depressed . . . you said take the Demerol . . . I said I would almost rather take the whole bottle of Seconal . . . I felt rejection and denial . . . I know you are very, very busy, but you did not say, "Shirley I am just too busy to take time out to give you Pentothal" . . . The pain is now and the test and class is tomorrow . . . tomorrow is too late to take the Pentothal . . . I know you care . . . What have I done? . . . I am scared . . . I keep crying inside . . . I'd better take the Seconal and go to bed . . . I took half a Dexamyl and a fourth of a Demerol . . . I wrote four pages about how I felt.

Still Connie withheld Pentothal, and Shirley struggled to earn more injections. For a few weeks she stopped splitting into alters who knew nothing of each other's existence. Instead, she reported that she sometimes sensed the different personalities right by her side, and she understood they were elements of her own psyche, not people separate from her. Sometimes, she said, she had feelings that were not Peggy but merely "Peggyish." Connie was delighted, and in mid-1957 she pronounced Shirley "integrated"—cured of her multiple personality disorder.

But she still wouldn't give her Pentothal, and Shirley's integration disintegrated. Like a hydra, she sprouted additional alter personalities. Soon there were eight: the Peggys; Vicky; Mike; Mary; and now a sad eleven-year-old named Shirley Ann; a bookish teenager, Clara; and Marcia, a snooty student.[7]

In the midst of this proliferation of alter selvers, Walter traveled from Michigan to New York City to visit his daughter. Connie met with him and asked him a few questions about his deceased wife. Mattie, Walter replied with embarrassment, had always been "nervous," but he said he knew nothing about her physically abusing Shirley. Connie didn't inquire about sexual abuse—she seemed so convinced it had happened that she saw no point in asking. She sternly told Walter Shirley was sick and needed money for her psychoanalysis. Walter did not see any of Shirley's other personalities during the visit. But he promised to send her a hundred dollars a month, to cover her rent and phone bill.[8]

Almost four years had passed since Shirley first walked into Connie's office as an upbeat graduate student with nagging but bearable emotional problems. Now, after hundreds of hours of therapy and countless pills, shots, and machine-induced convulsions, she was a thirty-five-year-old junkie who spent most of her time in bed and who, when she did get up, checked her mail box for money from her father, or walked the streets muttering to herself. When Jean Lane called to say hello, Shirley sounded so drugged that conversation was difficult.[9] And her roommate, Willie, was a problem. On the one hand she watched out for the alters: Peggy Ann, Peggy Lou, and the rest. On the other hand Willie was possessive. She didn't like Shirley talking to other women. When Shirley was in bed, Willie sometimes crawled in and tried to grope her. Willie was a lesbian, and Shirley wondered if she was, too.[10]

But she was afraid to ask her psychoanalyst, who was co-authoring a book calling male homosexuality perverse and mentally disturbed. Connie also had opinions about lesbianism: It was usually caused by a domineering mother and a weak father, and it was unnatural and bad.[11]

Shirley twisted between Adventism and psychoanalysis; faith and science; barbiturates and Benzedrine; her male self, Mike, and her females Peggy, Vicky, and the rest. Almost four years had passed since she started therapy and she had entered a maze of multiplicity that fractured more and more as time went by. Dr. Wilbur had promised to make her better. Instead she felt much worse.

She agonized about what to do. In late spring she made a decision.

On a warm afternoon toward the end of May, 1958, she walked into Connie's office for her appointment. In her purse was a typed, single-spaced letter that ran to five pages.[12] At first glance it looked like the dream and self-analysis diaries she usually brought to therapy. But this one was different.

From the first paragraph, it was clear the letter was a confession of wrongdoing. It began with Shirley admitting that she was "none of the things I have pretended to be." She had tried before to tell Connie the truth but could not "hold out very long when you showed doubts, and an actual desire to believe I was . . . the fine things you admire."

"I am not going to tell you there isn't anything wrong," the letter continued. "But it is not what I have led you to believe . . . I do not have any multiple personalities . . . I do not even have a 'double' . . . I am all of them. I have been essentially lying."

The rest of the letter explained how Connie had misdiagnosed her, and how Shirley had abetted the error. Before coming to New York, she wrote, she had never pretended to have multiple personalities. She hadn't even done so years ago when she ran around Connie's office in Nebraska and pounded on the window.

"I was only distraught and desperate the day I acted 'like Peggy' . . . I had injured my hand as I sat cutting a linoleum block and dwelling morbidly on the fact you had told me the week before that you would be leaving Omaha sometime within the next year or so . . . I was trying to show you I felt I needed help."

As for her tales about "fugues" to Philadelphia, they were lies, too.

"I make certain successes in art or teaching or music or whatever, momentarily, but I cannot seem to 'take' any success and I then get the tremendous . . . and uncontrollable . . . urge to do some fool thing. The last few years . . . the fool thing turned out to be to disappear and make people think I had no knowledge of what I had done or where I had been. Quite thrilling. Got me a lot of attention."

Pretending only made her feel worse, but she was scared to come clean, she told Connie, afraid "you would be angry when you found out I had been untruthful and then you would not let me come to talk with you anymore." Shirley knew she had a problem. It wasn't "dissociations," but it was something extremely worrisome and debilitating. Now, she "very, very, very much" wanted Connie's help to identify her real trouble and deal with it honestly.

To do that, Shirley wrote, she and Connie needed to stop demonizing Mattie Mason. There was no denying her mother had been anxious and overly protective. It was true Shirley had started acting "funny" at age seven or eight, and her parents scolded her to try to cure her. Even so, the "extreme things" Shirley told Connie about Mattie—the rapes with the flashlights and bottles—were fictions. "I did not exactly make them up ahead of time," she explained about her invented accusations. Somehow, probably from working in a mental hospital and reading psychology books, she had known the symptoms of schizophrenia and retrofitted them to her mother in a way that sounded convincing. Too, Shirley wrote, her descriptions of gothic tortures "just sort of rolled out from somewhere, and once I had started and found you were interested, I continued." The details "made a good story," and the embellishments were lubricated with Connie's intravenous barbiturates. "Under Pentothal," Shirley noted, "I am much more original."

Having admitted she'd spent years lying to her therapist, Shirley had no idea how her beloved Dr. Wilbur would react. Would she curse her and refuse to ever see her again? Or would she forgive, and start the treatment and the friendship anew?

"I don't know what next . . . I guess that is up to you," Shirley concluded. With great trepidation, she handed the letter to Connie.

Connie read the letter without blinking. There was no way she was going to accept a recantation of her diagnosis of multiple personality disorder. Shirley was the most important patient in her entire professional career, not to mention in the history of psychiatry. Connie was discussing the case with psychiatry students and with world-famous doctors like Sandor Lorand. She was preserving the tape-recorded narcosynthesis interviews she was doing with Shirley, and speaking about the case at conferences. She had no wish to give all this up.[13]

"A major defensive maneuver," Connie told herself about the recantation.[14] Shirley's denial was simply a metaphor. What her letter really showed was that she was progressing in her treatment and, paradoxically, trying to avoid the harder work that lay ahead. She was ready to go deeper. But first she needed a good talking to.

Connie sat her patient down and launched into an argument that mixed psychoanalytic talk with mistaken, if common, ideas about the workings of Pentothal.

Mattie Mason, Connie insisted, was undoubtedly schizophrenic. She howled when she laughed. Her constant attempts to protect Shirley showed she actually meant her harm. Further, the Peggys hated Mattie. Connie knew this because they told her so while Shirley was under Pentothal. In fact, the Peggys and the other personalities spoke about many things which Shirley never remembered when the barbiturate wore off. So how could she claim it was she, Shirley, who'd done the talking? In point of fact, Connie insisted, it was Vicky, Peggy, and the other alters who came out under Pentothal.

Further, Connie said, Shirley's recantation letter was merely a form of "resistance." Resistance, she explained, was the ego's attempt to trick itself into thinking it didn't need therapy. But Shirley did need it, badly. She was denying now that she'd been tortured by her mother. This showed she really *had* been tortured.[15]

No matter that people injected with Pentothal recall little or nothing afterwards. No matter that Shirley's recantation letter, far from renouncing therapy, desperately pleaded for more. Sitting across from her doctor on this warm afternoon in May, Shirley understood that she could continue being a multiple personality and keep Connie in her life, or she could reject the diagnosis and lose her beloved doctor's therapy sessions, not to mention her friendship. The choice was hers, Connie implied.

Shirley went home, sat at her typewriter, and composed a new communication. This one blamed her earlier missive on a pesky, unnamed alter. "One Friday," Shirley wrote to Connie, "someone stalked into your office, imitated me [and] had a paper written about how she had now become well and was confessing . . . that it had all been put on. Well, you knew better."[16]

Connie instructed her secretary to schedule five sessions a week with Miss Mason. She started the Pentothal again.

Soon Shirley had two additional multiple personalities, and her "memories" about Mattie's torture were flowing. Each recollection was more chilling than the last. One had to do with Mattie marching Shirley to her father's carpentry workshop in a small garage next to the house, where Mattie bound her with rope, hung her upside down from the ceiling, and administered enemas. There also, she led little Shirley upstairs to a loft, stuffed her in a crib—a big storage container—full of grain, and left her there. Shirley was suffocating in the grain when, by chance, her father walked into the workshop and freed her. He assumed an adolescent boy, the town bully, had done the mischief. No one realized that schizophrenic Mattie had tried to kill her little girl.[17]

Connie didn't know that in Minnesota in the 1920s and 1930s, "cribs" were the size of silos, much too big to fit into Walter's tiny workshop. There was no corn or wheat crib anywhere near the place. Instead, Connie took Shirley's horrific tale as truth and fixated on it. She rummaged through her patient's mind for more horrendous abuse, doing most of the talking during the Pentothal sessions, and continually cuing Shirley and her "personalities" about what she wanted to hear.

Connie tape-recorded a session that occurred in late 1958. The patient was not Shirley but her alter Clara, and Clara was complaining that Shirley still was doing poorly in chemistry. She couldn't study because "her back hurts so."[18]

"I think her mother hit her on the back," Connie suggested. *"Do you remember?"*

"Stand up by the wall," Clara answered groggily. When Connie responded with an encouraging *"Yes,"* Clara continued this train of thought.

"Like when you kick?" she queried Connie.

Connie eagerly put two and two together: Mattie plus assault. *"When did mother kick her?"* she asked. *"When did mother kick her? When she was going down the stairs?"*

"Big girl," murmured Clara.

"Oh, when she was a big girl . . . And what else?"

"Throw the shoe at her."

"Yes," Connie reinforced the answer. *"Throw the shoe at her. What else?"*

"Throw the book."

"Throw the book. And what else?"

"She hit her and knocked her out and she fell down."

"Oh dear. What else? Standing up by the wall made her back hurt. Did her mother ever bump her or push her when she was standing against the wall, and bang that door in her back?"

The weapon was a broom with a *"big handle,"* Clara answered.

"*Yes!... That's it then,*" Connie responded excitedly. "*When you whack... right across the back and hit ... it hurts like the dickens for a long time afterward... Yes, yes it hurts. That's it. That's it.*"

With the "memory" of assault finally recovered, Connie told Clara, her back pain would disappear and Shirley would learn her chemistry.

But the back pain wasn't disappearing, Clara complained. Shirley still hurt.

Connie renewed her search for memories.

"What else?" she demanded.

When Clara kept silent, Connie switched from words to the one thing Shirley craved from her as much as Pentothal: her touch. "Here, turn over. Now, we'll make the broom handle, the book and the shoe all go away and instead we'll feel nice, soft hands." Connie stroked Shirley's body. "There. Doesn't that feel good?"

"You're so nice," Clara swooned. She recovered a memory of Mattie threatening to chop up her hands in a meat grinder.[19]

The pain did not go away, and neither did Shirley's problems with chemistry. She studied her textbooks, went to lectures, and promptly forgot everything she heard and read. The obvious explanation was drugs. Sitting in class, she was under the influence of far more mind-and-body-altering medications than were most patients in the intensive-care unit at a hospital. She told Connie she felt "weak all the time." And her back hurt.

"*Did mother hurt your back in the carpenter shop, too?*" Connie asked.

"*Yes,*" Shirley answered. And now she introduced a shocking element: her father had pulled the rope she hung from when her mother raped her with enemas. Walter was a new character in the horror story, and Connie was surprised. She knew Shirley loved her father. So she ignored this new accusation and refocused on Mattie.

"*Where did she hurt your back? Besides with the broom stick.*"

"*In the attic.*"

"*What did she do in the attic?... How did she hurt your back in the attic?*"

"*She put me in a trunk.*"

"*Oh, and she slammed the trunk lid on your back? Were you afraid when you were shut up in the trunk?*"

"*It was dark in there... I was afraid I couldn't breathe... afraid...*" Shirley's speech halted, became garbled. The very word "afraid" triggered loud sobbing. Suddenly another voice took over.

Water, water everywhere,
And all the boards did shrink.

Startled, Connie realized Shirley was performing Coleridge's "Rime of the Ancient Mariner," just as she had recited it as a child with her mother in the sunroom in Minnesota. Connie chimed in:

Water, water everywhere,
Nor any drop to drink.

Shirley next took up "Invictus":

Out of the night that covers me,
Black as the pit from pole to pole,
I thank whatever gods may be
For my unconquerable soul.

Eventually Shirley ended up in a hospital in Harlem, not for multiple personality disorder treatment but to break her of her barbiturates addiction.[20] She lay in bed thinking about her current situation. All her life, she realized, she had put her troubles into divine hands, but lately she had turned to a psychiatrist and her drug. Now God had taken the drug away and was punishing her, even as her roommate, Willie, was urging her to terminate therapy because Connie was manipulating her.

Instead of heeding the warnings of God and Willie, however, Shirley left the West Side and found a tiny place across town where she could live alone, just a few blocks from Seventy-seventh and Park Avenue. Connie helped with the move. She paid the deposit on the new apartment and showered Shirley with gifts: old rugs and drapes from her office, a seven-foot Christmas tree, a fur-trimmed winter coat, an electric frying pan—even a cat.[21] And once, when the rent was overdue, Connie fronted Shirley the money. "You can pay me back," she said, "as soon as your father's check comes."[22]

Shirley knew she could give up Pentothal. She could give up her roommate, too, and even something of Adventism. But she could not give up Dr. Wilbur.

CHAPTER 10

CLINICAL TALES

WHILE SHIRLEY SLOGGED THROUGH ENDLESS therapy with Connie on the Upper East Side, Flora was busy freelancing across town for women's magazines, at first churning out pieces such as "Vitamins Can Help You Live Longer."[1] By the late 1950s she was tired of this apprentice fare and eager to write articles that would connect her with the famous and the powerful. In late 1959, she contacted the office of Vice President Richard Nixon, and asked if she could spend a week with Nixon's mother.

The Republican Party was planning to run Nixon for president, and the article Flora proposed was "My Son: Richard Nixon." It would use seventy-five-year-old Hannah Nixon to characterize her son to women in a "very warm" and "persuasive" way. Nixon's people approved and Flora went to Hannah's stucco house in California. Hannah was a quiet Quaker woman who prayed in front of Flora and drove her 1946 Chevrolet to the store for groceries. All the while she talked about her son Richard while Flora took notes.[2] Then Flora wrote the piece for *Good Housekeeping*.

"Many days I had nothing to serve but cornmeal,"[3] Hannah told Flora, describing a period when the Nixon family was financially strapped. She added that one of Richard's brothers had died of encephalitis when Richard was young, and another succumbed to tuberculosis. Richard's character had been forged by these adversities. As a teenager he attended church four times a week. He was always close to his mother. She never heard him swear. Though he was vice president and could eat all the fancy food he wanted, Hannah served him cherry pie and rump roast, his favorite foods, when he came home to visit.

Did this sweet, all-American mom think her good boy should be President? "If that's what he wants—and I think he does—I hope he gets it,"[4] she answered humbly. On that campaign note Flora ended her article. It came out in June 1960, a few weeks before the Republican convention, and it was chock full of the "overtly favorable corn" Nixon had told advisors his campaign needed from "a good article on my mother."[5]

Soon Flora got an assignment from *Family Weekly* for an article about the wife of John F. Kennedy's running mate. "Lady Bird Johnson: What Kind of Second Lady?" the resulting piece was titled. After Kennedy defeated Nixon, she wrote, for *Good Housekeeping* again, a piece called "What Jackie Kennedy Has Learned from Her Mother." (Answer: How to be tactful and elegant. How to compete in horse shows.) Then Kennedy was shot and Lyndon Johnson became President. Flora followed with "Mrs. LBJ: Our 32nd First Lady" in *Cosmopolitan*, and "Ladybird's Secrets of Successful Outdoor Entertaining." (Those secrets were barbecues and garden parties. "And what Lady Bird can do at the White House or the L.B.J. ranch for 400 to 500 guests, *you* can do for 10 to 20.")[6]

The Johnsons loved these apolitical articles and Flora loved that they loved them. She basked in the glow of the famous, political loyalties be damned. One day she was in Congress gathering prized dessert recipes from the wives of liberal men in power, while the next day she ghost wrote "What Women Should Know about Conservatism, by Senator Barry Goldwater." ("Heartfelt advice to his daughter—and to every woman—on right thinking and right living in a world she must help to manage.") She didn't get much money for that piece, but she got a chance to have lunch with Goldwater. That was pay enough.[7]

At age thirty-seven Flora lived in Manhattan with her parents. She was single and childless—a spinster. She hardly fit the profile of a *Ladies' Home Journal* reader but no matter. In the 1950s all kinds of writers freelanced for the women's magazines. The pay rates in those days were breathtaking by today's standards. *Redbook* offered $1,750 for an article. At *Cosmopolitan*, $2,000 was not unusual. A cover story for *McCall's* could fetch $4,000.[8] In

113

today's dollars that equals $32,000. With only three or four pieces a year, a women's magazine freelancer could live it up in Manhattan or buy a house in the suburbs and comfortably raise a family.

For writers who didn't mind hustling, freelancing was great fun. Reams of carefully thought-out story proposals were often turned down before one was accepted, but the preliminary wheeling and dealing with an editor—usually a male—often happened at elegant bars and restaurants. Lunches on the magazine's expense account at the Algonquin, drinks at '21'—these were the perks for a freelancer in New York. Travel was often required for a story, and the magazine footed the bill. Writers of both sexes were eager to pen articles, even for female readers. In fact, most freelancers for the women's magazines were men.[9]

The magazines were filled with pictures and articles that reinforced the gender divide between men and women during the Cold War. Ads showed housewives in high heels and white gloves stroking washing machines. In one typical piece, a male obstetrician described a typical work day with the "girls"—his word for his patients. One, a mother of three small children, was accidentally pregnant again. She didn't know how she would cope with a fourth baby, and her pregnancy was causing her to vomit nonstop. The obstetrician told the woman's husband her illness was all in her head, but he seemed confused by the diagnosis. The doctor shrugged. "Will men," he asked himself rhetorically, "ever really understand how different women are from men?" He prescribed a day in the hospital for the vomiting woman, "away from house chores and children." He was sure she would recover "miraculously."[10]

Willy Schreiber was proud of his daughter for making herself into the writer he'd never dared become. He helped when she worked on articles, editing her grammar and taking pages of notes for her at the New York Public Library. Then, in 1958, Willy checked into the hospital for minor surgery. In a freak outcome, he expired on the operating table.

His death made Flora feel dead.[11] At age forty-two she began mourning as deeply for Willy as she had eight years earlier for her "almost husband," Gene. O'Neill had been her lover, but Willy, Flora wrote shortly after he died, was her brother, her companion, and her audience. He had realized himself through her, and she struggled to keep him alive by realizing more. She moved herself and her newly widowed mother into a smaller apartment, installing twin beds in the single bedroom. And she went back to full-time teaching. That would have been job enough for most people, but Flora's mind and body were running on nerves and a desperate urge to tend her father's memory. In addition to the teaching, she dove deeper into freelancing.

It was getting harder, however. American magazines still looked shiny and lively, but by the early 1960s writers like Flora were sensing trouble. With television's exploding popularity, more and more people were staring at screens instead of turning pages. Big corporations like car manufacturers were pulling their advertising dollars out of print and spending them on the airwaves. Magazines were bleeding ad pages and readers, and editors scrambled to balance budgets by retooling audiences. Their efforts were creating "upheaval," according to the Society of Magazine Writers in 1961.[12]

At meetings of the Society, Flora heard colleagues fret that inflation was rising but freelance rates were flat. Worse, publications were folding, and the staffs of those that survived were writing articles themselves instead of hiring outsiders like Flora. "There is a shrinking market for the freelance magazine writer," Society member Alvin Toffler warned at an early-1960s meeting.[13]

The changes were severe. Editors at *Good Housekeeping* were asking for celebrity profiles. *Cosmopolitan* had once featured articles such as "Why Keep Paroling Sex Offenders?" Now it preferred "unusual first-person pieces." *Coronet* had concentrated on modestly informative pieces like the health-and-science article "Goodbye to Rabies." By 1960 the magazine was in trouble and its editors wanted "warmth of style rather than reporting."[14]

While these changes were taking place, a speaker at a Society for Magazine Writers meeting cautioned members to "expect a decline in editorial integrity over the next year or two as editors and publishers, hungry for the advertising dollar, sell their souls for space."[15] Despite the warning, some writers sold their own souls. They started injecting fiction into their work and passing it off as fact.

The pioneer of this Faustian development was a Manhattan woman named Terry Morris, whose son, Dick, would later serve as a Republican Party strategist, then flip to advising Bill Clinton when he was president, and flip again to become a conservative television pundit. Terry Morris had started her career in the 1940s as a novelist and short story writer, then switched in the early 1950s to doing freelance journalism for women's magazines. Her specialty was "as-told-to" articles, including "I Was a Crooked Tax Official," "We Bought a Black Market Baby," and "I Gave My Son Away." By 1960 she was vice president of the Society for Magazine Writers.[16]

"I have never permitted myself to become too fettered by the 'facts'!" Morris cheerfully wrote in *Prose by Professionals*, a guidebook to magazine writing that she edited in 1961. "Frequently, I take considerable license with the facts that are given me and manipulate them, as a writer of fiction does."[17] Morris notified her interviewees in advance that she was making things up about them. Most approved, and when they heard Morris's falsehoods from naïve fact checkers who phoned them to review the copy, they claimed everything was correct. No editor was the wiser.

Morris spun whole stories from her imagination and populated them with pretend men and women. She called the results nonfiction. For "We Bought a Black Market Baby," she lolled on a deck one summer in a bathing suit, keeping one eye on her son and the other on law journals about people prosecuted for selling infants. From this legalistic material, Morris later confessed, she "conjured up a married couple who had vainly tried to have a baby, bearing much in mind that their ages, education, place of residence and occupations suited that phantom which every magazine creates for itself—their own unique readership."[18] The fictional story was touted by *McCall's* as true.

Betty Friedan was a freelancer and a member of the Society for Magazine Writers; she was also finishing a book that would soon be published as *The Feminine Mystique*. In the same year that Morris was pushing prevarication, Friedan was advising fellow writers "never to make up a quote or case history," because "[r]eal people and their own words are much more powerful."[19] That Friedan issued this warning suggests that lying was already widespread in the industry.

Flora Schreiber and Terry Morris had a collegial relationship—Morris once invited the actress Helen Hayes to her home, for instance, where

Flora interviewed her for a freelance article she was working on.[20] Flora had a chapter in *Prose by Professionals*, with tips on how to win article assignments from editors. In 1961, she decided that she would do "as-told-to" pieces about attractive, well-spoken people with emotional problems. To find them Flora contacted Mel Herman, a former ad man who was now secretary of the National Association of Private Psychiatric Hospitals. The organization's members ran luxury institutions with big trees, lush lawns, and good meals for their mentally ill occupants—places with gentle names like Charter Oak Lodge, Northside Manor, and The Brattleboro Retreat. Many of their directors were eager to talk to the media. They knew publicity was good for their reputations, and it was scot-free advertising for their exclusive sanitariums. Herman's job was to introduce these medical directors to journalists.[21]

To help Flora's foray into mental health writing, Herman lined up meetings with psychiatrists like Holocaust refugee Dr. Lorant Forizs, head of a private hospital on the Gulf Coast of Florida. While New York shivered in winter slush, Flora luxuriated under palm trees, interviewing a beautiful young schizophrenic woman and her mother whom she called "Norma" and "Claudia." The resulting article was perfectly titled for a women's magazine suffering from marketing angst: "I Committed My Daughter." It came out in early 1962 in *Cosmopolitan*. Much of the dialogue in the story was cheesy and obviously made up. But Norma and Claudia really did exist—Flora conducted careful correspondence with them to make sure she got her facts right when she wrote her piece, and she felt that her work was well within the bounds of journalism ethics[22]—at least on this assignment.

Then Mel Herman introduced her to Dr. Murray Bowen, a psychiatrist at Georgetown University and a pioneer in family therapy. Dr. Bowen served as the male authority for another psychiatry article Flora wrote for *Cosmopolitan*.

In this piece, the troubled characters were a public relations executive named Henrietta; her husband, Stephen; and their daughter Ellen, who had repeatedly been hospitalized for her paranoid fears that, for instance, the family's phone was tapped. In family therapy, according to Flora's article, Henrietta learned she was "overadequate" as a wife and mother. Stephen realized he was "passive." As for Ellen, she suffered from "overattachment to her mother." These problems had rendered her insane. The family's therapist summed things up by asking, rhetorically, "Is the patient schizophrenic, or is the family schizophrenic?"[23]

That therapist was supposedly Dr. Murray Bowen. But Henrietta, Stephen, and Ellen probably never existed. Among Flora's papers at John Jay College is correspondence with Bowen about his theories of family therapy, and some letters talking about the *Cosmopolitan* story. But none mention any family in therapy. Nor is there an iota of discussion about how a particular mother, father, and daughter might have felt about appearing in a magazine, or what they thought of the work in progress.[24]

The Henrietta-Stephen-Ellen trio appears to have been invented by Bowen. They were characters in what psychiatrists call a "clinical tale"—a fiction pieced together from dribs and drabs of various bona fide cases. Ever since Freud's day, clinical tales have been a popular way for psychiatrists to tell each other stories about patients and treatment. The result is often metaphorically true, yet factually as false as a fable by Aesop.

But Flora was a journalist, not a psychiatrist. She was supposed to interview people in order to tell their stories—or at least make it clear that she was getting her information indirectly. She failed to warn her readers that she had spoken only with Dr. Bowen and could not verify that Helen and her parents existed. Meanwhile, Mel Herman, her liaison to the psychiatrists, assured clinicians that if they worked with Flora they wouldn't have to tell her about actual people.[25]

The pop psychology articles she wrote with Herman's help were big hits with the editors at *Cosmopolitan*, and Herman decided to direct Flora to another psychiatrist, one who was not a man but a woman. Her name was Dr. Cornelia Wilbur.[26]

Before Flora called Connie for details, it's possible she put out feelers among her psychiatrist contacts in Manhattan to learn who this woman doctor was. She might have heard that Dr. Wilbur enjoyed a tad of celebrity among her colleagues. Everyone knew that one of her patients was the actor Roddy McDowall.[27] On television he was a regular on the sci-fi thriller *The Twilight Zone,* and in 1960 he starred in the Broadway musical *Camelot,* where he belted out pieces like "The Seven Deadly Virtues."

"I find humility means to be hurt," McDowall sang lustily onstage. "It's not the earth the meek inherit—it's the dirt!" Connie adored that line. McDowall adored her. He enjoyed telling friends Dr. Wilbur was his psychoanalyst. She told people, too.

Flora was forty-four years old when she met Connie, with a voice like a loudspeaker, dark painted lips, and a body beyond zaftig—her waist was disappearing and she'd taken to adorning her boxy shape with big capes. Connie, meanwhile, was fifty-four, tall, still regally built, and had begun dying her graying hair as red as Lucille Ball's. But she sounded nothing like the *I Love Lucy* star. Connie's voice was soft, weighty, and flinty all at once—a voice for the couch but also for radio and TV.

When the two first talked, Connie said nothing about Shirley. Instead, she told Flora about a new book she'd co-authored with several other therapists. Its title was *Homosexuality: A Psychoanalytic Study*,[28] and it was nine years in the making by the time it was published in 1962. In over three hundred pages it expounded the authors' theory that male homosexuality was an illness generated during childhood, in the home. The data showed that the cause was boys' parents—usually their mothers.

The most dramatic finding was that men could be "cured" of their homosexuality. After therapy with psychoanalysts like Connie, the book boasted, 27 percent of patients became "exclusively heterosexual."[29] This was an amazingly large "cure" rate, and Connie aimed to gain some laurels.

Of course, *Homosexuality: A Psychoanalytic Study* was grotesquely unscientific—"a joke," as a former president of the American Psychiatric Association would call it years later. Though they were in Manhattan and could easily have found men who were happy as homosexuals, the investigators studied only people who were seeing psychiatrists. Of the 106 gay research subjects, twenty-eight were schizophrenic, thirty-one were diagnosed as neurotic, and forty-two were said to have character disorders. Using this very limited sample, Connie and the other researchers had concluded that all gay men were emotionally disturbed. To make things worse, some could be identified in the book. One was Roddy McDowall. From a series of details in the text, it was clear he was "Case 129."

Case 129, according to *Homosexuality*, had a father who did maritime work and a mentally ill mother who pushed her young son into voice lessons and show business. As the son got older, he told his mother he was gay, and in response she brought men to the house and invited them to bed down with her boy. Eventually he moved far away, found success in show business, and fell in love with a promiscuous older man who was a raging alcoholic. When this man called off the homosexual affair, Case 129 "collapsed," emotionally. He consulted a woman psychiatrist. [30]

The public knew that Roddy McDowall's father had worked on ships. They know his mother had pushed him into voice lessons and Hollywood, and that he'd later moved to New York and found success in show business. What McDowall never talked about openly was that he was gay and that after arriving in New York he'd begun an affair with the charismatic, bisexual actor Montogmery Clift, who was eight years his senior and a raging alcoholic. When Clift called off the affair, McDowall tried to kill himself. These facts did not become widely known until after McDowall died in 1998.

But to anyone paying attention in 1962, when *Homosexuality* hit the stands, it was easy to see that McDowall had been outed as gay by Connie and her coauthors.

Flora may not have noticed. Regardless, she unquestioningly accepted the book's claims about curing homosexuality, and she pitched a story to some magazines. *Cosmopolitan* assigned an "as-told-to" piece about a mother with a young homosexual son who was eager to help him go straight. Flora asked Connie for a clinical tale from her practice.

The best Connie could offer was Case 129, and Flora was flummoxed. The hero of that story was an adult; she needed an adolescent. In addition, she wanted a mother who was flawed but not a moral and psychological basket case. Case 129 was no good.

So flora made up her own clinical tale. First she turned Case 129 back into a teenager. Then she christened him Don. Next she had Don sobbingly confess one night to his mother, "Eve," that he had a boyfriend. Don didn't want to be gay. "Mother, I'm afraid," he implored. "Help me." [31]

The make-believe Eve obligingly sent Don to see Dr. Wilbur, then Eve found her own therapist to help with her problem. The psychiatrist told her Don was afraid of girls because she smothered him. She agreed that she'd been a bad mother because she refused Don a bicycle when he was young, and she'd taken him with her to the beauty salon. She confessed they'd shared a bed when they traveled for his performances.

According to Flora, Dr. Wilbur said Don might recover from homosexuality. "He is very young," she reassured Eve. "He wants to change." Don did improve. He started visiting the home of a girl named Ellen. One night they listened to symphonies by Wagner, and Don later told his parents that "Ellen was coming closer and closer. I drifted as one floats on a wave."[32]

He was still gay, but Eve swooned with hope.

A *Cosmopolitan* staff editor was disgusted by the obvious artifice and penciled derisive comments on Flora's draft: "Oh come on!" "Ugh!" "I still don't understand why he was homosexual. I can't believe boys become fairies just because they have possessive mothers."[33] Despite the silliness of the piece, *Cosmopolitan* scheduled it for a special, upcoming "Women and Immorality" issue. Among other articles were "Why VD Is on the Increase," "The Life of a Kept Woman," and "Case History of a Demoralized Town," about prostitution in Texas.

One afternoon just before press time, Flora was summoned to *Cosmopolitan*'s offices on Fifty-seventh Street. When she got there she was informed that her piece was not acceptable. Eve, the homosexual boy's mother, was overly intelligent, and her son, Don, seemed too sophisticated. The editors and printers ordered Flora to do an immediate rewrite. She sat down and worked as fast as she could.[34]

The "Women and Immorality" issue was on the newsstands by January 1963, featuring "I Was Raising a Homosexual Child, as told to Flora Rheta Schrieber."[35] The piece had undergone radical surgery. As a result of Flora's rewrite, Don's awful secret was revealed not while he sobbed to his mother one night, but after police arrested him in Central Park for hugging another male. As in the earlier version, Don revealed he had a boyfriend, and he did therapy with Dr. Wilbur. Eve, however, now realized she'd dominated Don because she got no attention from her husband, Arthur. At the end of the piece, Don and his boyfriend broke up and Don turned definitively straight.

"I think it's going to be all right now," he assured his mother.

"Bunch of guys're going to the movies tonight," his heterosexual brother said. "Wanna go?"

"Sure," said Don. "I might bring a date. Being with girls is a lot more comfortable than the other thing. I never really wanted to be that way."

Finis, except for two photos accompanying the article. Each showed the same limp-wristed youth in a man's shirt and jacket, with slicked-back hair, gleaming lips, and deep, sulking eyes. Each was the same model, a young woman in drag.

Connie was delighted with the article. Years later she would tell people that before she worked with Flora, she'd had difficulty with reporters "leaving things out or changing the meaning." But Flora "had gotten things right" Connie said.[36] In *Cosmopolitan* she'd "written everything absolutely correct." Connie was so pleased that she contacted Flora about working together again. The new project she proposed was a huge one, a book. It would be about an astounding patient Connie had been treating for years, a woman with sixteen multiple personalities. If Flora wanted to, she could speak with her.[37]

A few weeks later, the three women met for dinner in an Upper East Side restaurant that Shirley thought was "swanky." She couldn't stop worrying as she ate her meal. Was she placing her elbows in the right place at the table? Holding her fork correctly? Using the proper spoon? This was Manhattan, where everyone had fun and made deals in nice restaurants. But Shirley hadn't been in one in years. It had been so long that she feared she'd forgotten her manners.[38]

She needn't have worried. Flora was struck by Shirley's shyness, fragility, and extensive knowledge of poetry. She was a dead ringer for Emily Dickinson, Flora told herself, charmed.[39]

She would consider writing a book, Flora said. But even if she opted to do so, she would not be able to start until a cure was effected—until Shirley's sixteen alters were all "integrated" back into one. Flora needed to wait because a book about a woman with multiple personality disorder would never sell unless it had a happy ending. Connie guaranteed a happy ending sometime in the future. Good, Flora replied, because currently she was very busy. On top of all her freelance magazine writing, she was about to start a new teaching job at a city college, and she needed time to settle in. She couldn't begin a book now. She would be ready in 1965.

Shirley would also be ready in 1965, Connie predicted.

Shirley went back to her apartment to wait.

There was nothing else for her to do. She had started graduate school with thousands of dollars in savings. Now her money was depleted and she was too ill to work except occasionally, when she picked up pin money by stitching doll clothes in a sweatshop run by a toy company. Her main "job," however, was the fifteen to seventeen hours she spent being psycho-analyzed each week, and the fourteen to sixteen she slept each day as a result of the treatment. Her health seesawed. Some days her sinus trouble disappeared and she felt relaxed. Her appetite got so good that her weight waxed—from barely ninety pounds to a hundred and eight, she wrote her father and stepmother, complaining cheerfully that her face was getting round.[40] Other times she had such severe anxiety attacks that she had to pop pills and go to bed. "I have a way to go with Dr. Wilbur," she wrote to her father and stepmother in early 1962.[41] She was entering her eighth year of analysis with no end in sight.

She had a baby doll in the new apartment to keep her company, a little girl with red hair whom Connie had encouraged her to buy. Brenda, Shirley named the doll, and she busied herself with sewing Brenda's clothes—fancy dresses, cozy pajamas, and coveralls to wear in Central Park. She took Brenda there and put her on a bench to watch "the other children" play. At home, she held her in her lap to enjoy the kiddie shows on television. She sat Brenda at the kitchen table and spoon fed her while eating her own breakfast. She put the doll near her while she painted with oils and water colors, explaining her technique as she went along. At night she fluffed the bed covers and read to Brenda from books of her favorite children's stories. One followed the life of "Lonely Lottie," an only child who passed her time in solitary contemplation of nature. But another hero was happy and going places: "The Little Engine That Could" was his name. Shirley read that story over and over, and sometimes, after Brenda's eyes were closed, she shut the book and penned greeting cards to Dr. Wilbur.[42]

"Shirley, Inc.," she signed the cards, poking gentle fun at her multiple personalities, yet hoping against hope for their literary and marketing success.

CHAPTER 11

CONVALESCENCE

B Y 1962 SHIRLEY HAD RUN up over $30,000 in psychoanalysis bills.[1] If she'd been working as a teacher at the time, that amount would have equaled six years of salary. Yet Connie expected no payment until the book about Shirley and her multiple personalities came out—the book Shirley had agreed to collaborate on seven years earlier in exchange for the therapy.

Nearly four decades after this period in the two women's relationship, in the early 1990s, the American Psychiatric Association would publish a long list of ethics rules. Among them: psychiatrists should never "make exceptions" for a patient by altering treatment costs, creating unusual treatment schedules, or engaging in extensive gift exchange. Nor should they engage in business deals. Nowadays, such misbehavior can trigger disciplinary hearings and the yanking of medical licenses.[2]

Ethics rules were not so clearly codified for psychiatrists when Connie was treating Shirley. Even so, Connie most likely would have been disciplined if her colleagues had known she was giving a patient free treatment, clothes, a house pet, rent money, and even furnishings from the apartment where the patient's analysis was taking place. The psychiatry community would also have been shocked to know that part of Connie's treatment of Shirley involved having the patient work for her.

The job involved secretarial duties, dog walking, and care for a family member. To do this work Shirley went into Connie's home at all hours, unannounced—she even had her own key. "Spent Sunday at Dr. W's office helping her sort out and file papers and typing letters from the Dicta-phone," she proudly wrote home in 1962.[3] In another letter she described working "mornings from about 9 to 2 in Doctor's office . . . I was supposed to make new files for the new patients and put her notes and case histories in them." While doing the job, she read the records of psychiatric patients such as Roddy McDowall.[4]

Connie even employed Shirley as a companion for her husband's el-derly mother. "I was of course very, very busy," Connie would recall years later about a day when she had no time to go with her mother-in-law to a flower show. She asked Shirley to take Mrs. Brown. "She said she would love to," Connie continued. "And Mrs. Brown found her absolutely enchanting. Later she said to me, 'You don't mean to tell me that that girl *needs* a psychiatrist!'"[5]

Shirley often spent whole days in her doctor's orbit. Mornings she walked the dogs. Early afternoons she went to libraries to do psychiatry research for Connie. Later she returned to Park Avenue to walk the dogs again. Then she had a psychoanalysis session that frequently lasted two or three hours. It would be nighttime before she got back to her own apartment.

Shirley didn't complain. "It is good to feel needed and worthwhile," she wrote. "When I am not busy and am alone I feel so worthless."[6] In a note to Connie, she told her that "I love you, I'd do anything for you."[7]

She took to staying overnight at Connie's when she and her husband went out of town. In a letter to her stepmother, Shirley described how she once "took my pajamas, a sheet and pillow slip and light weight white cotton blanket" to Connie's "and slept on her couch." "I left a note on her living room door, where she'd come in about midnight," Shirley added, "telling her I was in the office." Shirley needn't have worried that Connie would disapprove of this Freudian slumber party; the next morning she found "a note slipped under the door." "By all means okay," it said. It was signed, "Dr. Connie."[8]

The two women went for weekend jaunts. Connie often drove to Brook-lyn to get her hair done, and she would take Shirley along. "We ride in the convertible with the top down," Shirley wrote to her stepmother. "Nutty? Some of the things Doctor Wilbur and I do, you would not believe . . . I hardly do." The women even went out of town together. For Labor Day weekend in 1962 they took Connie's car from New York to Michigan and back. When she returned, Shirley excitedly described how they'd "stopped at a roadside table and had tomatoes, cookies, cake, rolls (we'd bought for sandwiches) and peaches." They slept in a motel room with twin beds, she added. "Doctor is fun to travel with." [9]

Connie knew she was violating the rules of her profession. According to a transcript of one of their recorded therapy sessions, she told Shirley that their socializing was "not good analytic technique." But she didn't care: "I'm willing to violate the rules for you," she said. [10]

She did so, apparently, because her relationship to Shirley and her multiple personalities felt so beautiful, so much like those days in the 1930s at the mental hospital in Michigan, when she helped heal her hysterical girl patient by walking hand in hand amid tall trees, dissolving the walls of their souls. Now, a generation later, Connie was equally smitten, with maternal feelings so strong that they bordered on the erotic. "[Y]ou know what I have been through in not having children," she told Shirley during a therapy session, adding that she wished she could have been her real mother. Too, Shirley was beautiful. She had "a nice, trim little figure . . . nice hands," and "the cutest nose" Connie had ever seen. Her lips were full and "open to some kind of contact." Her face was "well shaped"—a face, Connie said, "that I like having around. This is the face that I like to be with." [11]

Her colleagues were not privy to these declarations. All they heard were generalities which echoed a controversial theory about how to conduct therapy, one which fascinated Connie. Chicago psychoanalyst Franz Alexander was already renowned for his theories about psychosomatic illness: the idea, for instance, that asthma, arthritis, and even diabetes were manifestations of neurosis caused by bad mothering. Alexander promoted what he called "corrective emotional experience," recommending that therapists socialize with their patients, including outside of the office, in order to take the place of inadequate parents and encourage psychological healing. Alexander urged that the corrective experience be completed quickly, in just a few sessions. [12]

But Shirley's therapy stretched on, and Connie seemed intent on making their "correctives" permanent.

"God sent you to me," [13] she told Shirley, and Shirley, too, thought God was involved. She was convinced that her psychoanalysis was part of a divine plan to convert Connie to Seventh-Day Adventism. Shirley took her Bible to therapy sessions and did exegeses on the Book of Revelation. "My! Things are moving fast these days, just as Mrs. White prophesized," she remarked after astronaut John Glenn orbited the earth three times in early 1962. "It certainly cannot now be far from the end of time." [14]

Connie would later recount that she was repelled by the fundamentalist ideas her patient expounded, and she had no interest in the evangelical camp meetings Shirley invited her to when she made plans to visit her father and stepmother in the Midwest. But Shirley had a different understanding of Connie's response to Adventism. "She has now acknowledged the seventh day as Sabbath," she wrote to her stepmother. "Dr. W. has come to the place where she says she believes Sister White was a prophet and really did have visions from God." [15]

During this proselytizing phase of her psychoanalysis, Shirley often walked the streets of Manhattan "praying silently for guidance." [16] The praying seemed to fill her up. She gained weight and felt calm and optimistic.

Those good feelings were quashed, however, by Shirley's obsessive efforts—abetted by Connie—to go to medical school and become a psychoanalyst. In 1960, after Shirley had taken various noncredit chemistry classes at institutions like Columbia Teachers College, Connie decided she was ready to matriculate as a premed student at Columbia University proper. Shirley registered for summer courses in subjects such as zoology and inorganic chemistry. [17]

But Shirley was a terrible student now, and by the next year she had missed so many classes, failed so many tests, and made such bad grades that she was expelled. Connie was indignant and wrote to Columbia's dean, demanding Shirley be reinstated. The dean refused, politely but firmly assessing as nil Shirley's chances of ever becoming a doctor. Shirley was sick to her stomach and paralyzed with misery. [18]

Connie got another idea about how to help Shirley. She had just taken a part-time administrative job at Falkirk, a private mental hospital in the Catskill Mountains, upstate from New York City. Falkirk was a luxury facility. Its clientele were well to do, and they received their treatment on a veritable estate, whose mansions sat amid hills and pine forests. Connie used her influence to get Shirley hired at Falkirk to give private art therapy classes to depressed and schizophrenic patients. [19]

Shirley was thrilled to have a regular income. She earned $30 to $40 a week which, added to her father's stipend, gave her enough to buy toiletries, art books, clothing, and even an occasional milkshake at the fountain of the drugstore where she got her Librium and Thorazine.

Her favorite pupil was a society woman and longtime schizophrenic named Margaret. Thirty years had passed since she had last spoken, and she usually shuffled around Falkirk in a daze or stayed in her room screaming. But she seemed to connect with Shirley, who talked to her in soft, gentle tones. On art therapy days Margaret came to the crafts room early and grabbed the paintbrushes. Once she even uttered a few words. Delighted, the staff predicted she would soon speak normally again, thanks to her new teacher. Shirley nearly burst with pride.[20]

Walter Mason was in ill health during this period, and in spring 1962 he died. Despite this unquestionably traumatic event, Shirley grieved normally—she wrote letters to friends talking about how sad she felt, she continued to teach Margaret, and she did not split into alter personalities. Soon, though, she was facing a real crisis: penury. For years Walter had been sending her $100 a month, in a time when Shirley's apartment rented for $90. Now her father's stipend was gone, and she desperately needed to make it up.

Hoping to raise money by selling her paintings, she took several to a vanity gallery on the Upper East Side where artists paid to display their work to audiences who sometimes commissioned artwork to match the colors of their dining room and kitchen walls. The gallery owner said Shirley could get up to $400 for an oil or watercolor of her favorite themes: nature, skyscrapers, and boats.[21] But she hardly sold anything. To help, Connie bought some paintings for herself and continued to take orders from friends. She hired Shirley to decorate her kitchen with hand-painted wallpaper.[22]

By the Christmas season after her father's death seven months earlier, Shirley was so indigent that she could not afford to send gifts to her closest friends. She suggested exchanging long letters instead. One, from her old Mankato classmate Luella, made her especially happy, for it contained cash. A thank-you letter Shirley wrote makes clear how financially bad off she was. "Used your $1 for nylons," she told Luella, and "$1 for milk, food, butter."[23]

Connie again swooped in. One of her former psychiatric patients, a woman named Karen, wanted to open elite gift shops on Madison Avenue and in East Hampton, a resort area of Long Island. Eager to go the extra mile with another emotionally needy but ambitious woman, Connie bankrolled Karen's venture. She did so with the proviso that Karen hire Shirley to work in the Manhattan shop. Shirley knew of the arrangement, but in her mind the job "came through God."[24]

Karen paid Shirley $1.50 an hour plus commissions for items she sold. In addition, Shirley was to create inventory by purchasing baby dolls wholesale and outfitting them with hand-sewn clothes. Connie gave her $100 to buy the raw materials,[25] and Shirley was excited about the chance to play with dolls once again. She visited a neighborhood dressmaker's shop and begged scraps: silks, crepes, and satin. She spent hours in the shop, her apartment, and Connie's car en route to Falkirk, stitching tiny "slips, panties, housecoats, nighties, [and] coats with hoods trimmed in imitation white fur."[26] Life became a cross between Santa's Village and a sweatshop—complete with sweatshop money. Karen never got the shop off the ground, and within a few months she had dropped Shirley's wage to $1.25. She shuttered the business soon after. Shirley was as poverty stricken as ever, and just as dependent on Connie.[27]

"You may hear [from me] a little less often," Shirley wrote her stepmother in early 1963, after the price of an airmail postage stamp rose from seven to eight cents. It sounded like a joke but she was serious. "I am counting pennies, literally," she wrote. She could afford to eat only two meals a day, and one was toast and milk.[28] Florence Mason, now a widow, maintained a regular and very affectionate correspondence with Shirley— in letters the two discussed Seventh-Day Adventism, prayer, and their respective problems with loneliness. Now Florence was horrified to hear of Shirley's hunger. "I am sending you $5," she wrote, "and I want you to get some food with it."[29]

These alms did not keep Shirley from looking eccentric when she stepped out of her apartment wearing overshoes even on dry, sunny days. The shoes gave her a bag-lady air but she had to wear them, she wrote Florence, because she couldn't afford new nylons and didn't want people to see the runs in her tattered old stockings.[30]

She still had her part-time work at Falkirk, but it was becoming less and less satisfying, and more and more unreliable. For every session that Margaret spent painting peacefully, there was another time that she vomited on the art table.[31] Shirley's miracle therapy had not turned out to be so miraculous: After months of art instruction, Margaret was as mute and deranged as ever, and one day in spring 1963, she failed to show up for her lesson. It was the first time she had ever skipped class, and Shirley was terrified about being laid off from Falkirk. She was "worried half sick" Margaret would never paint again. "I prayed," she wrote to Florence.[32] It was all she could do.

Oddly during these days of destitution, Shirley was taking taxicabs.[33] They were paid for by Dr. Herbert Spiegel, a New York psychiatrist known for his dapper bow ties and his stellar ability as a hypnotherapist. During years of research, Spiegel had discovered that 5 percent of Americans are so highly hypnotizable that they often go into trances on their own, without even knowing it. "Hypnotic virtuosos," Spiegel called these exceptional people. Their tendency to enter trances spontaneously is so marked that sometimes they temporarily lose their sense of identity. The last thing Spiegel thought therapists should do was reinforce these people's sense of splitting. Instead, he recommended techniques to quickly help them regain the sense that they are one person. As far as Spiegel was concerned, Shirley was this type of patient.[34]

He had learned about her special abilities in 1959, when Connie asked him to check Shirley's capacity to be put into a trance. When he hypnotically regressed her to earlier ages, she sometimes said her mother hurt her, but Spiegel knew that people often fantasize during age regression therapy. What he did not know was that during her hypnosis sessions with Shirley, Connie was asking extremely leading questions, the kind that are notorious for causing false memories.

Spiegel had encountered Vicky, Clara, and Marsha when he hypnotized Shirley. But he did not consider them alter personalities. He always called them Shirley's "roles." He thought of them as enactments by a woman who expressed anxiety by behaving as though she had other people inside her.

During his hypnosis testing with Shirley, Spiegel found her to be such a virtuoso that he recruited her to serve as a model in classes where he taught other doctors how to do hypnosis. She would ride in cabs to medical schools like Columbia University, and there audiences would watch as she sat onstage in a chair—exactly as Dr. Jean-Martin Charcot's patients had sat before audiences at the Salpetriere hospital in Paris almost a century earlier—and went into her trances.

Connie left town frequently, for American Psychiatric Association meetings and other professional events. Shirley often threatened suicide during these absences, and Connie asked Spiegel if he would take over when she was gone. He saw Shirley a few times in his office.

During one session she posed an odd question:

"Well, do you want me to be Helen?" she asked.

"What do you mean?" Spiegel replied.

"Well," said Shirley, "When I'm with Dr. Wilbur she wants me to be Helen."

"Who's Helen?"

"Well, that's a name Dr. Wilbur gave me for this feeling."

"Well, if you want to it's all right but it's not necessary."[35]

Shirley did not mention "Helen" again. Spiegel concluded that Connie was pressuring her to come up with alter personalities.

Spiegel continued to conduct hypnosis research on Shirley in his office, and he sometimes let Connie stay in the room and watch. Once Shirley produced a new personality named Natalie. Where had that name come from? Spiegel's wife was Natalie Shainess, also a psychiatrist, and she often came into her husband's office. Shirley had run into Shainess not long before being hypnotized, and that is undoubtedly how she came up with her Natalie role.[36]

No one took her Natalie seriously, not even Connie. But Connie was present once when Spiegel hypnotized Shirley and told her to be a baby. She complied, and later, back in her own office, Connie defined the baby as a newly appeared alter. She asked for a name. "Ruthie," Shirley said, and Ruthie joined Peggy Ann, Peggy Lou, Mary, and the rest.[37] Dr. Spiegel, meanwhile, never knew that he had served as midwife for one of Shirley's alters.

Though he probably didn't have as much information as he would have liked to about Shirley, Spiegel knew that hypnotic virtuosos are exquisitely sensitive to suggestion and that they constantly scan their therapists' postures and utterances to guess what they were thinking and what they want to hear. In addition, they demand constant attention, and if they do not get it they can become more ill. None of this behavior is conscious. But, Spiegel cautioned, it can create serious problems for a psychiatrist suffering from "grandiosity strivings." Urges to be heroic or famous can suck an unwitting doctor into the seductions and exactions of a hypnotic virtuoso.

Apparently, Connie did not attend the segments of Spiegel's lectures that discussed these risks. Either that or she ignored the warnings.

Using hypnosis as a substitute for the Pentothal during therapy sessions with Shirley, Connie would drone, "Your eyes are getting heavy, your eyes are getting heavy. Your eyelids are very heavy, they're very heavy, your eyelids are very heavy, your eyelids are very heavy. . . . Just relax. Just relax. Just relax, just relax."[38]

Shirley did relax. Soon she was in a trance and calling herself "Peggy."

"Now what were you afraid of today?" Connie asked.

"Well, I see all these animals," "Peggy" answered. "Camels in the desert, a mule's head."

". . . Did you ever see a man's penis?" Connie probed.

"No. I don't know . . . I can just remember up to it."

"What do you remember up to it?"

"Daddy came upstairs in the morning, to tell me that grandma died, and he had on a nightshirt."

"And you looked over and you could see down the nightshirt, and you could see his penis then . . . Well, Daddy had pubic hair, remember you thought the penis was hidden in feathers?"

"But I don't remember . . ."

"But I'd like you to remember now, Sweetie . . ."

"I didn't see it."

"Well, of course you did, Sweetie. And his penis wasn't very big."

"Now I remember."

During other sessions Shirley recalled "primal scenes"—her parents having sex in front of her. And once, she said, she saw her mother pull up her skirt and sit down. "Did she urinate or defecate?" Wilbur cued. "She did that at different places all over town,"[39] Shirley replied. From this Wilbur deduced that Mattie had sneaked around neighbors' homes in Dodge Center at night to foul their lawns with her feces. No matter that Shirley didn't remember any details. Connie assured her that under hypnosis, she would eventually remember them "like a dream."

Soon Shirley developed images of Mattie raping babies and holding secret, lesbian orgies with teenaged girls. Connie responded by stressing that Mattie was "wicked, bad, cruel." "If you don't hate her," she told Shirley, "you ought to," and "there is something the matter with you if you don't."[40] Hearing this, Shirley wrote an essay about Mattie on pink stationery. "I hate her," the essay repeated seventeen times. "Shit," it added. "I want to kill my mom."[41]

Connie finally had her breakthrough.

Shirley's $90-a-month home was in Manhattan's Yorkville section, a few minutes' walk from luxurious Park Avenue and Connie's office. The apartment was a garret. A fourth-floor walkup, it had only one room, though it was slightly indented in the middle to suggest separate rooms. The whole thing was two hundred and fifty square feet, about the size of a foyer in Connie's apartment. A bed and bookcase took up half the room; a kitchenette and table filled the rest.[42]

Shirley found solace in letter writing. She spent hours with stationery, greeting cards, and postage stamps, penning missives not just to Florence, her stepmother, but also to her art teacher from childhood and many former classmates from college in Minnesota—Alice in Albert Lea, Neva in Vernon Center, and Merlaine in Cokato were just a few. The letters talked at length about the weather but were cryptic when it came to exactly what Shirley was doing with her life. Some mentioned her "dear friend," a doctor she'd met back in Omaha and run into years later in New York. Others alluded to her dreams of being a child psychiatrist.[43] Many letters said she was sick but left the details vague. She was close-mouthed with Florence, as well, though the women mailed each other one or two letters a week.

She wrote every day but Sabbath, when writing was forbidden to Adventists. Her boredom and loneliness on Saturdays were unbearable, and in May 1963, after Connie flew to the Far East to lecture Filipino psychiatry students about how to cure homosexuality, Shirley called Dr. Spiegel and threatened to commit suicide. Spiegel called Connie's mother-in-law, and she took Shirley to Park Avenue to live there for several days until Connie came back. Shirley passed the time by kneeling and praying: "Let not thy heart be troubled, neither let it be afraid."[44]

When Connie returned she decided it was time that Shirley start thinking seriously about getting well, and she arranged another restaurant date with Flora. Not long after, she summoned Flora to her office to show her Shirley's panoply of personalities. As Flora looked on, the doctor chanted to the patient to relax, relax, relax. Shirley's face loosened, her eyes fluttered, and Peggy Ann came forth, then Peggy Lou, Vicky, Sam, Mike, Helen, Ruthie, Shirley Ann, Mary, Clara, Nancy, Lou Ann, Marcia, Vanessa, and Marjorie. Each emerged for a few seconds before being replaced by someone else, while Flora stared at their shape-shifting postures and listened to a theater of voices, astounded.[45]

She felt as though she'd fallen into Shakespeare's play *The Tempest*—the scene where Miranda declaims, "O wonder! How many goodly creatures are there here! How beauteous mankind is! O brave new world / That has such people in't!"

Then and there, she vowed to write the book.

CHAPTER 12

CURE

T HE SUN HAD JUST COME up one Sunday in November 1964 when Robert Moulton, of southeast Minneapolis, heard a knock at his front door. He opened it to a redheaded woman with steely eyes and a younger, shy brunette. Moulton recognized neither, but the younger one introduced herself as Shirley Mason, from Dodge Center. Astounded and delighted, Moulton waved her and her companion inside. Almost thirty-five years had passed since he had sat in the Mason family's home crafting Elizabethan stages from scraps, and sewing costumes for the members of Shirley's doll collection who would play Puck, Romeo, and Hamlet.

Everyone called him Bobby back then, but he had long since abandoned his childhood nickname. He had gone on to become a professional dancer, actor, play director, and choreographer, and now he was a professor of theater at the University of Minnesota. To people who didn't know him well he was Dr. Moulton.

To Shirley he was just Bobby, and the two old friends settled over breakfast to gossip and reminisce. They remembered Bobby's visits to Shirley's Seventh-Day Adventist church, her reciprocal attendance at his Methodist congregation, and the way the two children, inspired by their friendship, each kept two Sabbaths: Saturday and Sunday.[1]

Bobby glanced curiously at the woman with the bright red hair, asking with his eyes who she was. "Dr. Wilbur," he was told, Shirley's psychiatrist. Bobby was amazed; he had always considered Shirley to be a typical

Dodge Center girl and had never imagined she had emotional problems. No one in the room that Sunday morning mentioned multiple personality disorder, and Bobby tried to make light of the fact that his old friend was in therapy. After all, he chuckled, Shirley's mother always *had* been strange. Connie's ears perked up; she waited for more. But Bobby changed the subject, the reunion wound down, everyone said goodbye, and Connie and Shirley got back in their rented car. The morning had been delightful for Shirley, but it had not taught Connie anything.

The women were on a weekend jaunt—they'd flown to Minneapolis the day before and were doing a quick trip through Shirley's childhood haunts before returning home. In a café in Dodge Center they ran into Hattie Halmbrecht, Shirley's eighth grade teacher from twenty-nine years ago. Hattie was delighted to see Shirley all grown up. But who was the woman with her? A doctor friend, Shirley said. Connie again listened intently as the elderly teacher reprised old times with her student. Not a word was mentioned about a schizophrenic mother.

Nor was anything revealed in the modest home of Dessie Blood Engbard, the woman who had worked as the Masons' maid and lived in their household when Shirley was a child. Dessie, a plump, uneducated woman, fussed over her prodigal guest, hugging her, calling her "daughter," and pointing to drawings by Shirley that hung on the walls. Clearly, Connie could see, Dessie adored Shirley and had been in a position to see and hear Mattie mistreating her when she was young. Yet she seemed to have witnessed nothing remarkable. For Shirley's mother Dessie had only sterling words.[2]

Connie had thought about talking with Dr. Otoniel Flores, the cigar-smoking family physician who'd cared for Shirley when she lived in Dodge Center. Under Pentothal and hypnosis, Shirley had recalled Dr. Flores treating the fractured larynx, bruised ribs, and other injuries she said Mattie inflicted on her in the 1920s and 1930s. Dr. Flores could corroborate Shirley's memories of abuse and open her medical records.

And there was Shirley's home, ground zero for Mattie's tortures, including her attempts to suffocate her daughter in the corn and wheat crib. The property was close by, just a few feet from Main Street. But Shirley refused to go near the house. Her memories were too awful, she said. Besides, she wanted to visit a public park she'd frequented during summers when she was a child. Connie drove her there, and by the time they finished looking around, night was falling and it was time to get to the airport for their return flight. The women left Dodge Center without looking for Dr. Flores or viewing Shirley's old house.

Back in New York City a few days later they mentioned their Minnesota visit to Flora but gave few details.[3] That was fine with Flora: she was much too busy to pay attention. The popular magazine *Science Digest* had started a psychiatry section and appointed her co-editor.

But she sometimes saw more than she wanted to of Shirley, who was desperate as ever for mothering. She was as anxious as always about money, too, because shortly after meeting Flora, Connie had decided to quit her director's job at Falkirk and buy her own mental hospital.[4] Left in the lurch without a ride from New York City, Shirley soon resigned from her art therapy position. She was blithe about leaving at first; Connie had her eye on a private sanitarium upstate on the Hudson River, and she promised that as soon as the sale was clinched she would hire Shirley as a therapist and pay her well.[5]

But the hospital deal fell through, and by fall Shirley was frantic. She made endless rounds of employment agencies, hunting for work teaching English or art to normal children. She proved unemployable despite her earlier years of experience. Due to modifications in New York's teacher education requirements, she was a few college credits short of a certificate.[6] The change had been announced long ago, but during her time on the couch she had completely lost touch with the world. Her time in psychoanalysis now comprised more than a quarter of the years she had been alive.

It had finally become obvious to Connie that Shirley would never make it into medical school, and she might never get well. Connie started wondering what to do with this perpetual patient, who might be mentally ill—and materially dependent on Connie—for the rest of both of their lives. Money from a book by Flora was Shirley's only hope for financial independence. But as Flora had earlier demanded, the book needed a happy ending.

Connie had already predicted Shirley would be cured by 1965, yet here it was, already the end of 1964. She tried to get the wheels turning by telling Shirley to get a job—any job. Shirley obeyed, first sewing doll clothes again, then working as a desk clerk at a hotel.

The work filled her weekdays, but the loneliness of her free time still tormented her. She telephoned Connie and Flora in the early morning hours of Saturday and Sunday, and in the too-late hours as well. Flora accepted these intrusions with major help from her mother. Esther Schreiber, now seventy-eight, had been a widow for six years, and her life's work had always been to attend to Flora's every need so her daughter could concentrate one hundred percent on her career. Now that work included entertaining the subject of her daughter's potential book. It was Esther who stayed on the phone when Shirley made her Sabbath phone calls. Esther chatted patiently for hours and invited Shirley for dinner. She answered the door when Shirley dropped by unannounced.[7]

Connie, meanwhile, spent much of her free time looking for a way to leave New York, which in 1964 seemed anarchic and threatening. In Queens early that year, a middle-aged woman, Kitty Genovese, had been stabbed to death by a stranger outside her apartment building, and the newspapers reported that thirty-eight neighbors witnessed the homicide in progress but did nothing to stop it. Months after that, just blocks from Park Avenue and close to Shirley's apartment, a disturbance broke out after a policeman confronted a fifteen-year-old black student engaged in horseplay with friends and fatally shot the boy. Harlem and other black neighborhoods erupted in riots and ominous graffiti such as "Burn Baby, Burn!"

The last straw came when Connie hired a teenager to care for the dogs after Shirley became unable to do so because of her new jobs. Out on a walk one day, the girl was mugged at knifepoint for the sum of a dollar and thirty cents.[8] It was too much for Connie. Again she looked around for a mental hospital, if not to buy then at least to work in. This time she found one a world away from New York, in rural West Virginia.

Weston State Hospital was not for sale in 1965, but it desperately needed a new superintendent. Opened during the Civil War, it boasted nineteenth-century asylum architecture in the grand style. Inside its lovely buildings, though, Weston was a hellhole. It housed over two thousand residents, more than twice the recommended capacity. This enormous population was served by only two psychiatrists. Patients seldom got treatment. Mentally ill men spent their waking hours, as a journalist reported, "milling in a narrow hallway." In another hallway women moaned and huddled. At night in the crowded wards, the beds were jammed so close that they looked like one gigantic mattress.[9]

Still, Connie was frantic to move. If she took the job it would start in October 1965. Her husband, Keith, would remain in New York as a lawyer for Lloyds of London, and visit on occasional weekends.

But if she went to West Virginia, what would Shirley do? Over the years she had made some progress managing her sixteen multiple personalities and their disordered behavior. Coming out of hypnosis sessions with Connie now, she often remembered what Peggy and the others had said during the trance. Before, she had been completely amnesiac, so remembering seemed an improvement. And her body did not ache so much as before. Still, she continued to split into Peggy, Mary, and the others when she was with Connie. And she often felt paralyzed with anxiety. How, Connie wondered, could she possibly leave this patient on her own?

For a year Shirley had been waiting for Connie to set her up with a full-time job at a mental hospital. Meanwhile she'd taken menial jobs, including the desk clerk position at the St. Regis, a five-star hotel on Fifth Avenue. There, a Brazilian accountant named Mario started flirting with her. Soon they were dating, something she hadn't done for ten years. Mario was on temporary assignment at the hotel. He was not an Adventist, but he was a gentleman, never demanding sex from Shirley.[10]

The two got along well and Mario knew nothing about Shirley's diagnosis of multiple personality. But why should he? She'd never split into different identities in front of anyone unless she had first talked about the illness, with Flora, for instance. To Mario, Shirley seemed perfectly normal. After several dates he announced he would soon be moving to California for his work, and he wanted her to go as his wife. He presented Shirley with a diamond and ruby engagement ring.

Shirley was thrown into a quandary. She felt love for Mario, and she had accepted that she would never go to medical school. Still, she wanted to do a book with Connie about her illness. Besides, she wanted to work with mentally ill children, and if she stayed put she was sure that with Dr. Wilbur's help she could land a job at a hospital. That would not happen if she went to the West Coast with Mario.

Connie was away when he proposed. Shirley did not wait for Connie's return to make her decision. She broke up with Mario, and from that time on, she would never have another boyfriend. For years afterward she would miss Mario and deeply regret her decision not to marry him.[11]

With Mario gone, no choices remained. After 1964 ended, more months passed, and Connie began searching for a way to take Shirley to West Virginia with her. She found a means by telling the head of West Virginia's mental health department that, as a condition of her employment, a second person would also have to be hired—Shirley—to do art therapy with children.

The health department accepted the package deal but could not place Shirley at Weston. Instead, she was assigned to another facility: Lakin State, just across the border from Ohio. Formerly the West Virginia Hospital for the Colored Insane, Lakin was an egregiously substandard institution. The previous year, a grand jury had decried the hospital's "filth," "stench," "sex problems"—probably referring to rapes—and general neglect of patients.

But Lakin had its good side. A unit for juveniles had recently been opened, and the hospital had a long tradition of providing arts and crafts activities to patients. Shirley was given a job working with children. She was to begin in late October, the same time Connie moved to Weston.[12]

It was now early summer, three months before the women were scheduled to leave New York, and Connie knew things had to change between Shirley and herself. After all, she would not just be running a very large and troubled hospital; she would also be teaching psychiatry part time at a nearby university. Lakin and Weston were a three-hour drive from each other through the mountains. Weekend visits would only occasionally be possible.

She told Shirley she would simply have to get well. For over a decade, being a mental patient had been the reason Connie paid attention to her. Now, the only way to get more of that attention was to move to West Virginia and work full time at a state mental hospital. But that would be possible only if she "integrated" her multiple personalities—and soon.

So she did. In addition to the tranquilizers she was taking, Shirley upped her ingestion of antidepressants, past the recommended dose. This caused a medical crisis, and on a Wednesday in early July, Flora got a call from Shirley begging her to come to her apartment immediately. She was lying on the floor when Flora arrived, weak, trembling, and bruised. She gave a strange explanation. She'd been in her tiny living room, she said, when suddenly she felt a spasm, jumped several inches off the floor, slipped on a rug, and pitched ten feet forward.[13] As she was describing this seizure to Flora, Shirley's face suddenly went blank and her voice became unrecognizable. "I'm the girl Shirley would like to be," she intoned. "My hair is blonde and my heart is light." Then, as suddenly as the voice emerged, it disappeared. Shirley got up off the floor and Flora hurried to call Connie and tell her about this new identity, whom Flora christened "The Blonde." But The Blonde made no more appearances.[14] Shirley never again dissociated into an alter personality.

Four weeks later, Connie wrote a final notation in Shirley's file: "All personalities one." The date was September 2, 1965, almost eleven years after their first psychotherapy session on Park Avenue. Having been declared cured, Shirley packed her things. She gave up her apartment at the end of the month and spent several days at Flora's, waiting for the Lakin job to start. Then she left New York.

Flora had her happy ending, exactly when she wanted it. Now she could do the book—and not just a potboiler, but a work of moral and literary heft. Writing about multiple personality disorder would free her from the surface, she told herself. It would take her to the deeps, to that place in her writing where she'd always yearned to go. She felt terrific about the whole thing.

It's harder to know Connie's reaction. A photograph from the period shows her face strangely smooth, waxy, and devoid of emotion even though she is smiling. She was fifty-seven years old the autumn Shirley was cured, and she would later confide to a relative that she availed herself of plastic surgery to refresh her appearance.[15] It's not clear when Connie went under the knife, but perhaps she felt she needed a pick-me-up before departing for Appalachia with Shirley in tow.

CHAPTER 13

IMPATIENCE

S HIRLEY AND CONNIE WERE STILL in town when Flora started writing her proposal, christening the book *Who Is Sylvia?* and strategizing about finding a publisher. As she talked about "Sylvia's" case to friends, she found that many were skeptical about whether multiple personality disorder really existed, and suspicious that the patient was faking it. Others had read *The Three Faces of Eve* or seen the movie almost a decade earlier. They weren't interested in sequels.

Flora herself wasn't sure why "Sylvia's" story was different from Eve's, or if it could be made as exciting. Eve's three personalities had strikingly defined characters. "Sylvia," on the other hand, had sixteen personalities who were mostly the same age—preteens—and who hardly seemed to have bodies: they only occasionally talked about what they looked like. Even Connie had trouble telling them apart.

Flora realized she had too many people and not enough characters. This was a dilemma for a writer attempting to create sharply etched heroes and villains, with a powerful supporting cast. She tried to flesh out "Sylvia's" alters by grilling Connie about them:

Which are the strongest of the personalities? Vicky? Peggy? Mary? . . . Are any of them ugly? Can you describe the body image of each? . . . Are some brighter than others, kinder than others, more impetuous than others; do they agree on religion, books, music, painting; do they like the same people, hate the same people, have the same politics, enjoy the same things? If S. goes to the theater do they all see the play? . . . When S. paints, do they all cooperate, or do they obstruct the process?[1]

Connie had not thought about these questions and neither had Shirley. Over the years, it had become clear that some personalities seemed angrier, calmer, or more depressed than others—but not always, and in other respects they rarely distinguished themselves, except for "The Blonde," who may have emphasized her hair color simply because, by the time Shirley had the "seizure" preceding her personalities' final integration, Flora had already told her what information she needed about the alters in order to write a book.

Still, it was hard to imagine people as young as Shirley's alters having enough "personality" to interest adult readers. This problem was "a very serious commercial point," Flora warned. She didn't really think of the alters as selves anyway. She told Connie she imagined them more as "extensions of moods, personality traits, family connections, periods of life, repressed desires, fantasies, abilities, character traits, et al.—but not as physical entities." [2]

"NO, NO, NO," Connie insisted, "We cannot think of them as fantasy selves." [3] She told Shirley to come up with physical descriptions and Shirley complied. Two personalities were blonde, she said. One was a redhead and the rest had brown hair. All were blue-eyed and thin. And some were adults after all.

In ensuing months, Connie and Shirley prepared a document describing each alter by age, height, weight, hair color, coiffure, and favorite clothes. An enormous *dramatis personae* was being created, over five times the number as in *The Three Faces of Eve.*

The cast was in the making when Connie and Shirley started packing to leave Manhattan. A few days before they departed, in late September 1965, *The New Yorker* ran Part One of *In Cold Blood*, Truman Capote's book about the stabbing and shooting murders of a Kansas farm family by two nihilistic, psychopathic punks. In an unprecedented publishing move, the magazine used four installments to print the book-length account of the killers and the plainspoken, rural community affected by their crimes. [4]

Capote's work eerily reflected the national sense of giddiness and doom, idealism versus malevolence, that haunted the country after the

Kennedy assassination and during the years when the Civil Rights Movement rumbled, the sexual revolution revved up, and the Vietnam war spun out of control. Bus riders hunched over the magazine, glued to its pages and missing their stops. Married couples with subscriptions fought over who went first. Reviewers praised the author's ability to turn journalism into something that read like a novel.

In Cold Blood was a new genre. Like the novel, it used narrative tools such as plotting, foreshadowing, and scene juxtaposition to give fictional heft to reality. The details, however, were all true, even if they fit together so elegantly that readers suspected they were made up. In one scene a mangy dog trots by a Kansas road. In the next scene one of the punks swerves his car to kill the dog: he's always enjoyed killing dogs. The twinning of these scenes seemed too perfect, too fortunate, and an interviewer for the *New York Times* asked Capote if he hadn't really taken two distant events, each involving a separate dog, and mashed them into one. "Absolutely not," answered a piqued Capote. "One doesn't spend almost six years on a book, the point of which is factual accuracy, and then give way to minor distortions."[5]

He called his book a "nonfiction novel." Novelists couldn't pull it off because they didn't care enough about journalism, journalists were unable because they didn't know how to write novels. Possibly, Truman Capote implied, the only person who could successfully tackle a nonfiction novel was Truman Capote.[6]

Flora had never written a novel, but she had tried her hand at radio and television plays. Though none had ever been produced on major stations, she understood plot, character development, and the other elements of drama. And as a journalist, she knew how to gather facts. Reading Capote, she became convinced that Shirley's story could be turned into a nonfiction novel.[7]

She had barely started working on *Who Is Sylvia?* when she was overwhelmed by a death almost as random as the ones Capote described. In October, she and her mother attended the bar mitzvah of a nephew. A festive dinner followed, within hours of which the guests were doubled over with food poisoning. Esther was stricken, and though everyone else soon recovered, she died in a hospital on November 1. Flora was five months short of her fiftieth birthday. For forty-eight years she had lived with her mother, including continuously over the past three decades, and for seven years the two had shared a bedroom. Thanks to Esther's fanatic caretaking, Flora knew nothing about cooking, cleaning, or mending the holes burned in her clothing by cigarette ashes. She was so devastated that she was unable to think much about *Who Is Sylvia?*

Instead, she did what she always did when she grieved: She threw herself into busy work, including more journalism from the nation's capital. "The Johnson Girls: A Study in Contrasts," was typical of her writing from this period. *"Luci has strong maternal feelings. She wants a large family . . . While Luci's bathroom contains an infinite variety of lipsticks, Lynda's has no such display. . . . It took her father to persuade her to include fashion magazines on her reading list."*[8] It was typical Flora celebrity mongering and puffery. But stars and fluff took her mind away from death.

Things were much cheerier down south. When Shirley arrived at Lakin State Hospital, Connie took her to the nearest town, Point Pleasant, a picturesque riverfront hamlet of seven thousand people. The women looked at houses and when Shirley found a red-and-white-trimmed cottage she liked, Connie supplied the down payment. Shirley was overjoyed to finally have her own home.

Her new job made her equally happy. Under a federal grant, she worked with Lakin's forty child residents, doing art therapy and planning their school studies, play time, and visits with social workers and psychiatrists. To do this she scrutinized the children's medical and psychiatric records, a task laden with responsibility. She delighted in staying late at the hospital and running an evening story hour. She had the children make masks, puppets, and a puppet stage. And of course, she set up a dollhouse.[9]

She stayed just as busy at home. In Point Pleasant she organized private art classes for children and adults. She was invited into the local chapter of the American Association of University Women and asked to give talks on subjects such as Chinese art.

Point Pleasant's coziness reminded her of Dodge Center, Minnesota, except that there she'd been a sullen adolescent who locked herself in her room and felt snakes crawling up her arms. Now, her doctor had diagnosed her as having gotten well, so she suddenly *was* well—no snakes, no more alter personalities. People in Point Pleasant noticed that she was twitchy in a birdlike, nervous way. Other than that, she was so functional, so normal, that her eleven years as a psychiatric invalid seemed like little more than a bad dream.

She didn't even have a psychoanalyst anymore, and sometimes she forgot to call her former one "Doctor." She switched to "Connie," who after all was just her friend now. Their connection was still strong; Shirley got a car and made the three-hour trip to Weston on holidays and weekends. Connie's husband was seldom there, so the two women took road trips, sometimes as far as Florida. Or they stayed home and passed the time styling each other's hair and playing with their dogs. Connie still had her toy black poodle. Shirley had a silver one to match.[10]

And they talked about *Who Is Sylvia?* which—a year after Shirley's cure—was bobbing aimlessly in the mire of Flora's inertia. In early summer 1966 she sent a draft chapter to West Virginia.

Connie fumed when she read it, and so did Shirley. The chapter was "lousy," they complained in a joint letter sent to New York on the Fourth of July. Not only that, they couldn't fathom why she had written that Shirley's alter "Peggy" liked to listen to TV with the volume too loud. That description was all wrong and "out of character." Flora had better get things right and do some more work immediately. Otherwise, they would find a new writer.[11]

Flora answered that she was trying to sell *Who Is Sylvia?* to the prestigious publishing house Knopf.[12] Connie was only partly mollified. She needed cheering up, for things were not good at work. When she'd first arrived at Weston State Hospital she'd been welcomed as a star from the big city, an expert who would change a dark, backwards hole into a clean, well-lighted place. Connie was blamed for a series of misfortunes, some of which she was involved in and some she was not—a tuberculosis outbreak, a mass escape from the hospital by violent patients, rumors that others were having sex on the hospital lawn. By late 1967 she was out of a job, and irate about it.[13]

Then the University of Kentucky offered her a post in the psychiatry department of its medical school. She accepted, left West Virginia, and soon became a popular if controversial professor in Lexington. Young women at the medical school appreciated her passion for recruiting and mentoring female psychiatrists at a time when there still were very few of them. Young men, too, felt appreciative. Connie was respectful to medical students, always addressing them as "Doctor" when few other professors bothered. She tried to build up confidence.[14]

She was also admired for her passion for treating patients. "She would take on anyone, no matter how complex their problem," one colleague remembered years later. "She didn't think about money or about the time it would take to treat them." And she listened.[15] Other psychiatrists might give patients fifty-minute hours and drug prescriptions. Connie talked with them for hours, abandoning her hard-charged, abrasive persona and shifting to her deep, gentle self.

As usual, her warmth got out of hand. That became apparent as she developed strange relationships with some of the medical residents. "Connie's children," is how they are remembered today by old-timers in the psychiatry department. "The lame and the halt," a faculty member called some of them,[16] because everyone could see they had emotional problems. Connie should have encouraged these troubled residents to seek treatment with therapists who weren't on the faculty. Instead, she took them on as patients—a clear violation of boundaries in psychiatry, since she was also working with them daily as their superior.

The lame, the halt, and even some better-adjusted residents clustered around her. There were about eight of them, mostly men, and all became practicing psychiatrists. In the coming decades, half would be accused of having sex with their patients. Most of these would lose their licenses, temporarily or permanently. One, charged with having sex with teenaged boys, would shoot himself to death. Lexington psychiatrists who had not been "Connie's children" would follow these shocking events and speculate about the extent to which they'd flowed from Dr. Wilbur's bad behavior. Had her boundary violations with the young residents encouraged their own violations against patients? People chewed over the question, which had no firm answer.[17]

One thing was certain, however. During Connie's tenure at the university, Lexington, Kentucky, became as efficient at manufacturing multiple personalities as it did at producing race horses.

The process started soon after she arrived at the university, when she showed residents how to test for the condition. She recommended that a patient be hypnotized, then encouraged to look into a mirror until some-one different appeared. The patient was then asked if the person in the mirror had a name and an age. If the answer was yes, the diagnosis was multiple personality. Connie did not seem to realize what recent studies have shown: many people, even normal ones, will see different faces in a mirror within minutes of gazing.[18]

Lexington's first case of multiple personality was diagnosed in early 1968, after a woman came to the campus hospital appearing to be a para-noid schizophrenic. But when she was hypnotized she sucked her thumb and produced a parade of alter personalities she called "Allison," "Baby," "Bitch," "Bethany," "Pam," and "Clod." Under further hypnosis she recov-ered "memories" of severe childhood abuse. In short order Connie hypno-tized four additional female patients and decided that they, too, had alters.[19]

But a man named Jonah would become Lexington's star multiple. He came into the hospital complaining of violent spells that he could not re-member later. Connie hypnotized him and evoked a personality Jonah called Usoffa Abdulla, an angry "god." Two additional alters followed, and Connie turned Jonah over to Dr. Arnold Ludwig, chairman of the Depart-ment of Psychiatry.

Ludwig already had a history of aggressive experimentation, including with LSD, and he was known as quite the showman. Once, after a patient said she was "demon possessed," he dressed up as a priest, gathered the residents around, and went through the motions of a Catholic exorcism. He taped Jonah going in and out of his personalities. He decided to scien-tifically measure the alters' existence.[20]

Ludwig gave Jonah some word-memorization tests, hypnotized him, and tested the alter personalities to see whether information taken in by each had "leaked" into the others' consciousness. It seemed there was no leakage; each alter really appeared to have amnesia for the others' learning. They seemed like separate people.[21]

Ludwig hooked Jonah up to an electro-encephalograph—an EEG—to measure each personality's brainwaves. The readings all came out different. Ludwig gave Dr. Cornelia B. Wilbur a byline, and the study was published in 1972 in a prestigious journal.[22] Jonah joined *The Three Faces of Eve* as a famous case, and Connie became a recognized expert in the field of mul-tiple personality.

Shirley, meanwhile, was thriving by herself in West Virginia. She had gotten a new job after Connie left the state, as an art professor at Rio Grande, a small college just over the border, in Ohio. She'd found the position on her own, without drawing on any of Connie's clout or connections. Fourteen years had passed since she'd lived independently, and now here she was, back on her own and teaching art again, just as she had been before going into therapy so very long ago. Not only was she self-sufficient, she loved her new work. Today, former Rio Grande students still remember "Miss Mason" as shy and austere but warm in her teaching, supportive of everyone's efforts with canvas and paint.[23] She got tenure and reactivated her membership in the National Art Education Association, which she'd let drop for years while immobilized in therapy. Her old fantasy of becoming a psychoanalyst faded. She was forty-three years old and it looked as though she would be a college art professor—a very contented one—for the rest of her working life.

She probably would have been if not for *Who Is Sylvia?*

The book was still on Flora's back burner in late 1968, rejected by Knopf and several other publishers, who—as Flora would later recall to reporters—dismissed it as "trash." But with Shirley and Connie busy acclimating to new jobs, no one was thinking much about *Who Is Sylvia?*—Flora least of all. Her life was more frenetic than ever, piled not just with work but with something she'd forgone for over a decade: a lover.

He was forty-six-year-old Leonard Reiser,[24] president of John Jay, the New York City public college where Flora had gotten work in 1965, first teaching speech and English, and later also becoming the director of public relations. A Columbia Law School graduate and former deputy police commissioner, Reisman cut an elegant figure, with deep-set, soulful eyes and wide, soft lips. He was considered an adroit and self-confident man, but he was haunted by a lack of self-confidence, and he was not getting along with his wife. Soon he was meeting weekly with Flora for two hours.[25] They were supposed to be discussing ways to promote the college, but more often they talked about Reisman's problems. He and Flora began an affair.

They sneaked around, according to Ben Termine, Flora's best friend at the time and head of the Speech Department. "They would meet for dinner away from the college. Reisman's wife suspected, and once things almost came to a head when Flora choked on a chicken bone at a restaurant and he had to take her to the emergency room. That almost gave the whole thing away."

Very early in the morning on the first Friday of December 1967, Reisman was hailing a taxicab on the Upper East Side when he suffered a massive heart attack. He died before the ambulance could get him to the hospital.

Flora was in Washington, D.C., that day, attending the weekend wedding celebration of President Johnson's daughter Lynda Bird. She was in the bathtub at her hotel when the news of Reisman's death reached her by phone. She rushed back to New York, ostensibly to handle the press but really to mourn her lover.

She would always regret missing what she called "the wedding of the year,"[26] for she adored First Family parties. "I went to Richard Nixon's inaugural balls with her," Termine remembered. "She was so attracted to the lights of Washington that when she got there she was suddenly brighter, faster—everything seemed heightened. And her diction! She talked more theatrically in Washington than she did in New York!"

"Politics?" Termine added rhetorically. "Flora wasn't out for politics or political change. She was out for Flora."

Accordingly, after Nixon's 1968 electoral victory, she informed his staff she'd voted for him, then submitted an application for a job in the presidential cabinet (she never heard back from Nixon's people).[27] After she realized she wouldn't be relocating to Washington, she took on more work: doing public relations for her college and working on a nationally syndicated newspaper column with Stuart Long, a liberal Texas journalist who looked like a cross between Abraham Lincoln and Buddy Holly. Cavern-faced, bespectacled Long traveled the country writing about politics, and Flora added a psychology slant: they called their joint effort "Syndrome USA."[28] Soon the two were sleeping together and Long was writing Flora notes filled with sexy double entendres and paeans to her nipples. As college president Reisman had been, Long was married with children. His family lived in Austin, though, so Long's wife was fuzzy about what her husband was up to in Manhattan.

Shirley and Connie were also in the dark about Flora's pecadillos. As long as she reported regularly to them about her attempts to sell *Who Is Sylvia?*, they felt sufficiently informed.

Finally, in late October 1969, an editor bit. Gladys Carr worked at a small publishing company, Cowles. She was intrigued by multiple personality, and she already had heard of Dr. Wilbur. A friend with emotional problems had received psychotherapy from her, and as far as Carr was concerned, Connie had saved the woman's life.[29]

But when Carr asked if she could meet the real "Sylvia," Shirley got cold feet. She wasn't even sure she wanted to do the book anymore; she said she was worried her identity as a mental patient would be revealed. Flora and Connie swore they would keep her identity secret, and to reinforce that vow, Connie offered to make a huge sacrifice. Though it meant she would achieve no fame from *Sylvia*, she, too, would appear in the book under a pseudonym. Shirley finally relented.[30]

Flora signed a contract with Cowles.[31] The advance was $12,000, as much as she was making each year doing full-time teaching and public relations work. She got a third of the money immediately. Another third would come halfway through the writing, and the final third on completion of the manuscript, which was due in only eleven months.

The book's title morphed slightly, to *Sylvia: The Many Multiples of One*. Flora started working on it in earnest. Very quickly, however, she discovered problems with the story, problems so profound that she would wonder if she could write a book about Shirley.

PART IV

CASE STUDY

CHAPTER 14

THE EDIT

FLORA'S MAIN DILEMMA, THE FLATNESS of the multiple personalities, had seemingly been taken care of with Shirley's and Connie's list of sixteen sets of likes, dislikes, and hairdos. But as she more closely examined that inventory, Flora saw that she still had problems. She was preparing to write an action-packed, "nonfiction novel," yet the personalities didn't *do* much of anything. Even when rebellious little Peggy first appeared in Connie's office, she didn't run or yell or bug her eyes out—she simply knocked on the office door and matter-of-factly announced herself as an alter personality. Connie had acted equally ho-hum during this introduction. And when Shirley was first told she had multiple personalities, she'd barely blinked an eye.

For years Connie had made tape recordings of her therapy sessions, and now she gave them to Flora. Listening, Flora heard sobbing, screaming, and confusion: *"Let me out! Let me out! The people, the people, the people! It hurts. It hurts. My head hurts. My throat hurts. The people and the music. The people and the music. I want to get out! Please, please!"*[1] The reel-to-reel mayhem dragged on for hours. The distress it conveyed was incoherent, monotonous, and for all its horror rather boring.

But during conversations Flora had with Connie and Shirley as she prepared to write the book, they told her about the many childhood atrocities Shirley had remembered after Connie helped her dissociate into Peggy, Vicky, and the other alters during drug and hypnosis sessions. Flora was amazed by Mattie Mason's assaults. Describing them, she realized, would boost *Sylvia*'s appeal to readers, especially because Americans were growing increasingly concerned about a newly recognized phenomenon: the battered-child syndrome.[2]

That's what pediatricians were calling the recent discovery, by radiologists in the 1960s, that, when x-rayed, many children showed evidence in their bones of having been severely beaten by their parents. Experts were trying to figure out why in the world people would deliberately injure their offspring. Some thought poverty was the underlying problem: when fathers and mothers led mean lives marked by too much work, too much stress, and not enough money for a babysitter, they got frustrated and swung their fists, including at babies.[3]

Other experts focused on individual rather than socioeconomic causes. They thought people who assaulted their children were mentally ill. By the early 1970s, policy makers had become interested in this possibility, including Senator Walter Mondale, who a few years later would serve as vice president under President Jimmy Carter. Mondale was working on a package of child-protection legislation that would fund abuse prevention and treatment programs, and require teachers, doctors, and others to notify authorities if they suspected maltreatment in children they worked with. Mondale soon realized that his colleagues in Congress would be friendlier to those reforms if they believed child abuse was caused not just by minority parents who were poor, but also by white mothers and fathers who were middle class but emotionally disturbed.[4]

Policy makers who were trying to solve the child maltreatment problem also realized that sexual abuse was even more compelling a public issue than was physical abuse. That fact was even reflected in the literary world, in a book by an outspoken woman lawyer. Lisa Richette was a former Philadelphia assistant district attorney who had gone on to specialize in defending children accused of crimes. Her book *The Throwaway Children* was first published in 1969 and promoted as a critique of the country's juvenile justice system. True to marketing strategy, it contained many anecdotes about children unfairly sentenced in the courts and inappropriately locked up in detention centers. But the real draw for readers was the book's titillating bizarreness, which was based on actual cases Richette had dealt with as a prosecutor. One chapter told of a group of children coaxed by a neighbor man and woman to copulate with the couple's pet German

Shepherds. In another chapter, a paranoid schizophrenic woman made her young son fondle her breasts and genitals. A third case history featured a thirteen-year-old who murdered his parents after seeing them having sex and discovering his mother's collection of hard-core pornography.[5]

This salacious material could have competed with the sleazy offerings of Times Square; it certainly had never appeared in mainstream media. Now, with *The Throwaway Children* available in bookstores and public libraries, even women could read about mind-boggling lewdness perpetrated against boys and girls. Such reading was not only legal, it was noble, a kind of obscene civic duty. Richette's book sold briskly and was soon reprinted as a mass-market paperback. That happened in 1970—the year Flora began writing her own book.

She decided that *Sylvia* would be a "whodunnit" about severe child abuse—especially sex abuse. The heroine's psyche would be fractured by her lunatic mother's mistreatment, as severely as a child's bones would be split if they were hit on the street by a truck. But thanks to Dr. Cornelia Wilbur's dedication and brilliance, Shirley-aka-Sylvia would be healed. Her sixteen alters would knit together, making her whole again. She would accomplish this feat by remembering Mattie Mason's hideous crimes, as catalogued in Flora's nonfiction novel.

Flora began planning the book's abuse scenes. Connie had told her that while Shirley was under Pentothal, she had remembered Walter and Mattie Mason keeping her in a crib in their bedroom until she was nine years old. There they often staged what Connie called "primal scenes"—the Freudian term for having sex in front of one's young sons and daughters. According to Freud, primal scenes invariably traumatized small children.[6]

In addition, Connie said, Shirley had recovered memories of Mattie engaged in lesbian sex with young women in Dodge Center. Shirley remembered witnessing these acts when she walked in the woods near Dodge Center with Mattie and Mattie's "three teenage friends," spying on them as they sneaked behind bushes. Flora had also heard about Shirley being dragged around the neighborhood at night while her mother defecated on lawns. Worst of all were Peggy's accounts, preserved on audiotape, of Mattie hanging Shirley with ropes, splaying her legs apart, and raping her with utensils and enemas.[7]

Flora began having doubts about these stories, however, after she read autobiographical entries in Shirley's old therapy journals that diverged radically from what she was being told. Homosexual orgies in the woods with three teenagers, for instance: In a 1956 journal, Shirley had described her mother babysitting girls who were not teenagers but only eight or nine years old. Mattie had taken these children into the woods to play, Shirley wrote, but Shirley, herself, never saw anything improper. She'd only began to visualize images of gyrating bodies when injections of Pentothal, coupled with questioning by Connie, got her to thinking about Mattie's sick mind. She had realized then that it was Peggy who'd seen Mattie having illicit sex in the bushes.[8]

Flora knew nothing about forensic research into Pentothal and other supposed "truth serums." Nor was she aware that, far from eliciting truth, barbiturate injections commonly provoked wild fantasies. She did understand that hypnosis was risky. For an article she'd done four years earlier for *Science Digest,* she'd interviewed psychiatrists talking about innocent men who had falsely confessed to murders they had nothing to do with when hypnotized during interrogations at police stations. And she'd found a doctor who once hypnotized a man to cure him of asthma. While in a trance state the patient said he had killed his sister, and everyone believed him until it was revealed he never had a sister.[9]

But when Flora expressed skepticism about Mattie's perfidy, Connie pooh-poohed her doubts: "You are being naïve about this," she wrote in a letter, "if you can't imagine what an intelligent, intellectual, talented sadistic schizophrenic might dream up to torture her daughter."[10] Shirley reinforced Connie's position. She complained to Connie when Flora questioned her about the abuse. Flora backed off.[11]

Focusing on other motifs in Shirley's history besides abuse, she was especially eager to write scenes in which the Peggys, Vicky, Vanessa, and the rest of the alters left home and interacted with the public. After all, the book required glances, handshakes, and conversations with other people: in school, in stores, on the street. What had Shirley's friends done and said when they saw her acting like an eight-year-old, a baby, or a boy? Once, as Peggy in Trenton, New Jersey, she'd tried to break into a car she thought was her father's. Hadn't anyone noticed? Had she been arrested? She talked of marching many times into gift shops as Peggy and smashing goblets. Could any saleswoman remember a diminutive, staidly dressed woman acting deranged? Did anybody ever call the police, or an ambulance?[12]

No, Connie said, and she added that, oddly, no one in public had ever noticed Shirley dissociating into alter personalities. Her friends didn't notice, either, except for her former roommate Willie, who herself had been in psychoanalysis with Connie and was prepped about Shirley's multiple personalities before she started seeing them.[13]

Flora decided to write a fugue scene about a trip to Philadelphia. But as she researched Shirley's trips there, she discovered that most sounded less like amnesiac fugues than like the pleasant, out-of-town jaunts any artist might make for a quick change of scenery. Often Shirley returned to New York with a notebook full of charcoal and pencil studies, fully aware of everything she'd done all weekend.

Of course, the one trip that really did sound like a fugue was murky in detail because Shirley really didn't remember what had gone on in Philadelphia. She recalled catching the train from Manhattan and later calling Connie from a pay phone, confused and anxious. She had found children's pajamas in her hotel room in Philadelphia, she said, and didn't know how they got there until she found a receipt showing they'd been purchased from a store called The Mayflower Shop. She couldn't remember being in the store, which was frightening. But she'd always known she was in Philadelphia, and she returned to New York without incident. It was not a very interesting story.

Flora soon learned of a much better one. After she'd explained that she needed a good fugue scene, Shirley described an extraordinary event whose memory she said she'd repressed for the last three decades and just remembered.

It was a Saturday in early April 1942, Shirley said. She was a nineteen-year-old freshman at Mankato State Teachers College in Minnesota, and had dissociated on that day into nine-year-old Peggy. Peggy was wandering by the big post office downtown when a large-breasted woman approached and asked if she wanted to make a quick $100. Peggy said yes in her childish voice, and the woman led her to a black car. They drove north for two hours, to the Minneapolis airport, and got onto a jet. It was bound for someplace in Europe. Peggy didn't know exactly where.

Hours later they disembarked in Amsterdam. There, Peggy—who no one seemed to notice was a child in a woman's body—was handed a sheaf of papers identifying her as a British citizen. The buxom woman quietly told her to walk by her side so it would be obvious that the two women were together. That was necessary in order for them to be recognized by a young man, an officer in the British Army, who was trying to spirit his wife out of the country. The airport was occupied by German Nazis who were not allowing Dutch citizens to leave. Peggy, who looked English, was to switch places with the wife, and if the Nazis guessed the trick they would kill her, not the Dutch woman. But if Peggy made it through with her fake papers, she would give the documents to the wife and herself return to America.

It dawned on Peggy that she was part of a cloak-and-dagger operation to rescue people from the Nazis. More excited than frightened, she marched through Immigration and Customs. She passed muster without a hitch and handed her papers to the husband, who melted into the crowd. The buxom woman slipped her a return ticket and the $100 she'd earned, and she flew back to Minnesota. There, Peggy reverted to Shirley, who had no memory of the four-day trip overseas or her contribution to the struggle against fascism. All she knew was that, back in Mankato, she found $100 in her purse and had no idea where it came from. Not only that, but for years she felt funny whenever she heard the word "Amsterdam." Only recently had she begun having dreams about the place. Connie told her the dreams were memories, and one day, after Flora started planning the book, Shirley suddenly recalled everything.[14]

Flora could barely contain her excitement about the Amsterdam story, which would make a gripping opening chapter. She would bring it to life not just with Shirley's memories, but by gathering more details. She wrote a friend in Amsterdam asking him to tell her exactly what the airport there looked like. She also made plans to visit Mankato to see the post office where the full-breasted woman had approached Peggy.[15] And she would take the opportunity to investigate Shirley's childhood by spending a few days in nearby Dodge Center.

But when she told Connie and Shirley about her upcoming trip, they begged her not to go.[16] Flora's papers don't name their reasons, but the two women probably told her that Shirley was worried about Flora showing up, and the people in her hometown learning that Shirley was mentally ill and a book was being written about her condition.

To minimize the possibility, Flora came up with a scheme. She would represent herself as a journalist doing an article about "Tiny Towns in America," and claim she'd chosen Dodge Center because she had a friend named Shirley Mason who just happened to be from there. Then, when people started talking about Shirley, Flora would discreetly fish for details about her past. She expected stories about Mattie's deranged and revolting exploits to be part of the town folklore. Without anyone suspecting her motives, she would retrace Shirley's youthful footsteps.

She arrived in Minnesota in mid-June, and sure enough, there was the grand, limestone post office in downtown Mankato, just as Shirley had said. She headed to Dodge Center, sixty-eight miles away. The little town had barely changed since the Masons' time there over a generation earlier. White wood houses sat in the shade of great elm trees, flanked by flower and vegetable gardens tended by sun-bonneted old women with ramrod-straight posture. Main Street abutted two railroad tracks. Hulking, nineteen-sixties-model cars with fins were parked in the shopping district, which had never grown beyond two blocks: it was still possible to walk the length and width of the town in a half hour. Flora checked into a down-at-the-heels hotel and set out to find people who had known the Masons.[17]

The first person she ran into was Genevieve Crouch, Shirley's childhood piano teacher. "A gracious, cultivated lady," Flora wrote in her notes.[18] For a rural woman, she seemed exceptionally intelligent and sophisticated. If she had seen pathology among the Masons, Flora was sure that Crouch would remark on it, but she said nothing of the sort. Shirley had seemed moody, Crouch said. Mattie was aloof but dignified. Flora waited for tales about defecation on lawns. Nothing came.

Next on Flora's list was Grace Sorenson, a distant Mason cousin by marriage whose voice and mannerisms Mattie had taught Shirley to imitate many years ago. Sorenson was elderly and half deaf now, but she struck Flora as energetic and "peppery." She described Mattie as "odd," and when Flora asked why, she told a story about Mattie once walking into the hardware store where Walter worked and taking over her husband's job selling to customers.[19] Odd, indeed; and Flora waited for what would follow. Sorenson said no more.

Next she visited Mrs. Howe, who had once run a maternity home in Dodge Center, where she'd delivered many babies; she'd also been Mattie Mason's "good friend." Mattie was "lively" and "full of fun," Howe told Flora. And "nervous," too, but when Flora asked her to elaborate, she said merely that Mattie used to bite her nails.[20]

Even more frustrating was Dessie Blood Engbard, the Masons' former maid. Shirley had visited her in 1964, accompanied by Connie, and now, six years later, Engbard had even more photos of Shirley hanging on her walls, plus letters from Shirley, new paintings and drawings, and a housecoat she'd sent as a gift. The two were so close, Engbard told Flora, that she considered Shirley her oldest daughter. Finally, Flora thought, she'd found someone who knew the family intimately—who had lived for years with them behind closed doors—and who loved Shirley without reserve. Engbard would have seen child abuse and battering. She would not keep it a secret now.

But Engbard had nothing critical whatsoever to say about how Mattie Mason treated her daughter. On the contrary, she was full of praise, swearing that she had "never met such kind people as the Masons."[21] Flora waited for at least a hint about domestic torture and defecation on neighbors' lawns. Nothing.

And nothing from anyone else, either.

Flora went for a walk, passed the Masons' old house, and was invited inside. She stood in the sunroom, where Shirley remembered her ribs being broken. She went down in the basement, where Shirley recalled Mattie squatting shamelessly in front of Walter's workmen and fouling the floor with her feces. Outside, Flora noticed the so-called "carpentry shop and wheat crib" in the backyard. But it was only a squat little coal shed, much too tiny to have served as a horror house where a homicidal schizophrenic could leave a child to die.

Flora also searched Dodge Center for the forested area and the bushes where Mattie was said to have conducted lesbian orgies with Shirley in tow. As hard as she looked, she could not find any woods. There was only flat Midwestern prairie.

Had orgies really happened? Was Mattie Mason actually mad? Or were her crimes merely her daughter's fantasies gone awry? Mulling these questions, Flora felt uneasy.

To erase her doubts, she planned to interview Dr. Otoniel Flores, the Masons' old family physician. Surely he would have noticed a little girl's broken bones and her damaged genitals. From his office file cabinets he would pull manila folders with yellowing records, corroborating Shirley's most terrible memories. Then Flora learned that Dr. Flores had been dead for twenty-seven years.[22] His records were gone.

There were plenty more people in Dodge Center to talk to, but Flora didn't feel up to further frustration. As she was heading out of town she passed a small, white building with a lintel over the door. It was the Seventh-Day Adventist church. "Made of wood," Flora wrote in her notes. "Victorian in feeling. Neat as a pin."[23]

Back in Manhattan, Flora anxiously contacted two of her closest friends, Aubrey and Val Winsey. Aubrey had met Flora during their days on Madison Avenue, where he'd been a prize-winning copywriter. Now he worked in the public relations department at John Jay College. Val was an anthropology professor.[24] They invited Flora to their apartment in mid-summer after she asked them to listen to some recordings she was using to write *Sylvia*. The material was beginning to confuse her, she said, and she wanted their opinion. The three of them spent hours reviewing tapes of Connie's old Pentothal and hypnosis sessions with Shirley. Then they talked for hours more.

Both of the Winseys expressed profound skepticism about Shirley's mental problems, not to mention the reasons she claimed she was ill. Val and Aubrey could not believe so many horrible crimes could have been perpetrated by Mattie Mason without anyone's noticing.[25]

"The fact that the mother was defecating on the lawns," Val asked Flora. "Wouldn't the town people get to know about this?"

"I didn't pick that up," Flora said. "I doubt if they would have withheld it . . . it seems to me that if she had done that she would have been committed or hospitalized." Connie had also told her Mattie had "homosexual affairs with girls in the woods." Yet in Dodge Center, Flora confessed, she had not been able to find "where the hell the woods are." Val asked if anyone there had confirmed the lesbians-in-the-forest story. "Absolutely not," Flora answered.

"What the hell!" Val exclaimed. "You're dealing with a psychiatrist who is obviously having a homosexual relationship with this girl. And you are dealing with a girl who has been diagnosed time and again as a hysteric." Flora was quiet; Val continued. "Unless you have some of the evidence, I don't see how you can take this whole thing on faith."

Aubrey hypothesized that "Sylvia's" stories of abuse were fantasies, and he offered Freudian explanations for their origins. Sylvia's father, he reminded Flora, "was such a serious, religious person," much more so than her mother. In Sylvia's oedipal stage of early psychological development, when she wanted her father all to herself, she might have tried to "reject in the mother" what her father disapproved of in his wife. Yet Sylvia loved her mother, and she might have had "strong feelings of guilt" at identifying with Mattie's vestigial Methodism and relative lack of devotion to the tenets of Seventh-Day Adventism. Maybe, Aubrey speculated, the little girl had unconsciously "desired to be punished" for being like her mother. Hence her fantasies of being raped, and her obsessions with vaginal assaults and enemas.

But why was her mother the culprit? Perhaps, Aubrey mused, little Sylvia wanted to hurt Mattie but couldn't admit it. So she turned her unconscious urge into fantasies about her mother hurting *her*.

"Say that again," Flora said. "I'm not sure I fully understand."

"Projection," Aubrey explained. "It's a simple projection of your otherness onto someone else, so you can take it out on them rather than on yourself."

"You know," Val added, "the thing I think is very important is for you not to get trapped, Flora, into the psychiatrist's diagnosis."

"I can't simply be an echo for Connie and Sylvia," Flora agreed. Still, she told the Winseys, Sylvia's stories of her mother's insane behaviors were essential to the book, whose structure, she explained, "has already been established. It's official."

Val could sense Flora's unease. "So you feel very motivated about doing this book?" she asked.

Yes, Flora answered, she did. But she wasn't sure what she had left in the way of compelling facts—except for Amsterdam. She told the Winseys the story about Shirley's spy-versus-spy trip there on a plane in 1942.

They were singularly unimpressed.

"1942?" Aubrey echoed, incredulous. "But wasn't Holland at that time occupied by Germany? Weren't we at war with Germany?" His implication, of course, was that Holland's airports were under military control by the Nazis during the time Shirley said she'd gone there. The idea of her arriving from Minneapolis was absurd.

Flora left the Winseys more confused than ever. Some weeks later she had her secretary's husband drive her to Lexington, Kentucky, to meet with Connie and Shirley[26] and try to do damage control. What followed was an *Alice in Wonderland* conversation about Amsterdam.

"I inquired from a friend," Flora announced, "and found out it would be impossible for an American to come there in April 1942 because we were at war then. You could not come on a commercial plane."[27]

"It wasn't a commercial plane," Connie interjected, though Shirley previously had said she traveled on TWA. Shirley chimed in and reported that the flight was full of British soldiers.

"What was a British transport plane doing in Minneapolis?" interrupted Flora.

Shirley didn't know, but she insisted she was in Amsterdam "a day or two before the actual occupation" and "Nazi soldiers were in the airport."

When the group attempted to fix an exact date, however, they realized that Shirley had always said her fugue to Europe occurred while she was in college. But Holland had already been invaded by the time she finished high school.

"Did you go back on the same plane?" Flora asked.

"No. I went back on an American plane."

"You couldn't have gone on an American plane. There were none flying," Connie allowed.

"Well," Shirley concluded blithely, "one thing I know for sure: I got back, because here I am."[28]

Things only got worse after Flora told Connie she wanted Shirley's and Mattie's old medical records. Flora knew that Mattie had been treated decades earlier at the Mayo Clinic, and Shirley had, too, when she'd been hospitalized at age three—for malnutrition caused by the enemas, Shirley and Connie said. This was the period, presumably, when she'd been so traumatized by Mattie that alter personality Peggy had first appeared.

Connie had never bothered to request these records, but at Flora's insistence she asked for them now. When they arrived, Flora noted with alarm that Mattie had been diagnosed with "asthenia"—what today would probably be called depression—but never with schizophrenia. As for Shirley, the records showed that her hospitalization at age three had lasted for only a few hours, and it was due to tonsillitis—there was not a word about malnutrition.[29] If Flora's archives are an indication, no records regarding the gynecological surgery ever came. Or if they did, Connie never passed them on.

If the discrepancies in the medical records weren't disturbing enough, Flora also leafed more carefully through Connie's therapy materials and found Shirley's five-page, single-spaced letter from 1958 denying she had multiple personality disorder. Reading the completely believable recantation, Flora was stricken with the realization that *Sylvia: The Many Multiples of One* was, quite possibly, one big lie. No, it wasn't, responded Connie— Shirley had falsely repudiated her illness simply because she'd been "apprehensive" about having her case written up for public consumption.[30] Many patients issued fake denials at the end of analysis. It was a trivial matter, and there was no reason for Flora to include Shirley's letter in her book.[31]

Issuing her demurrals, Connie seemed as oblivious as Shirley had been about Amsterdam. Flora's sinking feeling sank deeper; she was tempted to trash the project.

Yet how could she? Not only had she told her friends, her colleagues, and all the famous psychiatrists she knew that she was writing *Sylvia*, but she had already accepted an advance for the work and was contractually obligated to deliver a finished book within just five months. Yet every time she checked one of Shirley's abuse claims, it came up questionable. Was it possible that her diagnosis derived from her psychiatrist's suggestion? What if Shirley had never had alters before she met Connie?

But she *had* possessed alters early on, Shirley insisted, even when she was a teenager, and there was solid evidence. She handed Flora her journals from high school and college—from before she'd been exposed to psychiatrists. In the journals, Shirley said, Flora would see evidence of multiple personalities long before Connie or any doctor could possibly have planted ideas in her head.[32]

Flora opened a sheaf of papers labeled "1941 Diary," penned neatly in Shirley's hand. Its dozen or so pages each contained several brief entries.[33] They began in the voice of a normal teenaged girl:

Feb. 20—I went to the basketball game but we were so late we couldn't both sit down front so I sat in back and Lois went down.

Feb. 26—I got B+ on my autobiography . . . I am reading Patricia *by Grace L. Hill and I think the story is good.*

Some entries brimmed with angst that sounded self-pitying but typically adolescent:

March 17—I have such overwhelming feelings of being alone, and how I wish someone could understand me!

But other entries, dated after Shirley's graduation from high school, were darker, hinting at serious mental distress. These passages strongly suggested she was battling alterations in consciousness, as though something or someone else controlled her. There was even evidence of fugue states.

Oct. 7—Four days. Oh what will I do? I was in and out of the dorm—didn't eat here but came back nights. Am very tired. Can't find out much.

Oct. 8—I must be very careful so no one will know. They would put me out and I just love it here.

Oct. 25—Started for class yesterday a.m. but didn't get there . . .

One entry must have particularly struck Flora. It was dated late in 1941, when Shirley had moved from Dodge Center to Mankato and was finishing her first semester at the state teachers college. According to the diary, however, Mankato did not yet exist for her.

Dec. 31—Almost through high school. Am I ever glad! Only go so I can go on to college. I want to learn. Care nothing for social life.

It is as though an alter personality had written these sentences—one whose consciousness was trapped in the calendar of a year before, back in Dodge Center. The diary was proof that Shirley's mind had fragmented long before she met Connie. Flora refastened the loose pages with a paperclip. She must have felt tremendously relieved.

She wouldn't have if she had looked into the diary more carefully. A closer examination might have stopped her at this entry:

Sept. 29—Been reading A Surgeon's World *by Max Thorek—he is a Jew.*

Max Thorek was a famous American physician in the 1940s. He developed a new technique for removing gall bladders; he was also one of the first doctors to do cosmetic operations on women. And Thorek wrote a *A Surgeon's World*, a popular account of doctoring, which Shirley's diary had her reading in 1941.

But she could not possibly have read *A Surgeon's World* that year. The book was not published until 1943. Furthermore, according to forensic document specialists Peter Tytell and Gerry LaPorte, who examined the diary during the process of researching this book, Shirley's "1941" entries were written in ballpoint pen. But ballpoints were not used in the United States until 1945.

The diary was a fake.[34] Most likely Shirley and Connie had cooked it up together in order to trick Flora into staying with *Sylvia*. She fell for it.

And she decided that, while the details of Shirley's case history were confused and often patently false, the story as a whole was "emotionally true," which was all that mattered. Truman Capote's rules were irrelevant, Flora rationalized. She could make *Sylvia* into a nonfiction novel even if she took tremendous liberties with the facts.

Soon she had completed her opening chapter. It dealt with a fugue from Columbia University to Philadelphia that was said to have lasted from January 2 to January 7.

Five days lost, Flora wrote in eye-catching italics. She continued in spell-binding language reminiscent of her style in the women's magazines, piecing together a narrative based on Shirley's accounts of several different trips to Philadelphia, including the incident with the children's clothing.

[I]n a corner of the dresser, was something that she hadn't noticed before: a receipt for a pair of pajamas purchased at the Mayflower Shop, 5007 Wayne Avenue, telephone Victor 3-7779 . . .

Pajamas! Where were they? She searched the drawers and the closets, but she couldn't find them.

She searched the bathroom. At first she saw nothing; then she saw the pajamas on a hook behind the door, hanging like an accusation.

The pajamas were rumpled, slept in. Had she slept in them? They were loud and gay and bright orange and green stripes. Not her style. She always chose solid colors, usually in varying shades of blue. The pajamas she found were the sort a child might select . . .

Her knees sagged. The self-recrimination she had felt upon discovering that she had lost time was suddenly intensified . . . She had to get back to New York while she was still herself.[35]

In subsequent chapters, Flora changed Mattie's name to Hattie and concentrated on her cruelty and sexual perversions.

She wrote a grain-crib scene: *Then the mother placed the child in the wheat and left, pulling the stairs up into the ceiling. Encircled by wheat, [Sylvia] felt herself smothering and thought that she was going to die.*[36]

She included sex in the woods with teenagers: *Their dresses, pulled up, were tucked above their waists. Naked from the waist down,* she continued, *mother and the girls were lying on the ground, their hands intermingling, their buttocks visible. Fingers moving. Palms stroking. Bodies gyrating. Ecstatic expressions.*[37]

She created a primal scene, too: *The shades were usually halfway down in the twelve-by-fourteen bedroom. The crib was placed so that a street light shone in the bedroom window, silhouetting the penis . . . until she was nine years old, parental intercourse took place within her hearing and vision . . . the various selves had different reactions . . . Marcia feared for mother's safety. Mary resented the denial of privacy. Vanessa was revolted by the hypocrisy . . . Peggy Lou . . . sobbed all night.*[38]

In a scatological-walk-in-the-neighborhood passage, Flora described how Hattie *pulled down her bloomers, squatted, and with ritualistic deliberateness and perverse pleasure defecated on the elected spot.*[39]

Finally, she wrote an especially long section detailing the way Hattie would separate her daughter's legs *with a long wooden spoon, tie her feet to the spoon with dish towels, and then string her to the end of a light bulb cord, suspended from the ceiling. The child was left to swing in space while the mother proceeded to the water faucet to wait for the water to get cold. After muttering, "Well, it's not going to get any colder," she would fill the adult-sized enema bag to capacity and return it to her daughter. As the child swung in space, the mother would insert the enema tip into the child's urethra and fill the bladder with cold water. "I did it," Hattie would scream triumphantly . . .*[40]

Flora also included riveting yet wholly fictional portrayals of "Sylvia" first presenting herself to Connie as Peggy, then reacting to Connie's revelation that she suffered from the presence of multiple personalities. In reality, Peggy had announced herself quite calmly, and Shirley had seemed calm, even pleased when she found out about her diagnosis. But Flora knew these behaviors would bore readers, so she changed them. The face of the emergent Peggy, she wrote, contorted with fury as she *jumped up from the desk chair . . . She headed with rapid, spiderlike movements toward two long casement windows. Swinging the green draperies aside, she clenched her left fist again and pounded with it at a small windowpane. "Let me out,"* she screamed. *"Let me out!" It was an agonized plea—the call of the haunted, the hunted, the trapped . . . there was a crash. The pounding fist had gone through a windowpane.*[41]

And after learning she had multiple personalities, Flora added, Sylvia exploded, toggling crazily from alter to alter: *She really blew . . . one moment she was a ranting child, walking on the furniture, leaving her fingerprints on the ceiling. The next moment she was a self-possessed and knowing woman . . . then . . . quaking . . . lying inert on the bed.*[42]

Then, to assure readers that this outrageous behavior was caused by real abuse, perpetrated by an actual maniac, Flora wrote a scene in which Connie got Walter Mason to confess that his wife was, in fact, psychotic. Nothing of the sort had ever happened. But the passage was narrated in the third person as an interrogation, with Connie relentlessly grilling Walter, whom Flora called Willard Dorsett:

Had he been aware that Hattie's behavior was peculiar?

He moved jerkily in his chair and became defensive . . . "At times she was difficult . . . nervous . . . she had some spells . . . Hattie was odd."

"It was more than odd, Mr. Dorsett . . ." Was he aware that as a child Sybil sustained an unusual number of injuries, the doctor wanted to know . . .

"Why yes," he replied, screwing up his thin lips . . .

Did he remember the burns on his daughter's hands, her black eyes?

"Yes," he replied slowly . . .

The wheat crib over his carpenter's shop? . . .

"Oh, merciful Father, not Hattie!" . . . Then he told Dr. Wilbur about his having taken Hattie to a psychiatrist at the Mayo Clinic . . . The doctor there had diagnosed Hattie as a schizophrenic.[43]

Shirley probably knew her mother had never been diagnosed as a schizophrenic. And she certainly must have remembered that her home had no grain crib. Yet she rarely objected to Flora's falsifications. Only two of them seemed to bother her. One involved an erotic scene with Mario, the Brazilian man she had dated in the 1960s. For the book Flora changed his name to Ramon.

Ramon caressed her. Her head moved against his chest. He embraced her tightly. "When I have an erection," he told her, "I measure. It's seven inches. Good?" . . . He moved back toward her and began gingerly to unzip her dress.[44]

When Shirley read this passage in Flora's draft chapters, she swore she'd never acted sexually with Mario, and she asked to have the material deleted. She also objected strenuously to paragraphs about the "primal scene"—her parents having sex in front of her—though she had once described something similar to Connie while she was high on Pentothal. "Nothing like that went on!" she insisted now. "Oh, no, no, no, no, no!" She recorded herself demanding the passage be removed and sent the tape to Connie and Flora.[45]

For her part, Connie was thrilled by the work Flora mailed her, and she provided sneak previews to several women who did office work at the University of Kentucky medical school. "Gave [the manuscript] to my secretary who gave it to Linda (other secretary) to read then returned it—came to borrow it back to give to Judy . . . (another secretary), who wanted to read it after Marcia told her about it—and Judy gave it to Dotty who got excited about it . . . and Flora, there are *lots* of secretaries! They loved it."[46]

So did the book's new publisher. Cowles, the company that had bought *Sylvia*, had folded in 1971 and been bought by Regnery, a Chicago-based company. Regnery for years had been known as a publisher of weighty, politically right-wing books: its biggest seller was William Buckley's 1951 denunciation of liberalism in universities, *God and Man at Yale*. But in the late 1960s, owner Henry Regnery handed executive control to Harvey Plotnick, his young son-in-law, who was much less interested in politics than in making money, as he would later tell the *Chicago Tribune*. When Plotnick first looked at the *Sylvia* contract he'd just inherited, he'd decided to scrap the book. But he changed his mind after Flora's agent sent Regnery some chapters and Plotnick's wife started reading them. She couldn't put them down, and in the middle of the night she woke her husband up and told him he had to publish the book. After reading it himself, Plotnick assigned an editor to *Who Is Sylvia?* and told Flora to finish the manuscript.[47]

By late 1972 she was writing nonstop. For several weeks she shuttered herself in her apartment, where she commenced work early in the morning, broke only for meals, and picked up again until midnight. She wrote by hand, so intensely that she could barely bend her fingers. Finally she completed her last chapters, mystical accounts of the sixteen alter personalities, under hypnosis, gradually progressing in age to adulthood.

"In ten minutes I'm going to say it is five minutes of seven," Dr. Wilbur commented in one age progression scene to Ruthie, the baby personality. *"Between now and that time, you are going to grow up one whole year . . . and later all the others are going to grow up too . . . in ten minutes you will be six . . . now you are six years old" . . . "Will I have to go to church?"* Peggy Ann wanted to know. *"No, you won't have to go to church,"* the doctor replied reassuringly. . . . *"Would you still be my friend?"* Mary asked apprehensively. *"You bet your life,"* the doctor replied emphatically. . . . *"I won't leave you."*[48]

One by one thereafter, Mary and the others relinquished their identities and melded into Syvia's consciousness. In a neat stylistic counterpoint to her own brunette looks, the last alter to yield was "The Blonde." *"Do you know what it means to have a whole day ahead of you, a day you can call your own?"* Flora had Sylvia asking excitedly. *"It's still a marvel to me how much a well person can accomplish; I'm so lucky."*[49]

Putting the finishing touches on the manuscript, Flora decided to keep the juicy material about Mario, as well as the section about Sylvia's parents having sex in front of her. "I have already written the primal scene," she wrote Connie. "To revise its essential meaning would distort the truth."[50]

At Regnery, Harvey Plotnick had some ideas of his own about how the book should read. He demanded that the heroine's name be revised.[51] Sylvia sounded improper to him, possibly because most women in the United States named Sylvia were Jewish. Flora objected vehemently, but Connie and Shirley christened the book *Sybil* because it sounded more mythic yet more American, and more saleable.

Regnery had one more request: that Connie agree to have her real name appear in *Sybil*[52] in order to increase sales by gracing the book with realism. Connie was pleased; she had never been happy with the idea of concealing her identity. She agreed to reveal it, and by now *Sybil* was so close to fruition that everyone involved was feverish, unable to think about the risk that using Dr. Cornelia Wilbur's name would pose to her patient's anonymity.[53]

With the final edits done, Plotnick decided to put serious resources into promoting the book. He ordered a first printing of 40,000 copies—the largest Regnery had ever done. He also arranged for an advertising and promotion budget of $60,000. Today that would be well over a quarter of a million dollars. Plotnick even managed to interest the big publishing company Warner Books in *Sybil*. Surmising that it would be a hit, Warner paid $300,000 to publish the paperback edition a year after Regnery's hardcover came out. Warner's plans were lavish—they included promoting Flora and Connie for appearances on television shows such as *To Tell the Truth*.[54]

By early spring *Sybil* was typeset and bound, with a shiny cover featuring an image of a young woman's face in jigsaw-puzzle pieces. The book was scheduled for publication in late May. Flora activated prior connections with the *New York Times* syndication department, which sold work for reprinting in other newspapers.[55]

The *Times* decided to syndicate not just excerpts of *Sybil*, but the whole book, abridged, before it was published. Twenty-eight daily installments were scheduled to begin in late April, in cities such as Miami, San Antonio, and Springfield, Massachusetts. For a month, newspaper readers would be able to settle in with Vicky, Peggy, Mary, Mike, and Sam—and with scenes of Sybil's demented mother defecating on lawns, conducting lesbian orgies, and raping her daughter with kitchen utensils. This kind of sex and perversion had never before been published on the "Women's" pages.

Flora, Connie, and Shirley waited excitedly for public reaction. They hoped that the newspaper series would pave the way for positive reviews as soon as the book came out. They also hoped to garner interest from major television programs, and even from Hollywood. After almost twenty years of suffering and therapy and toil, they hoped that the fame they had dreamed about was on its way.

It was. And when fame struck, none of them would be immune to its lure—or its complications.

CHAPTER 15

THE BOOK

S YBIL WENT ON SALE ON May 22, 1973, and soon became one of the year's two top nonfiction books that weren't how-to guides or cookbooks—its sole competition was Alistair Cooke's *America.* Within a decade it would sell almost seven million copies in the United States and overseas, and be adapted as a television drama that would go on to be regarded as a classic. All this success created an intense buzz around the book's creators. Shirley strenuously avoided the limelight, but her collaborators embraced it, scheduling countless media appearances. Thanks to early interest created by the book's syndication to newspapers, Flora and Connie began making these appearances in mid-May, days prior to *Sybil*'s publication. Their debut was on the *Dick Cavett Show.*[1]

Cavett led off with jokes about the Watergate scandal, which had just gone into televised Senate hearings. He joshed with comedians Bob and Ray, and sang "Way Down Yonder in New Orleans" with Pearl Bailey. Then his voice grew solemn. His next two guests, he announced, would be talking about "one of the most incredible case histories in psychiatric history."

Flora was fifty-seven years old. Connie was sixty-four. Each walked onto the set in satin pumps and a full-length, low-cut evening gown. Flora's coiffure was sprayed to impossibly high bouffant, and the diaphanous sleeves of her snow-white gown trailed boas of ermine. The getup was her idea of glamour, but more than anything her appearance revealed the toll that writing *Sybil* had exacted on her health. She had developed deep bags under her eyes in the last three years, and her body had ballooned to at least two hundred pounds of avoirdupois—each one accentuated by her scoop-necked bodice and its feathery fluff.

Cavett grimly summarized the book. When the woman known as Sybil was young, her psychotic mother assaulted her with enemas and "penetrated her hymen with a button hook." Flora chimed in, adding that this violence wrought such a burden of anger—or "buhhhhhden of annnguh," as she put it in her "voice beautiful"—that Sybil had split into multiple personalities.

Cavett noted how bizarre the concept of multiple personality was and asked if anyone had suggested the story was a hoax. Most publishers had turned up their noses at the book, Flora said. "But true it is!" she insisted.

Connie told the story of how she had first noticed her patient's illness. It happened, she said, when Sybil charged into the window in New York City, cut her hand on the glass, and announced that she was Peggy.

Flora never smiled on the Cavett show, and neither did Connie. There was friction between the women, though they were trying to conceal it before the public. Flora was angry that she had to go on television with Connie. She wanted the stage to herself. But Flora's agent had advised her that TV audiences would want to see Dr. Cornelia Wilbur because her psychiatry credentials lent *Sybil* credibility. Still, the agent advised, there were ways to deal with Connie. "[S]he will try to hog the camera," the agent wrote. "But you've simply got to get in there and fight and interrupt her."[2] Flora's frown on *Cavett* reflected how hard she was working to cut Connie off—butting in with abstruse medical terminology, for instance, and launching into longwinded explanations of the nature of hysteria. Connie's frown evidenced her distress at Flora's behavior.

The critics weighed in several weeks later, and many panned *Sybil*. A *New York Times* reviewer wrote that the book made him "uncomfortable from beginning to end," giving him feelings of "nagging embarrassment and ultimately of anger." Author Flora Schreiber was "prurient," "voyeuristic," and displayed the main character's sixteen personalities like "freaks at a circus." Psychoanalyst Cornelia Wilbur seemed "both one-dimensionally patient" in the book, "and—with her barbiturates and her hypnosis—peculiarly intrusive."[3]

Time magazine wondered if *Sybil* was real.[4] The tweedy *New York Review of Books* was put off by the story.[5] But lesser publications loved it and found it perfectly believable. The Omaha *World-Herald* titled its review " 'Sybil' Bizarre but Still True."[6] Flora subscribed to a clipping service so she would not miss the favorable reviews, like this one, from smaller cities and towns.

Bookstores sold out quickly and reordered immediately. The Literary Guild and Psychology Today book clubs began featuring *Sybil* as selections. The hardcover climbed the best-seller list and settled in, alongside *Dr. Atkins Diet Revolution, I'm OK You're OK, The Joy of Sex*—and *America*. Foreign publishers bought the rights in various languages.

Flora responded in two ways to this heady success. For one, she started doing behind-the-scenes paperwork to nominate herself and *Sybil* for a Nobel prize in literature. (She did not win.) In addition, she began "spending like a drunken sailor," according to her cousin Stan Aronson—pulling out $20 bills for $3 taxi trips, for instance, and telling the driver to keep the change.[7] She upgraded her wardrobe with designer dresses, capes, and a full-length mink coat, and she began having her hair done at Saks Fifth Avenue. She bought an annual subscription, costing hundreds of dollars, for orchestra seats at the opera.[8]

Connie was already so well-heeled that the money she earned from the book's success had little effect on her life. But Shirley used her royalties to cancel her therapy debt. For years after she got a steady job, she'd been paying Connie $100 a month, but now she paid off the balance of the thousands of dollars she still owed.[9]

Sybil's astonishing triumph followed a savvy promotion campaign, to be sure. But Flora quickly became aware of other forces pushing it. By summer 1973 she was receiving bags of letters each week, and they weren't typical fan mail. They came from readers who had stayed up all night to reach the last page, and had been haunted by the story ever since.

"I was that young lady (and the rest of her selves) through the entire book," wrote Ruth, from upstate New York. "Never have I been so moved."

"Tears came to my eyes," confessed Patsy, an Avis Rent-a-Car clerk in Fort Lauderdale.

From Lynch Station, Virginia, Vicky gushed: "It was almost as though I was living her struggle."

And Sarina, with no return address, wrote, "I, too, dream about Sybil . . . although she is old enough to be my mother."[10]

Flora had worried that Sybil's multiple personality disorder would make her seem too alien for readers to identify with, and now she was ecstatic to find that the opposite was true. "There is a little of all of us in Sybil, and a little of Sybil in us!" she began exclaiming to audiences at events.[11]

At least one esteemed publication agreed. *Sybil* was a hit, wrote the *Washington Post's* Sonya Rudikoff, because her multiple personality disorder mirrored "the contemporary stereotypes that people often apply to themselves: The poorly assimilated psychological and sociological notions of the day have led many to think of themselves not as persons but as disparate assemblages of roles, without any reigning self."[12]

Rudikoff was on the mark except for one thing. She referred to "people" and "persons," yet Flora's torrents of mail came almost entirely from women. And they weren't just *thinking* of themselves as "disparate assemblages of roles"—they *were* confronting new roles, barrages of them. Profound social changes had recently opened up new spheres, at home, school, and work. It was hard for people to get used to those spheres, and they led to conflicting feelings. Searching for a sense of integration, women took up multiple personality disorder as a metaphor, thanks entirely to *Sybil*.

"I always had times when I wanted to be someone else," an unmarried young woman from Massachusetts named Delphine wrote to Flora. Inside, she explained, she had other selves, "struggling to escape."

Delphine said she cared for nothing except "being loved." But for women, to be both loved and unmarried required constant sexual willingness, lest a "chick" be labeled a cockteaser, a bitch, or even worse, "uptight." Many young women eagerly embraced the new, erotic zeitgeist. Many others felt pressured by men, who were still calling the shots: demanding sex on their own terms, paying little attention to their partners' desires or needs.

"As I was reading *Sybil*," Delphine wrote to Flora, "the question . . . "What is a whole person?" came to my mind. Another did also: "Am *I* a whole person?" She felt "torn in all directions," Delphine added, but she told Flora how "grateful I am for a book like *Sybil*, for it made me realize that I have to get myself together, learn to be me."[13]

Millions of women felt similarly—as though they harbored buried identities crying for discovery, expression, and integration via extraordinary and heroic ministrations such as the kind Dr. Wilbur had given to Sybil. And indeed, new psychotherapies claiming special qualities were springing up in the 1970s. Many aimed to help patients find their inner selves by thinking and talking about their relationships with their parents—often in aggressive and disturbing ways.

Primal therapy, for instance, theorized that unremembered psychic pain from early life caused illness in adults. Children were thought to be deeply traumatized by the experience of being conceived and born, and after that it just got worse, because parents rarely showed enough love.

Primal therapy encouraged people to sob, roll on the floor, and scream blood curdling accusations against their parents. "Daddy hates me. Stop, Daddy, stop!" "Mommy! You promised you wouldn't!"[14] The screaming was said to bring back repressed memories of trauma during childhood, birth, and even conception. These recollections freed the self.

Years down the road, primal therapy was dismissed by many psychiatrists and psychologists as quackery, but meanwhile, people flocked for treatment, including celebrities like ex-Beatle John Lennon. He incorporated his experience into the 1970 rock album *John Lennon/Plastic Ono Band*. One song led off with a lyrical rendering of primal therapy's founding principle: "As soon as you're born, they make you feel small / By giving you no time instead of it all." Another song wailed "Mama, don't go!" over and over and over. It's title: "Mother."[15]

Lennon could just as well have been singing about the hateful Hattie Dorsett.

Sybil, with its depiction of a psychotic, violent mother, became a poster book for national concerns about child abuse—which were skyrocketing during 1973, if media coverage is evidence. Americans were flooded that year with stories about infants and preschoolers whose parents assaulted them with weapons and—as Senator Walter Mondale put it—by "kicking, torturing, strangling, stabbing, scalding, burning, poisoning, dismemberment, starvation, imprisonment, freezing and crushing." Flora sent a copy of *Sybil* to Mondale; he wrote back that he looked forward to reading it.[16]

Meanwhile, many of the letters Flora received dwelled on abuse in families. A California woman named Karen wrote that the book "greatly facilitated the understanding of the most complex and horrifying results of wounds that can be inflicted on children in the name of love."

The letters kept coming, from readers moved by various aspects of the story. Some saw Sybil as a heroine and an inspiration. As one woman wrote:

I admire her courage against the seemingly insurmountable problems that she faced as I've never respected or admired anything or anyone before. When I am faced with my day-to-day problems, I hope I will always remember Sybil and realize how small my troubles really are.

Younger women, high school and college-age girls, focused more on Sybil's multiple personalities than on her suffering. Some wondered if they, too, sometimes split into different people, then reunited with no memory of the alternate selves.

Countless others took multiple personality more metaphorically and more seriously. Ellen, from northern Virginia, had just gotten a bachelors degree in math and had started looking resignedly for a "strictly math related" job that would mean "abandoning a part of me that was more concerned with people." But reading *Sybil* had made her realize she didn't have to be "just one person at a time for all my life." After all, "if Sybil can live with all her selves, I shouldn't have to give up any part of me just because of a job." Ellen changed her career plans, and her joy at her new "multiplicity" was visceral: "My body teems with excitement," she wrote Flora, "at having many different parts of its own. You have revived in me the feeling that each day is a new beginning."

Lois, from Los Angeles, felt mystical about her encounter with the book. "I find it utterly amazing that not everyone who has read *Sybil* sees the . . . fantastic probabilities of understanding not only themselves but the entire universe."

Others wrote Flora simply to thank her for a fantastic read. Janna, in Washington state, thought *Sybil* was "sensational." Lori admitted she'd cried while reading it. Suzanne, from rural Pennsylvania, was especially absorbed when Sybil's mother sexually tortured her: "When I read that part, I got deeply involved like I was there watching." Lori was eleven years old going on twelve, and so was Janna. Suzanne was in eighth grade.[17]

With letters like these pouring in, Warner Books knew it had a hit in its forthcoming paperback edition. The company scheduled two million copies for release in early 1974, each with a cover featuring a long-haired young woman's face in jagged slats, like an image in a smashed mirror.[18]

Flora, Connie, and Shirley decided to cash in on the book's success even further. They contacted a lawyer in Kentucky, drew up papers, and emerged with an enterprise for marketing *Sybil*-related products: *Sybil* tee shirts, *Sybil* lapel buttons, *Sybil* board games, *Sybil* dolls. Shirley started contacting manufacturers, and when she made calls and wrote letters, she always mentioned the new company. Its name was Sybil, Inc.[19]

CHAPTER 16

THE FILM

I N EARLY 1974 FLORA LEARNED that Lorimar, a made-for-television film company in southern California, wanted to produce *Sybil*. Contracts were signed and work on the project began. The first task was to recruit a writer to do the screenplay.

Stewart Stern took the job. He was the perfect Hollywood writer for *Sybil*, having spent years trying every therapy under the sun.[1] He also was one of the film industry's most highly regarded screenwriters; his most famous work was *Rebel Without a Cause*. Stern was a stickler for understanding his characters completely and for communicating, as he put it, "the deepest psychological motivation" for any action he portrayed.[2]

In early 1974 he started work on *Sybil* the television script, but after weeks of reading and taking notes, he realized there were major roadblocks. The characters made little sense—and in many ways neither did the story.[3] Flora was furious when she heard these criticisms. She had wanted to author the script, and she'd heard that Stern was writing his teleplay from scratch because he thought her book lacked dramatic conflict. She wrote him an incredulous letter. "No conflict in *Sybil*? Man against man," she suggested. Also "man against society . . . man against the elements . . . man against himself."[4]

Stern politely ignored her.

But he was so puzzled by the book that he typed out over two hundred questions[5] for Flora and Connie, including No. 24:

When Sybil had a "fugue" in Dr. W's office in Omaha and tried to jump out of the window, Dr. W said "I wasn't really disturbed."... Really? Seems to me Dr. W. would have been gravely disturbed.

As a maven of psychotherapy, Stern was also bothered that Dr. Wilbur socialized with her patient, even traveled with her. *"Where did Dr. W. and Sybil go on their 'frequent out of town visits'?"* he asked in Question No. 225:

If they stayed places overnight, did they share a room? Did this present problems for either of them? Was it very hard for Sybil to accept Dr. W. in the role of a friend ... a woman who had nightgowns, possibly creamed her face, brushed her teeth, went to the bathroom? In the light of Hattie's bathroom excesses, did the knowledge that Dr. W went to the bathroom on occasion present problems for Sybil?

Stern's biggest problem with the book was that he didn't believe its claims about Sybil's crazy mother hurting her. *"Hattie's shrill rising laughter when she tortures Sybil,"* he wrote, *"must have been heard by Grandma upstairs and the live-in maid, Jessie. How could it go on in the way described?"*

Further, given that Sybil came from *"a town whose hobby was to keep an eye on everyone,"* how could her mother possibly have gotten away *"with such excesses as public lesbian play, fooling around sexually with small children ... public defecation, and torture?"*

Stern's years of therapy had sensitized him to the fantasy life of children. In a string of additional queries, he asked if Sybil's horrific memories might, in fact, be *"the elaborate creation of a child warned constantly that if she didn't behave ... some awful and unnamed punishment would be meted out to her."* Furthermore, *"Has Dr. Wilbur ever had second thoughts ... ? Has she ever thought, as I did, that perhaps the tortures were invented by Sybil ... ? Isn't it possible that a badly given enema, even if given therapeutically, can be seized upon as the form of the torture to come when threats are made?"*

Looking for answers, he flew to New York and spent several days with Flora, asking her question after question from his list. Flora had never spoken at such length with a screenwriter, much less one as brilliant as Stern. After several conversations, she forgot her hostility and warmed up to him, admitting that she, too, worried that the torture memories were false. She confessed that she once considered scrapping the project.[6]

But she also played Stern some audiotapes of Shirley's old therapy sessions with Connie. Though he could barely make out the words, he was bowled over by the screams of terror in high-pitched, little girl voices. Sobbing and furniture crashing—that was Peggy trying to escape, Flora explained. Garbled pleas to some mysterious tormenter to "Stop! Stop!" Abject weeping. It made Stern want to weep, too.[7]

Stern didn't know that Peggy and the other child voices had never appeared except when Connie had "Sybil" in bed with a syringe full of Pentothal in her arm, or on a couch in a hypnotic trance. Still unsure of what to believe after his visit with Flora, Stern went to Lexington to talk to Connie.

She had reserved a room for him at a motel, and she showed up for their first meeting, as Stern remembered over thirty years later, driving "the longest convertible Lincoln Continental I'd ever seen. It was pink. Pink! And in [the] front . . . was this apricot colored hair on top of a face." Though it was only 10:00 a.m., she "was in full evening make up. Beyond evening—it was theatrical makeup. She had blue eye shadow on and she had these enormous false eyelashes."[8]

The visit lasted many days, during which Stern spent lots of time at Connie's house, going over his questions. Connie brushed aside his doubts. Of course Sybil had been tortured by her mother, she insisted. Hadn't Sybil's own father admitted he'd once found her suffocating in the wheat crib of his backyard workshop?

It never seemed to have occurred to Stern that Connie might be lying. She had "an incredible self assurance" when she talked about Sybil, he recalled years later, and her persuasiveness was buttressed by his impression of her as one of the foremost psychiatrists in the world.[9] Sybil's psychoanalysis constituted "one of the outstanding cases of all time," Connie proclaimed. Stern believed her, especially when he heard more therapy tapes, which were as indecipherable yet riveting as the ones he'd heard at Flora's.[10]

By the time Stern left Lexington he was enamored of Connie. Sometimes she used her flat, hard, professional voice with him. Other times he heard the tender, intimate voice usually reserved for people on her couch.

"I found myself wishing more and more that I too could have been—could be—your patient," he wrote Connie after he returned to California. If he'd had that good fortune, he added wistfully, "there might have been ultimate discovery and final resolution" of his psychological problems.[11]

He begged her to let him listen to more of the therapy tapes. She complied by packing them in a footlocker and catching a plane west. She and Stern spent three weeks at his home on the ocean, working tirelessly on an outline for the script.[12]

During breaks they took walks on the beach, where Connie talked and talked about everything—from the seaweed drifting through the water to the way she'd saved suicidal schizophrenics by putting them into overnight trances with Penthothal, rescuing them from death. Stern took her to one of his own therapy sessions, then asked for her professional opinion about his problems.

They hobnobbed with Hollywood celebrities, and Connie was star struck. Returning to Lexington, she dropped celebrity names nonstop. When she corresponded with Stern she called him "Stewart Dear."[13]

When Stern finally hunkered down to write his teleplay, he inserted fiction after fiction to smooth out the parts of Flora's book that seemed poorly motivated or downright illogical. Stern had his Sybil character dissociate and slog fully clothed through a pond in front of a group of shocked children in Central Park. He put her into raging, suicidal "Peggy" and "Marcia" modes while on dates with her horrified boyfriend. He made up a visit by Dr. Wilbur to the family doctor who treated Sybil as a child, inventing a shame-faced confession by the doctor that he had seen hideous genital trauma on little Sybil, but had done nothing about it.[14]

Stern was creating perfect sense through perfect fantasy. He added a spellbindingly creepy scene that had not appeared in Flora's book. It showed Sybil bound and immobilized with dishrags, suspended on ropes and hooks as her deranged mother cranked a pulley to raise the little girl into the suffocating "wheat crib."[15]

Stern had gotten this idea from one of the therapy audiotapes. "What did she do to Shirley that made Shirley's arms and legs so weak?" Connie could be heard asking on the tape, referring to the evil Mrs. Mason.

"Pumped 'em up and down," Stern heard the patient answer.

"Pumped 'em up and down how, Sweetie? . . ."

"Put the rope on her arms like this and pull her up on Daddy's pulley and she'd pull like this and make her go up and down and then up so—high— . . ."[16]

Connie was extremely skeptical of this story, but by the time she worked with Stern she had forgotten it was on one of the tapes she'd given him. She expressed her annoyance to Stern when she spotted this scene in his first draft.[17]

Stern stuck to his guns. "I really didn't invent this," he corrected Connie, and sent proof: a transcript of the tape.[18] Reading it, she was alarmed that she'd almost admitted that certain things Shirley said were not to be believed. She told Stern she'd forgotten the carpentry shop torture because it was too awful for *her*, Connie, to remember. "You are so right about the pulley session in the garage and I had completely repressed that," she wrote.[19]

Flora criticized the script,[20] calling it "frantic," "overwritten," "lurid," and suffering from "cheap stereotypes" and "lesbian overtone."[21] She did not object to most of the fictions Stern had inserted—the rope and pulley scene, for instance, or Sybil dissociating before the school children. But oddly, she was angered by a scene which Stern wrote that portrayed Dr. Wilbur addressing a group of male psychiatrists about her multiple personality case and being laughed at because she was a female doctor.

During all the years Flora and Connie had discussed the case, Connie had never described any such experience. Perhaps it had happened, perhaps not. Either way, Stern seemed to understand that Connie and her patient were the victims and heroines of a prefeminist era—and that this fact evoked great enthusiasm from women readers of the book. Still, Flora complained to Stern that his characterization of Dr. Wilbur "as a women's lib character fighting the male psychiatry fraternity" was "outrageous" and "invented."[22] Stern removed the scene.

With the script completed, Joanne Woodward—who two decades earlier had portrayed the multiple-personality-disordered patient in *The Three Faces of Eve*—was chosen for the role of Dr. Wilbur. Sally Field, twenty-nine years old and famous as a television sitcom comedienne, gave an impassioned dramatic performance at her audition and got the Sybil role.

She started listening to therapy tapes from Connie's collection, provided by Stewart Stern.[23]

Sybil aired as an NBC miniseries on two evenings in November 1976. It was seen by forty million people—almost a fifth of the country's population.[24] It won four Emmys, including one awarded to Field for her acting. Frequent reruns followed, and countless more viewers recoiled at scenes of a child being battered, hanged, and raped by her demented mother. They cringed as the victim, grown into an adult and a mental patient, keened and shuddered under furniture. And they wept as Joanne Woodward cradled Sally Field in her lap, murmuring "It's all right, Sweetie. It's all right."

The telemovie became so iconic that Scholastic, a company that produces educational magazines for students, developed a "Sybil" lesson plan for use in high schools. Teenagers were instructed to "Write a discussion in dialogue form between two or more sides of your personality. Name them as Sybil named her Selves. Try to indicate why you are more 'together' than Sybil."[25] Conclusive proof that *Sybil* had become a cultural obsession was a parody on *Saturday Night Live,* featuring a red-wigged Jill Clayburgh as Dr. Wilbur and Gilda Radner—beloved for her Roseanne Rosannadanna persona—playing a daft-faced Sybil. "We all have many people inside of us," Clayburgh lectured Radner. "I myself am a psychiatrist, a married woman . . . an *Unmarried Woman*! I'm a dancer. As a matter of fact I'm two dancers: I'm jazz and modern. . . . I'm four artists: an impressionist, an abstract expressionist and a primitive, and I'm a lot of gym teachers, and I'm at least one dental technician."[26]

No one in Hollywood, on *Saturday Night Live,* or at the Scholastic offices could ask Shirley what she thought of their efforts. They didn't know her real name, much less her phone number. Connie and Flora bent over backwards to conceal her identity, and not merely to respect her wish for anonymity. Even if Shirley had changed her mind and opted to go public, they would not have allowed it. As far as they were concerned, she had no choice. In order to maintain their claim that *Sybil* was nonfiction, she had to remain in the shadows. They struggled to make sure that she did.

PART V

RELAPSE

CHAPTER 17

COMMITMENT

T HREATS TO SHIRLEY'S ANONYMITY BEGAN almost immediately after
publication of *Sybil.* To Flora, at least, this should have been no surprise; after all, she had written the book in a way that practically
advertised Shirley's identity to anyone who knew her well. Perhaps out of
laziness or maybe because of journalists' innate discomfort with disguis-
ing facts, Flora had barely changed the name of anyone or anyplace in the
book.

Over and over, people contacted the three women saying they knew
who Sybil was. Some were mistaken, including a handful of patients in
mental hospitals who claimed *they* were Sybil. But others made the correct
identification. "Oh Shirley," wrote a childhood friend from Dodge Center
in a letter she asked Flora to forward. "I never dreamed of the torment and
unhappiness in your past."[1]

Shirley had known before the book came out that she would need to
give up some of her former life. Connie had instructed her that as soon as
Sybil went on sale, she would have to cut off communication with people
from her past. They included Dessie Blood Engbard, the Mason family's
maid when Shirley was young and whom the book called "Jessie Flood."
Dessie was an old, sick woman in 1973, and for years Shirley had been
sending her affectionate letters, as well as photographs, paintings, and gifts
of inexpensive clothing. But Shirley and Connie had visited Dessie less
than a decade earlier, and even more recently Flora had asked her endless
questions about the Mason family. If she got letters from Shirley after

Sybil became widely read, there was a good chance she would put two and two together—and reveal Sybil's identity. So Shirley stopped sending letters to Dessie.

She also stopped writing to Florence Mason, her stepmother in Michigan. For eleven years, ever since her father's death in 1962, Shirley had been corresponding regularly with Florence, usually once or twice a week. Their letters to each other were unfailingly warm, even loving.

Connie had always loathed Florence, however, and despite Shirley's affection for her stepmother, under Connie's influence she denounced Florence as vain, cold, and stingy. Flora elaborated on these character defects in the book. "Frieda Dorsett," as she called Florence, wore trashy spike heels, chased men, had a nose like "the large horny bill of a predatory fowl," and "disliked women"—including her husband's daughter.[2]

Shirley read Flora's draft chapters of *Sybil*, so she must have seen these vindictive passages. Even so, she seems to have assumed that Florence, a devout Seventh-Day Adventist, would never pick up a book about a woman who went into trance states and allowed herself to be hypnotized—for Adventists such literature was evil if not downright Satanic. Still, Shirley couldn't help bragging about *Sybil*. Writing to Florence a week before publication, she told her that a book about her psychiatric treatment was about to reach the stores and was headed for the best-seller list. "I'm so glad my name is in no way connected with anything," she wrote, adding that her main hope was that the book would help children in danger of becoming mentally ill. "This letter is just between you and me," she concluded. "But you have always known about my connection to Connie and years of treatment."[3]

Then she stopped writing, and Florence had no idea why. She would find out three years later, when she was at a grocery store and saw a *TV Guide* advertisement for the television movie. The ad mentioned Dr. Cornelia Wilbur, whom Florence recognized as her stepdaughter's psychiatrist. She got a copy of *Sybil* and was shocked to see herself insulted in it. Except for talking to her son and his wife, however, she kept quiet about her discovery.[4]

The rest of Shirley's long-distance friends were also mystified when her correspondence stopped. Her old college dorm mate Luella Odden, and Luella's daughter, Muriel, had been receiving letters for twenty-two years, beginning the week Muriel was born. Shirley's old art teacher, Wylene Frederickson, who had given her private art lessons in high school and helped her get into college, also stopped hearing from her.[5]

Many of these people sent mail to West Virginia and didn't hear back. They mailed again and still got nothing. Shirley Mason, inveterate letter writer week after week and year after year, had dropped off the face of the earth.

If going underground was traumatic for Shirley, it also came with a benefit: not having to write all those letters gave her more time to enjoy the people and places around her. She felt deeply fulfilled at Rio Grande Community College, where she taught art education, art history, art appreciation, and oil painting. She had recently gotten tenure and become very busy on academic planning committees and as a student advisor.[6]

And she loved her house. She delighted in painting the exterior a barn-red color with white trim; in laying new, sapphire-blue carpet; and planting young rosebushes in her yard. She planned to donate most of her *Sybil* royalties to charity rather than spend them on herself, and to keep her house and teach.[7] With her job, her students, her colleagues, and her home, she thought she could be happy.

But within weeks, these pleasures would be obliterated.

The first threat to Shirley's identity was fifty-seven-year-old Willie Price, who had shared an apartment while Shirley was addicted to Pentothal injections, and had warned her roommate about the dangers of therapy with Connie.

"Teddy Reeves" was the pseudonym Flora used for Willie in the book, and in it she wrote that Teddy "had one abiding remedy" when her emotionally disturbed friend felt ill: "To get into bed with Sybil." Teddy was a lesbian, the book explained, and Sybil always rejected her homosexual advances.[8]

Reading these passages a few weeks after *Sybil* was published, Willie Price was irate, not to mention terrified. She had a doctorate in early childhood education and a job as a professor at a teachers college in Manhattan. Whether or not she was actually a lesbian, Willie risked losing her employment and her reputation if she were publicly exposed as one. She wrote to Flora, threatening to sue her, Regnery, Connie, and Shirley for libel or invasion of privacy. Taking her case to court would uncover Sybil's true identity.[9]

Rushing to do damage control, Flora contacted attorneys. "Teddy Reeves" was not Willie Price, she told them and her editor. Instead, "Teddy" was a composite of several women Shirley had lived with over decades of sharing dorm rooms and apartments.[10] Composite characters, of course are fictions, and Flora's demurral was her first admission that, contrary to the marketing claims for *Sybil*, the book was not entirely a "true story." But to make sure Willie didn't sue, Flora excised the lesbian scenes with Teddy from the book so that readers of the second, corrected printing would never know they'd existed. Everyone involved with *Sybil* held their breath, hoping that Shirley's old roommate would be the last of their problems.

She wasn't. At the same time Flora was trying to keep a lid on Willie Price in New York City, a crisis was brewing ninety miles south—another one about lesbians. It started in late June 1973, when hundreds of thousands of people in Philadelphia picked up the city's biggest-circulation newspaper, *The Bulletin*, and began reading the syndicated version of *Sybil*, which was still running in some papers even after publication of the book. The first installment included Sybil finding herself in a hotel in Philadelphia with a pair of "loud and gay" pajamas "with bright orange and green stripes." She also found the receipt from the Mayflower Shop. The store's address and phone number appeared in both *Sybil* the book and *Sybil* the syndicated series.[11]

At the Mayflower Shop, calls started coming in nonstop. They came from customers and from strangers, all of them excited that the owners, a middle-aged couple named Joe and Marguerite Paris, had met Sybil. They even came from pranksters calling to ask, "Do you sell pajamas?"[12]

They did not sell pajamas—the Mayflower Shop was a neighborhood mom-and-pop florist that sold flowers and nothing else. There was no way "Sybil" ever could have found a receipt from that store for a purchase of clothing.

No matter. As the Parises' son Al remembered years later, his parents were struck by Flora's use of the word "gay" to describe the style of the pajamas, and Mrs. Paris hated the idea that people would think she'd sold bedroom apparel to some "sick"—i.e., lesbian—"girl." The respectable Mayflower Shop had been libeled and defamed by intimations of homosexual hanky panky, and the owners smelled money. The Parises decided to sue.

A civil complaint was drawn up. The defendants were *The Bulletin*, Regnery, Flora, Connie, and an unknown individual the lawsuit called "Jane Doe a/k/a Sybil." All were accused of maliciously portraying the Mayflower as a place "where sexually deviant and perverse women would congregate." The Parises demanded $280,000 in damages. There was talk of calling all the parties in to give depositions and testimony—including Jane Doe a/k/a Sybil.[13]

By late summer Shirley was in serious trouble, even as Connie and Flora toured the country telling talk show hosts and newspaper reporters that "Sybil" was "doing extremely well"—so well that her college had to "put a ceiling on her advisees" because "so many students wanted her as an adviser that she couldn't handle them." In one such interview, Connie went on to describe "Sybil" as a favorite with her colleagues.[14]

In fact, Shirley's colleagues were unwittingly terrorizing her. Decades later, Jean Lane, Shirley's old art-student friend from Mankato State Teachers College, would recall the gossip during the summer of 1973. "The book had just come out and everyone was reading it," she remembered. "People were going to National Art Education Association and other professional events. They were talking to each other about how 'Sybil' was really Shirley Mason."[15]

Some colleagues were shocked, Jean remembered. Many were not surprised, particularly those who had known Shirley in college. Some called the school nurse who had cared for Shirley when she was a student in Mankato. The nurse said she knew about Shirley's multiple personalities and that she'd been in treatment with Dr. Wilbur. She told the callers not to talk about this with Shirley, to leave her in peace. But other people would come up to Shirley and ask about her condition and the book. As word spread from close friends to not-so-close ones, even people at Rio Grande College began asking questions. Shirley became terribly upset, and Jean recalled hearing that she'd decided to leave town.

By fall she had resigned from the teaching position she adored, put her beloved house on the market, and fled from Mt. Pleasant with her toy poodle, Mimbe, in tow. She went to stay with Connie in Lexington.

Christmas was approaching and life seemed unbearably difficult, so Connie engineered a sun-and-fun-escape; she bought airplane tickets and the two women flew to Mexico City. Shirley tried to forget her troubles by climbing pyramids and exploring ruins, and in January she and Connie proceeded to Guatemala.[16] But Shirley struggled to accept that when the trip was over, she would have to settle for good in Lexington, refrain from teaching in schools, and otherwise take pains to hide from her friends and the public.

Back in the United States in late winter, Shirley tried to make a new life in Kentucky. She bought a cute Cape Cod-style house within walking distance of Connie's home. From early in the morning until late in the evening, she hung out at Connie's, cooking breakfast, lunch, and dinner, assembling jigsaw puzzles at the dining room table, and painting canvases with watercolors and oils. Connie fixed up a bedroom so Shirley could stay overnight. She often did.[17]

The two women spent a lot of time bickering long distance with Flora, who was trying to contain the "gay pajamas" lawsuit. As the old saying goes, truth is the best defense against libel, and Flora told her lawyer that years ago, she'd been shown the receipt she mentioned in *Sybil*, the one listing the purchase of children's pajamas along with the store's name, the Mayflower Shop. She couldn't find the receipt now, of course, and neither could Shirley. Eventually, Flora was forced to admit she'd never seen it and that Shirley might never have been at the Mayflower.

Flora was furious and scolded Shirley for fantasizing about the store. Shirley and Connie scolded back. Flora should have done fact checking, they said, for if she had she would have realized that the Mayflower was in part of Philadelphia that Shirley could never have gotten to on the subway.[18]

Besides Flora's records of her arguments with her collaborators, there aren't many records of Shirley's life during this time. She was basically in hiding, after all. Deborah Kovac, a niece of Connie's husband, Keith, remembered seeing her when she traveled with Keith and Connie to rural Illinois for days-long visits with Keith's kin. Deborah was a teenager then, and she recalled Connie sitting in living rooms and kitchens talking endlessly about her work with multiple personality patients—while Shirley said hardly a word.[19]

Another girl, Dianne Morrow, got to know Shirley a little better.[20] Dianne's mother, Jan Morrow, was married to a Lexington physician and had three children and a large, lovely home. Like many upper-middle-class women in the early 1970s, Jan had grown bored and frustrated with being a housewife, and unhappy that her husband failed to understand her discontent. Jan thought a psychiatrist might help, and she went into therapy with Connie, who taught at the University of Kentucky medical school but also had a private practice.

Dianne was in grade school then, and almost forty years later she remembered her mother as being "pretty normal" when she started seeing Connie. Their sessions together motivated Jan to study guidance counseling in graduate school, though she was in her late thirties when she enrolled. She tried hard to fit in with her classmates, who were ten to fifteen years younger. But the threats these new pursuits posed to her domestic existence made her "pretty crazy," Dianne recalled. "My dad just couldn't figure it out. She had a nice life. Why couldn't she just shut up and enjoy it?"

She couldn't do that, and in therapy with Connie, Jan lost the last vestiges of her equilibrium. "I don't know if she truly had a nervous breakdown, if she was on some kind of drugs or if she was ill with something else," Dianne said. "But she was hospitalized once. Another time she was bedridden and hysterical and crying and screaming."

When Jan got on her feet again, Connie offered her free therapy—on one condition. In the backyard of Connie's home was a swimming pool, roofed with a plastic bubble so it could be used even in bad weather. Over the years, Connie had become a fanatic about swimming. She calculated how much a lap in her pool measured, and rain or shine, she logged over two miles a week. But she liked company, and the therapy deal she offered to Jan, according to Dianne, was that "my mom had to go to Connie's every weekend and swim with her."

Dianne was nine or ten years old when this routine began. Her mother started taking her to Connie's, and there she saw that Shirley was "always around." She was rail thin, Dianne remembered, "and very nice but very shy." The quiet woman and the little girl rarely used the pool themselves. Instead, they lounged nearby and discussed subjects such as dogs and art while Shirley waited with barely disguised impatience for the swimming to end.

Jan's husband—Dianne's father—became jealous of his wife's social time with Connie. He protested that "If you paid as much attention to me as you pay to her we would be happier!"

"You don't understand!" Jan would reply. According to Dianne, her mother "could never say no to Connie. She felt as though she owed her tens of thousands of dollars."

Dianne felt confused and anxious by what she saw at Connie's house. Everyone said she was married to a man named Keith, yet Dianne never saw Keith and wondered if he existed. When she asked her mother, she got a lecture "about how these were modern times, and Connie loves her husband very much, and they don't have to live together to be married." The explanation worried Dianne. Connie was fond of the 1970s-era feminist quip "A woman without a man is like a fish without a bicycle." Dianne had the constant sense that Connie's answer to her mother's problems was "to get rid of my dad."

The Morrows did divorce. Dianne's father soon remarried. As for Jan, she "was miserable for the next many years," said Dianne—during which time she faithfully continued her weekend swims with Connie.

Dianne was even more confused about *Sybil*. "Oh Dianne, look," Connie would exclaim, pointing to a new edition printed in a foreign alphabet. "It's been translated into Greek!" Dianne asked what the book was about, and Jan said merely that "Sybil's mother had treated her very poorly and she developed different personalities to deal with the stress. And I'm like, 'Well what did she *do* to her?' And she said, 'Well, it would be the equivalent of if you walked by the coat rack and your scarf fell on the floor completely by accident and your mother blamed you and maybe beat you up.' And I'm, 'Oh. OK.'"

Shirley never mentioned *Sybil* to Dianne, not even during their long waits by the pool. And no one told her Shirley was the book's heroine. Still, Dianne just *knew*.

Oddly, Dianne noticed, Shirley talked affectionately about Mattie. "My mother used to play the piano," she would comment casually. "My mother used to cook such and such food." "Wow!" Dianne thought to herself about these offhand remarks. "Wouldn't you have blocked all this out if she'd done these terrible things? Or never, *ever* mention your mother's name again?"

She watched Shirley and Connie assemble jigsaw puzzles, play Scrabble, and putter with ideas for a "Sybil" board game. Sometimes they bickered about things such as whose turn it was to load the dishwasher. To Dianne they seemed like an old married couple. She wondered about this, too. But by now she knew not to ask questions.

Shirley occasionally spent time in her own home, and sometimes the phone rang—it was usually Flora calling. One day, however, the voice on the other end was not Flora. It was an unfamiliar man, asking "Is this Shirley A. Mason?"

"Yes," she replied, and his next question made her reel.

"Are you Sybil?"[21]

CHAPTER 18

EXPOSURE

T HE MAN ON THE PHONE was Monty Norris,[1] a reporter at the Minneapolis *Star-Tribune*. It was summer 1975, and for weeks a young intern at the paper named Steve had been telling a fascinating story. Steve had just married a woman named Janice, from the tiny town of Dodge Center, eighty miles south of Minneapolis and St. Paul. Janice's father had moved to Dodge Center to serve as the town's new physician shortly after the death of Dr. Otoniel Flores, the community's longtime general practitioner. Janice had spent her life in Dodge Center until coming to the Twin Cities with Steve. In July she told him she'd been hearing gossip from back home. People were talking about Sybil, the girl whose mind had split because of her mother's sexual tortures.

The Dodge Centerites were certain this girl was their former neighbor, an artistic, moody Seventh-Day Adventist named Shirley Mason, Janice told Steve. And the townspeople were in an uproar, some believing Shirley's terrible tales of abuse, others dismissing them as lies. Steve told his city editor, whose interest was piqued. He assigned Monty Norris to visit Dodge Center and come back with a story.

Norris drove down and poked around. The Dodge Center residents verified that in the 1930s their town had had a telephone operator with a facial tic, a mentally retarded iceman, and a retired doctor who made violins. These facts exactly tracked the book. Everyone recalled Walter Mason's work as a builder and a member of a religion that celebrated the Sabbath on Saturday—also mentioned in *Sybil*. They remembered Shirley's art. Norris got chills when he arrived at the Masons' old house and saw the porch where Sybil had moped as a girl, and the sunroom, with its wooden bench and bank of windows—all exactly as the book described.

Norris was further convinced when he talked to Dessie Engbard, the Masons' former live-in maid. She told him that years earlier Flora Schreiber had visited Dodge Center, interviewed her about Shirley, and instructed her to remain mum about a book that was in the works. Engbard told Norris of her worry at not having heard from Shirley for over two years. "Lord, I'd love to see her again," she said. "I love that girl like my own."[2]

Some townspeople remembered Shirley's mother as "flighty" and "a little odd." The fact that she'd walked Shirley less than half a block to school every day, even in high school, seemed peculiar. But no one remembered Mattie acting hostile, psychotic, or violent. Engbard categorically denied Mattie had mistreated her daughter, much less defecated on lawns or conducted lesbian orgies. "I just can't believe all that stuff about her," she said. "No sir, it just doesn't sound possible."[3]

Another old timer added her skeptical two cents' worth. Pearl Peterson Lohrbach had been Shirley's teacher in fifth grade. That was the same year when, according to *Sybil*, the little girl had awakened in school one day, utterly disoriented. The book said she didn't know where she was because she had just emerged from a two-year blackout, and that during that whole time her body was controlled by alter personality Peggy.

According to the book, Sybil's grades dropped drastically after she "came to" in fifth grade. This happened because it wasn't she who had learned things during the third and fourth grades. It was Peggy who had, then Peggy left, along with the multiplication tables and other knowledge she'd acquired in Sybil's place.

Nonsense, Lohrbach told Norris. She'd often seen Shirley Ardell Mason daydreaming, and sometimes she talked about her imaginary friend Sam, whose name she concocted from her initials. But Shirley had never exhibited sudden behavior changes, much less alternate personalities. Nor had her schoolwork varied. Term after term, her grades stayed just the same.[4]

In fact, everyone scoffed at *Sybil* while speaking with Norris. But privately, some were extremely unsettled. What *had* happened to their neighbor when she was a girl? People like Pearl Lohrbach and Dessie Engbard were haunted by the possibility that the story was true and they had been too ignorant or insensitive to notice Shirley's suffering.

Monty Norris didn't know what to think either, but he wasn't supposed to report on whether "Sybil" had really been tortured by her mother—his assignment was simply to determine if the woman in the book was Shirley Mason. He thought she was, and after finishing up in Dodge Center he made a series of long-distance phone calls. The first was to Flora Schreiber.

He was amazed by her reaction; it was good-humored and collegial, as befitted one journalist talking with another. "I guess you know why I never went to Minneapolis when I was on my book tour!" she told him with a chuckle. Still, she never directly admitted that Sybil was Shirley. She insisted she'd only been in Dodge Center to do the "Tiny Towns in America" story.

Connie's response was completely different. "People like you are doing irreparable harm to my patient!" she snarled at Norris. "Wait a minute!" he shot back. "Didn't you just write a book about her and make it perfectly obvious who she is? Do you think I'm the only person in the Twin Cities who knows?" He felt defensive about outing Shirley.

After calling her, he wasn't so sure of his ethics, either. Shirley was too polite to hang up, and though she never said she was Sybil, it was obvious she was by the way she answered Norris's questions about the book. Still, he felt sorry for her. She was painfully shy, with a timid voice. He worried his work could hurt her. Sitting down to write his article, he felt a little protective, even meditative.

Back in New York and Kentucky, the mood was anything but meditative. As soon as she'd finished talking with Norris, Flora realized this was no chuckling matter—if Sybil's identity hit the press, the book could be fact-checked and completely discredited. Flora typed a press release defending her right to protect her sources, and trotting out "Tiny Towns" as the reason she'd visited Dodge Center.[5]

She may also have pulled strings to pressure the national media to keep quiet. Norris's Minneapolis *Star-Tribune* article about the ruckus in Dodge Center came out on August 27 and filled two pages. Soon he heard from editors at the Associated Press and United Press International that their offices in New York thought the *Sybil* story was hot and they wanted to distribute it. Yet the editors soon cooled without explaining why. Norris knew Flora was well connected, and he wondered if she was rattling her sabers. He didn't press the issue. He still felt a bit guilty about exposing a psychiatric patient.

Lies and string pulling weren't the only tactics Connie and Flora employed to squelch the talk in Minnesota. They also used intimidation. Dessie Engbard got a call from a lawyer, possibly Connie's husband, warning that if she talked publicly about the Sybil–Shirley Mason connection, she could be sued. Engbard was terrified and promptly suffered three strokes. (She died less than four years later.) She never again spoke to the press. Others in Dodge Center also received threatening calls. They, too, kept their mouths shut.[6] With no AP or UPI coverage, the story did not leave Minnesota. Hardly anyone in New York read the Minneapolis *Star-Tribune*. Shirley's secret seemed secure.

Still, in her anxiety about being discovered, she became ill, and she was so afraid of being recognized as Sybil that she hesitated to leave her house. She had always been somewhat reclusive, and now she got worse. Connie tried to soothe her, and Flora sent messages of reassurance. "We've been very lucky that the story has remained local," she wrote days after the Minneapolis exposé came out.[7]

While in the thick of trying to control the situation in Minnesota, Flora traveled to England to promote the British edition of *Sybil*. The English version of *Psychology Today* had asked to interview her, and Flora met with a twenty-seven-year-old assistant editor named Charlotte Gray.[8]

Years later, when Gray was in her sixties, living in Canada and one of that country's most prominent historians and nonfiction book writers, she laughed about her youth and her cluelessness when she met Flora. She had no background in psychology or psychiatry, and she was wide eyed at this world-famous author. At the same time, she was skeptical about the existence of multiple personalities.

At the interview, which took place in an elegant restaurant, Gray mentioned that she had some doubts about the idea of alternate selves. Flora nodded. She was "obviously tired and stressed," Gray remembered. She said her feet hurt, and she asked Gray to come with her to her hotel room. It was a hot day, and Gray stared in growing amazement as Flora removed her shoes, then her dress and stockings. Walking around in her underwear, she picked up a newspaper article and handed it to Gray. It was the Minneapolis *Star-Tribune* piece revealing Sybil's real name.

Gray said goodbye to Flora and took the exposé back to her office.

If she had sent the article to her colleagues at *Psychology Today* in America, she might have launched an investigation into *Sybil* and changed the history of psychiatry. But she didn't think Monty Norris's piece was important. A few days later she sent it back to Flora with a letter thanking her for lunch and promising she would "not quote the name of the person whom they say is Sybil."[9]

"I am grateful," Flora wrote back.[10]

Why had she shown Gray the article in the first place? It was as though she wanted—consciously or unconsciously—to expose not just Shirley but herself. As Gray had noticed during their lunch, all was not well with Flora by late 1975. During media interviews she seemed self-confident, upbeat, even glamorous in the $1500-dollar dresses she now wore thanks to the enormous royalties she was earning. In private, however, Flora was worn out, anxious, and angry with most things related to *Sybil.*

She hated being upstaged by Connie, and she resented having to share book and movie money with her. She toyed with the idea of exposing Shirley, writing her agent that she was "fed up" with protecting her and tired of acting as Connie's "patsy." No longer, Flora vowed, would she be "the fall guy in relation to both these despicable women." The agent tried to calm her. Friends at John Jay College, and her cousin Stan Aronson—the one she had hit in the head as a child, and who was now a neurologist—became concerned about the stress she was under.[11]

Whenever she started thinking about the conflicts with her collaborators, Flora's mind turned to thoughts of sexual perversity. Just weeks after Connie's husband, Keith Brown, died in 1976, Connie and Shirley breezed into New York City and unceremoniously dumped Brown's belongings in the trash. Flora was struggling with the fact that her long time paramour, Stuart Long, was dying at the time of cancer, and the indifference that Connie and Shirley showed toward Keith Brown's death convinced her that the two women were lovers. She got it into her head that this had been true even back in the 1960s, when Connie had first approached her about writing a book. If she'd known they were together back then, Flora complained to friends, she would have proposed a fifty-fifty royalty split instead of one-third and two-thirds.[12]

She decided to find another big project, one that she alone would control.

Shirley Mason's childhood home in Dodge Center, Minnesota, where she claimed she was abused by her mother for years, yet no one ever noticed.

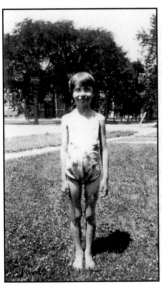

Shirley Mason as a young girl.
Courtesy Arlene Christensen

A 7th Day Adventist Camp, similar to one where Shirley worshipped as a young girl.
Courtesy Minnesota Historical Society

The future Dr. Connie Wilbur, as a young woman, from her 1930 University of Michigan yearbook.

A frail Shirley Mason, circa 1933. A close look reveals that her eyes are rolled back, suggesting that she is in a self-induced trance state. *Courtesy Arlene Christensen*

Shirley Mason and Jean Lane featured in their art classes in the college yearbook. *Courtesy Minnesota State University, Mankato*

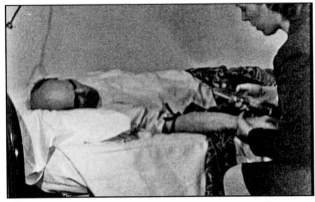

Dr. Wilbur injects a patient in World War II–era Omaha with barbiturates to induce "narcosynthesis." Note the enormous needle. *Courtesy The Nebraska Medical Center and National Library of Medicine*

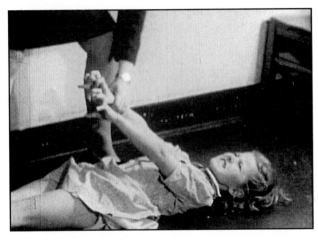

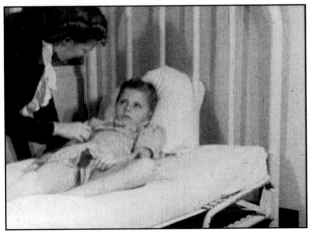

Dr. Wilbur compares the behavior of one troubled patient before and after treatment. *Courtesy The Nebraska Medical Center*

A young Flora Schreiber working at NBC in New York. From *Film and Radio Discussion Guide.*

The Schreiber family, who lived together for most of Flora's life. *Courtesy Sealy Library Special Collections, John Jay College of Criminal Justice*

The faculty of John Jay College, circa 1965. Flora Schrieber is third from the left. *Courtesy Sealy Library Special Collections, John Jay College of Criminal Justice*

A rail-thin Shirley Mason, looking posh and cosmopolitan, shortly before she moved to New York City in 1954. *Courtesy David Eichman*

A sample of Shirley's art during the time she was being treated by Dr. Wilbur. The name of this piece was "Good Mother/Bad Mother."

A sample of Shirley's journals from one of her therapy sessions, in which she writes about her mother "I hate her" seventeen times. In contrast to her beautiful script, the drug-induced writing is barely legible. *Courtesy Sealy Library Special Collections, John Jay College of Criminal Justice*

An idolatrous letter written to Dr. Wilbur by Shirley. In her gorgeous cursive, Shirley writes, "I think whatever you say must of course be right and it's intolerable ever to think you might be mistaken about anything . . ."
Courtesy Sealy Library Special Collections, John Jay College of Criminal Justice

The building that housed Open Hospital in Lexington, Kentucky, where Dr. Wilbur allowed patients the run of the slowly decaying space.

Dr. Connie Wilbur at the West Virginia University. *Courtesy West Virginia University*

Shirley Mason during a trip to Mexico in late 1973. *Courtesy Dianne Morrow*

Shirley Mason, Dianne Morrow, and
Connie Wilbur in Connie's home in
1989. The art on the walls behind them
is Shirley's. *Courtesy Dianne Morrow*

Flora Schreiber dressed in the
finery of her later life. *Courtesy
Jiro Kimura*

Dr. Connie Wilbur at a meeting of the American Psychiatric Association, circa
1965. *Courtesy Bentley Historical Library, The University of Michigan*

CHAPTER 19

BREAKDOWN

FLORA KNEW SHE NEEDED TO do another book after *Sybil.* Her friends urged her to fulfill her lifelong dream of writing something serious— a conventionally structured novel, perhaps, or a play—even though such work might not fly off the shelves. But she felt driven to produce another blockbuster: "You're only as good as your next best seller," she said.[1]

In early 1975 she chose her subject: a recent, bizarre crime spree on the East Coast. Joe Kallinger, a shoe repairman from Philadelphia, and his son Michael, were accused of breaking into suburban houses together and violently assaulting the people they found inside. Most were women, and the Kallingers were said to have gagged their victims, taped their eyes, and bound their bodies, often in grotesquely sexual positions. According to the charges, teenager Michael ransacked the homes while middle-aged Joe forced the women to fellate him. When one of them in New Jersey refused, he fatally stabbed her.

Flora believed that a book about a father-son murder team could be both serious and popular. She told her agent she intended to use feminist theory to analyze the crimes: " 'We are men,' the father seems to be saying. 'We are potent in both senses of the word—potent in sex, but also in subduing women' . . . Kallinger is a pathological representative of male chauvinism."[2] She contacted Joe's defense attorney and offered a deal: if his client would allow her to tell his and his son's story, she would give him twelve and a half percent of whatever she earned by publishing it, including from her book advance. Joe Kallinger agreed.

But the book rapidly turned into an echo of *Sybil*, as the feminist angle fell through—and as Flora, obviously influenced by Connie Wilbur's improper practices as a psychoanalyst, began violating the ethics of her own profession with the subject of her new work.

She broke the rules as soon as she heard from Joe Kallinger, by posing as his friend and confidant rather than as a reporter. In August 1975, he wrote his first letter to her. "My name is REV. JOSEPH KALLINGER," it began. "I am trying to develop THE HOLY SPIRIT in me its starting to get like the wind . . . God Bless You is my Prayer."[3]

"Dear Rev. Kallinger," Flora responded—though Kallinger was not a reverend. "I feel God wants my thoughts to be shared with you"—though for her entire life she'd been an atheist. "May the Lord bless you and keep you and make his light shine on you."[4]

Kallinger's lawyer was crafting an insanity defense for his client, who did have a history of mental disturbance. In court he once had testified that he talked directly to God and used to be a butterfly. But many psychiatrists who examined him thought he was a sociopath who was faking insanity.

Meanwhile, fourteen-year-old Michael Kallinger was a mystery to the public because his lawyer forbade him to speak with the press, Flora included. Unable to contact Michael, she realized she would have to scrap her "father-son male chauvinism" angle. The only saleable theme remaining was Joe Kallinger's craziness. As she waited for an offer from a publisher, she began thinking of herself as the next Dr. Cornelia Wilbur. She was determined to find extreme psychopathology in Joe—and horrific abuse from childhood which had caused his illness.

In July 1976 Flora got a book contract from the publisher Simon & Schuster, with an advance of almost a half million dollars. Soon afterward, Joe's lawyer went to court and cited Flora's work on *Sybil* to get her approved as a forensic mental health expert. This would make her eligible to interview Joe as a member of his defense team. She got the approval.[5]

Day after day thereafter, Flora visited Joe in jail, asking him to tell stories about his life that would explain why he was so violent. By summer 1977 she had spent hundreds of hours with him, and listened excitedly as his revelations became increasingly perverse and sadistic. Flora became convinced that Joe was, indeed, psychotic. She also believed he needed help—her help. She was eager to give it, and not just to acquire material for her book. She was becoming enchanted with Joe. Like Connie with Shirley, Flora felt the boundaries dissolving between herself and her "patient." He impressed her as "extraordinarily sensitive," as well as "verbal and analytical, charming, intelligent, and poetic."[6] Rather than a heartless rapist and murderer, he seemed like "a lost child." She let Joe call her Mama, Mom, and Mommy. In return, she called him Boomy Bum Boo.[7]

The relationship alarmed Flora's friends. Ben Termine, who ran the Theater Department at John Jay, warned her that she was dangerously overinvolved with Kallinger. She wouldn't listen, and continued to talk about "Joe, Joe, Joe," Termine remembered. "She felt people didn't understand he was a sweet guy who'd been abused."[8]

Yet almost three years after beginning her long talks with Joe Kallinger, Flora still had not found the Rosetta Stone of child abuse she was looking for. By then she was paying a staff to help with the search for trauma. Finally, in 1979, one of her investigators talked to a woman who'd lived near Joe when he was a child. The woman recalled a time when Joe was eight years old and and wanted to go on a school field trip. His mother insisted that he stay home, and when Joe protested, she beat him on the head with a hammer.[9]

Flora took this dramatic revelation back to Joe. At first he did not remember it, but eventually he added details and came up with yet another awful story, about a hernia operation he'd had almost forty years earlier, at age six. After he came home from the hospital, he remembered, his mother and father had told him the doctor did something to his penis with a knife so that it would never get hard for the rest of this life.[10]

Flora interpreted this strange conversation as the Kallinger parents' cruel attempt to frighten their son into avoiding innocent sex play with other children. She considered it a definitive clinical tale, with all the Freudian elements: a knife as phallic symbol, the Oedipal complex from hell, and castration anxiety. The story was sure to send goosebumps through—as Flora's agent put it—"major markets: women and all those frightened suburbanites."[11]

Simon & Schuster titled Flora's book *The Shoemaker: Anatomy of a Psychotic*. It came out in 1983 and made the best-seller list, but unlike *Sybil*, it remained there for only a few weeks. It never earned the publisher a profit and was deemed a commercial flop. Nor did *The Shoemaker* impress the critics. It was one thing to promote the mental illness of "Sybil," a tiny, anonymous woman who could not have harmed a flea. It was quite another to make a victim-hero of the infamous Joe Kallinger, who forced women at gunpoint and knifepoint to perform fellatio on him, who was a murderer.

One reviewer called *The Shoemaker* "pulpy." The *Los Angeles Times* joked that Flora had been fooled by Kallinger because she was an English teacher, not a psychiatrist, and probably "an easy grader." *Psychology Today* sniffed at her "mechanistic" castration-threat explanation for Kallinger's mental problems and her knee-jerk acceptance of his childhood abuse stories.[12]

Flora felt hurt and betrayed. But bad reviews were nothing compared with the next problem she faced. Flurries of civil actions were filed against her by the State of New Jersey and by Joe's robbery and rape victims, as well as by the survivors of people he had murdered. New Jersey was invoking its "Son of Sam" law, prohibiting criminals from making money by publishing descriptions of their wrongdoing. By extension, the state claimed Flora could not profit, either, from *The Shoemaker*. Using the same argument, the victims and families demanded Flora's profits. Some sued her for libel and invasion of privacy.[13]

Flora vowed to fight as a matter of pride, because even if the plaintiffs had won their lawsuits, she would not have had the money to pay them. Her $475,000 advance from *The Shoemaker* had vanished—spent long ago on investigators, book-related travel, and calls to Joe that had been running over $1500 a month for years. And now there were more lawyers sending invoices. Flora had quietly settled the "gay pajamas" lawsuit out of court in 1980, splitting the $10,000 settlement and the attorney costs with Connie and Shirley. Now, with the Kallinger litigation, she was amassing bills of up to $50,000 a year, with no three-way partnership to dilute the pain.[14]

By 1986 she realized that *The Shoemaker* had put her $100,000 in debt. *Sybil* had sold millions of copies in America by then and been published in nineteen foreign editions, yet Flora was utterly broke. Desperate to make money, she tried to sell *The Shoemaker* to Hollywood or television. There were no takers. She pitched spinoffs of the TV version of *Sybil*: a soap opera; a Broadway musical she proposed should be choreographed by Twyla Tharp, with songs including "The Peggy Part of Me," "Nobody Likes Girls," and "I Want to Be the Man I Marry." These efforts also bombed.[15]

She began a new book, a "psychobiography" about German Nazi leader

Rudolf Hess. As well, she planned to launch her own talk show. She was seventy-one years old, though most people thought she was still in her sixties because she almost always lied about her birth year. Sometimes she lied because of her identification with the venerable Broadway habit of never revealing how old one was. Other times, she may have worried that she would not get work if her true age were known.[16]

She still could barely stand her old Sybil, Inc. partners, and she seldom communicated with them. But in early 1987, illness, and a need for sympathy, overrode her hostility toward Shirley and Connie. "I was suffering from dehydration, starvation, total potassium deficiency, and electrolytes gone wacky," she explained in a letter she sent to Lexington.[17] Soon doctors discovered the cause of these symptoms: colon cancer. She had a tumor that was bigger than a grapefruit. Laser treatments over the next few months had virtually no effect on it.

By August she was in terrible pain but still traveling to Pennsylvania to see Joe. "I cannot tell you, Boomy Bum Boo, how much it meant to me to be with you," she wrote him after one such visit.[18]

In late September 1988, she was again hospitalized, for almost two weeks.[19] Joe wrote her telling her she had to get well because she was all he had. "I do think about our love," she wrote back, "which gives me the will to fight and become well again. . . . You, too, are all I have left in my life."[20] Days after returning home she collapsed.[21] This time she knew she was dying.

Her cousin Stan visited her and was surprised to see her hair askew, her face devoid of its usual fire-engine lipstick, and her voice gone slow and thoughtful.[22] Illness and painkilling drugs were no doubt partly responsible. But Flora may also have been reflecting on the riddle of her life: How had a serious young woman—one who had taken unpopular stands and wanted her writing to change the world—turned into an older woman obsessed with telling silly and salacious stories whose main purpose was to garner her as much fame and attention as possible?

On November 3 she died of a stroke and a heart attack.

Her will offered her voluminous, coffee-and-tobacco-stained personal papers to the New York Public Library,[23] where her father had worked for so many years. But the library did not want the papers. They eventually wound up where Flora had spent her own many years, at John Jay College.

Though the Public Library slighted Flora, another grand city institution honored her. The day after she died, the *New York Times* ran her obituary. It talked of the success of *Sybil* and the legal controversy around *The Shoemaker*. It mentioned her long teaching career. It alluded to her feisty independence and bucking of convention by noting that she left no husband or children.

This obituary from America's newspaper of record was accurate in all respects except for one: it stated her age incorrectly, saying that she had died at seventy when she was actually seventy-two.[24]

No one ever asked for a correction.

CHAPTER 20

CONTAGION

B Y THE LATE 1970S, CONNIE herself was in her seventies and had retired from the University of Kentucky. She had not slowed down,
though. On the contrary, she was busier than ever, on a crusade to
promote multiple personality as an illness that was much more common
than previously believed, and which required intensive treatment. She did
this promotion by continuing her *Sybil*-related media appearances. In addition, she started her own psychiatric facility, which she hoped would provide cutting-edge, humane treatment to multiples while keeping them out
of large, dreary institutions. She named her new treatment center the Open
Hospital. It was unsupervised by anyone but her, and it was unlicensed, cha-
otically managed, and possibly illegal. Yet the Open Hospital helped spread
Connie's ideas around Lexington and eventually throughout the world.

The facility consisted of two rundown old houses not far from downtown Lexington. One contained offices for Connie and three young psychiatrists, who were each paid $40,000 a year to work for her. The other
house was a dorm for patients who came from out of town for treatment—
mainly for multiple personality.[1]

There were many such patients by 1978, shortly after the "hospital"
opened. Typically they had been mentally ill for years before they heard of
multiple personalities and Dr. Wilbur. They had seen psychiatrist after psychiatrist and been diagnosed with schizophrenia, hysteria, manic depression, and borderline personality. They'd popped prescription pills, spent
time in institutions, and taken electroshock. They were still very sick.

Then they read or watched *Sybil* and learned that a brilliant doctor in Kentucky could explain the voices nattering within them, the black moods, the blank spells. Not only did this doctor know what was wrong, she knew how to make it right.

Letters poured into Connie's mailbox from people—almost all women—begging for treatment, and she invited them to Lexington. Arriving with backpacks and suitcases, each was assigned a room and a therapist. In a bizarre turn, Connie even gave some of these patients jobs.

One woman had a degree in nursing when she came from the Southwest to the Open Hospital. Connie appointed her as the facility's nursing supervisor, even though she had more than thirty alter personalities, and some of them got the urge to run off. Once she bolted from Lexington with no money or identification and did not return for weeks. While she was gone Connie had no nurse—though her other patients were smashing themselves with hammers, mutilating themselves with knives, and overdosing on drugs.[2]

A chronically suicidal patient, Marcy, became the Open Hospital's janitor. Marcy routinely tried to kill herself with pills, and she sliced up her arms with sharp objects. When Connie left town for a seminar or a conference, Marcy would starve herself, sometimes wasting to eighty pounds and ending up on feeding tubes in a nearby hospital. Meanwhile, the dorm's basement would flood and the "janitor" was not there to drain it.[3]

Marcy's numerous crises served as models for her roommates. There wasn't much entertainment in the old house: no television, radio, or record player; very few books or magazines, and no supervisory staff to talk to.[4] So, just as in Dr. Charcot's asylum in nineteenth-century Paris, and just like at Ann Arbor's Psychopathic Hospital in the 1930s, with its teenaged girls fighting over baby bottles, the women of the Open Hospital spent a lot of time hanging out together. They learned how to be ill by imitating each other.

After observing one of Marcy's alters cutting herself with knives, other patients developed alters who cut themselves. One of Marcy's personalities wouldn't eat; soon, everyone had anorexia. The patients even taught each other how to be sick outside of the facility. A woman walked downtown, smashed the windows of businesses like McDonald's, and told managers and police that it was OK because she was a patient of Dr. Wilbur's (the managers nodded sympathetically and the police drove her back to the Open Hospital). Observing how risk-free it was to let a destructive personality emerge in public, other patients discovered that they, too, had alters who were vandals. "I have the frightening feeling I'm getting worse," a patient from California wrote in a letter she sent back home. She had come to Lexington with a handful of personalities, but instead of "integrating" them, she developed additional ones.[5]

The Open Hospital's therapeutic focus, of course, was on identifying childhood abuse, and Marcy recovered memories of her mother tying her ankles to a stick and hanging her on a meat hook—exactly as Sybil's mother had done in the movie. The nurse remembered her parents raping her.

Heather, an aspiring writer and poet from the Midwest, had been diagnosed since late childhood with all kinds of psychiatric disorders, including paranoid schizophrenia.[6] It was not until the 1970s *Sybil* craze erupted that she started showing signs of having multiple personalities. After reading about Connie in a magazine, she wrote to her requesting treatment. In Lexington she was repeatedly asked if she remembered her parents abusing her. She didn't remember, but her Open Hospital therapist refused to take "no" for an answer—and Connie said she could help Heather get her writing published as part of her therapy. Heather was encouraged by this promise, and finally she recalled a mundane detail of family history: that both of her parents were only children. This, Connie decided, was the reason Heather was ill. Her mother and father had grown up without siblings, so they didn't know how to raise their own child.[7]

Under treatment Heather eventually came up with much more blameworthy accounts of trauma. One of her alter personalities remembered her father offering her to a business associate to be raped at his pleasure. That story competed strongly with the other Open Hospital patients' tales of parental rape.[8]

The three young psychiatrists on Connie's staff had deeply respected her when they studied with her at the University of Kentucky. But they were not happy at the Open Hospital, according to one of them, Rosa K. Riggs. She had been excited about multiples in the early 1970s, after learning about Jonah, the black man with the four alter personalities and the different EEG readings. But when Riggs joined Connie's staff, her excitement swiftly faded.[9]

The main problem was that Connie insisted that her employees act just as selfless as she had when she'd treated Shirley. Interviewed for this book thirty years after working at the Open Hospital, Riggs remembered how her boss demanded that staff take patients out to eat and accompany them to the movies. They were also supposed to give out their home phones, and answer day and night when patients (and their many alters) called to report a "crisis."[10]

If her staff neglected to do as she did, Connie would grow cold, disapproving, and distant. "You didn't argue with her," Riggs said, even though she and the other employees knew that Connie's treatment methods violated psychiatric ethics. Riggs would see patients who she didn't believe had alters, but Connie would insist that they did and order Riggs to do more hypnosis. Riggs did not disobey her.

Connie's facility folded in 1980, after the staff quit. By then, however, other psychiatrists and psychologists all over town were diagnosing people as suffering from multiple personalities. Thanks to Connie's influence, Lexington had become like one of those nineteenth-century European villages whose primary business was offering "rest cures" to neurasthenics and hysterics. For her part, Dr. Cornelia B. Wilbur now had dozens of new clinical tales about alter personalities—more stories, with more amazing details, than any other doctor in the field.

Using these stories, she worked with other psychiatrists to popularize multiple personality. She hoped her efforts would get the condition listed for the first time in the American Psychiatric Association's *Diagnostic and Statistical Manual of Mental Disorders*. It was popularly known as the *DSM*, and it was due for a revision soon. Politicking to list a new diagnosis typically begins a few years before a new edition goes to press, and to make sure the American Psychiatric Association—the APA—got on board to add multiple personality to the *DSM*, Connie began giving workshops about the diagnosis at the APA's national conventions.

One workshop was offered in Chicago in 1979. There, Connie mounted an exhibit of paintings by "Sybil," and she raved about how brilliant and talented Sybil's multiples had been, not just as artists but as writers, too. Virtually all her multiples were women with high IQs and tremendous creativity, Connie added. As a matter of fact, she was acting as a literary agent for many of them, sending their manuscripts to New York in search of publishers. The workshop was covered by the media, and an article about Connie's talented multiples was printed in newspapers throughout the country.[11]

Multiple personality became an official psychiatric diagnosis the next year. It was defined as "the existence within the individual of two or more distinct personalities" each of them "complex and integrated," with "its own unique behavioral patterns and social relationships."[12] As with every other diagnosis in the *DSM*, multiple personality received its own multidigit number. Therapists could now use it to bill insurance companies for their treatment of the newly recognized condition. Because multiple personality patients typically remained in treatment for years, their illness was worth good money.

Connie once again did a spate of media interviews, and she brought her patients with her. In 1980 she appeared on a New York City television news show with Marcy, the "janitor" who had always been trying to kill herself at the Open Hospital.[13] Marcy curled on the floor of the news studio, assumed the voice of a three-year-old, and recited the details of rope-and-meat-hook torture which she said her mother had perpetrated on her. Not only that, but both of her parents, as well as her brothers, her neighbors, and a dog had inserted toothpaste tubes into her vagina for sixteen years, beginning when she was six months old, and kicked the tubes farther inside her with combat boots. Marcy had not remembered any of this until therapy, when Dr. Wilbur managed to communicate with her alters. There were eighty-nine of them.

All of Marcy's claims were presented as fact. The reporter who narrated the program noted that she had not contacted Marcy's mother for her side of the story because Marcy had asked her not to. The show won a local Emmy award. Not long afterward, Connie went on *Good Morning America* and *20/20*.

With the Open Hospital closed back in Lexington, Connie asked Dr. Robert Kraus, chairman of the University of Kentucky Medical School's psychiatry department, if she could treat her patients at the University hospital. No problem, Kraus responded. But soon there were problems galore.

"She would sweep in" to the hospital to make rounds, Kraus remembered.[14] She would gather all the psychiatry residents and medical students around a patient she was treating for multiple personality. Then she would question everyone about the case. She seldom thought they got it right. "You're stupid!" she would scream, and "Thank God I'm here! I'll straighten you out!" Turning to the multiple, she would explain that "You've got to be patient with these people—they don't know anything." Pandemonium would erupt on the ward, with residents cursing, nurses trembling, and patients refusing to follow hospital protocol. "Dr. Wilbur said I can do this and I can do that," Kraus remembered them insisting. When the staff disagreed, the patients ordered them to "Go to hell!"

Kraus intervened, telling Connie that from now on he, rather than she, would call the shots about her patients' medications, privileges, and passes to leave the hospital. She agreed but soon afterward stopped making admissions to the hospital.

Connie's home was also a battleground. Years after the book *Sybil* had first appeared, she was still struggling to keep Shirley under wraps and under control. Shirley had grown furious that she had been forced to go into hiding, and Connie tried to keep her mind off the situation. She helped Shirley launch another business, "Mason Arts, Inc.," by "buying stock" in it—in other words, giving Shirley money with no payback date. Shirley tried to develop and sell her "Sybil" board game, but she had no luck.[15]

She exacted vengeance by throwing tantrums when Connie tried to socialize with others.

Connie's older brother Oliver was still alive in Canada. One of his daughters had gone through a divorce after Connie moved to Lexington and needed help putting her life back together. Ever eager to help a woman fulfill her dreams, Connie offered assistance if her niece would move to Lexington. She did, with her three teenaged daughters, Connie's grand-nieces. They all started coming to Connie's home to socialize with her. But Shirley wanted Connie to herself. She tattled that one of the grandnieces was having boys in the house when Connie wasn't there. The grandniece said that was a lie. She and her sisters and mother stopped visiting.[16]

Things got worse when eighteen-year-old Brenda Burwell, another grandniece, moved from Canada to live with Connie and finish high school. Brenda was having discipline problems in her own home and Connie offered to take her in. Brenda loved her aunt, and though Connie almost never talked about her past, she did confide certain things—that she'd had plastic surgery to rejuvenate her buttocks, for instance, and a touch-up on her facelift, no doubt to impress Hollywood. Connie also told Brenda that Shirley was Sybil. And Brenda learned about late-night calls from patients. Connie told her never to answer the phone when she was out of town, but Brenda did anyway, and found the experience mind bogglingly entertaining. She would chat for hours with women who switched into an array of voices.

Shirley hated having Brenda around. The first thing she'd told her when she arrived was that she, Shirley, "could get rid of anyone she wanted to, get them out of Connie's life," Brenda remembered years later.

Brenda tried to keep her distance but found it difficult. Shirley spent so much time at Connie's that she'd never bothered to furnish her own place with care. Only one room there reflected her personality: it was graced with natural light and filled with vintage dolls from her youth—all those Peggys and Peggy Anns. Otherwise, Shirley's home was bare inside, and she mostly stayed away from it. She showed up first thing every morning at Connie's to cook her breakfast. Later, she would cook dinner and wait for Connie's return from work. Brenda was usually there, too, and she never saw Shirley displaying any alter personalities. What she did see was a skittery, trembling woman, not just thin and anxious but shakingly, palpably angry.

One afternoon when Brenda came home from school she made the mistake of throwing her coat and books on a chair. Shirley scolded her. Minutes later Brenda went into the kitchen and started fixing herself a grilled-cheese sandwich in a pan on the stove. Shirley walked in and became enraged that Brenda had not first lined the pan with aluminum foil. She "flipped out," according to Brenda, and physically attacked her. Connie's housekeeper, an older black woman, witnessed the violence.

When Connie got home, Brenda and the housekeeper told her what had happened. Connie refused to believe them. Shirley would never do such a thing, she insisted, and she summarily fired the housekeeper. Brenda was evicted, too, and had to move in with a girlfriend.

Shirley was often alone in the house after Brenda was kicked out, while Connie spent days and sometimes weeks at meetings and conferences organized to turn the treatment of MPD into a specialty. In 1983, she was able to enjoy the fruits of her labors when a new professional organization was born: the International Society for the Study of Multiple Personality and Dissociation. The ISSMP&D held its first conference a year later, featuring presentations like "Inpatient Management" and "What to Do till the Friendly One Comes: Managing an Angry Alter."[17]

At the conference, Connie spoke about "Multiple Personality Disorder and Child Abuse: An Etiologic Overview." The title suggested that the talk would be a snooze: after all, her longtime axiom, that alter personalities were invariably created by severe child abuse, was by now so entrenched that her colleagues were starting to dub it "the post-Wilburian paradigm." But up on the podium, she launched into a circus of weirdness as she described a woman patient who'd recovered memories of her family as an organized cult of vicious assassins.[18]

That idea had been born in the popular culture in 1980, when the best seller *Michelle Remembers*[19] came out, a book about a patient who had suddenly recalled that her parents were Satanists who had led their coven in sexually torturing little Michelle when she was only five years old. It was co-authored by Dr. Lawrence Pazder, a Catholic psychiatrist in Canada, and Michelle Smith, Pazder's patient and later his wife.

Michelle Remembers told of ritual crimes in endless, gory detail. Marketed as truth, it became an instant bestseller. Seven years earlier, *Sybil* had awakened in many disturbed women the idea that they, too, possessed multiple personalities. Now, among this same demographic, *Michelle Remembers* evoked phantasmagoric memories of sexual torment by evil groups—everyone from devil worshipers to the Ku Klux Klan.

"How would you like to be exposed to multiple murders as an infant and a child, since your grandfather formed the first Klan and your father formed the second Klan and the family literally owned the town?" Connie asked rhetorically at the 1984 ISSMP&D conference. "I don't know how many murders this child saw . . . she tells me that a group of individuals in that part of the United States killed every single black person that came within their purview and they killed a great many . . . whites that were itinerant farm workers, including the children."[20]

The KKK had apparently been able to erase all evidence of their murders, Connie continued. They dismembered the corpses and put them "in these large burners on the farms that are used to burn trash from the harvest." During therapy, she added, her patient also remembered being forced by her father to slit victims' throats with a knife. "Blood was caught in jars and often times, everyone shared in drinking the blood," Connie said, adding that the killers would cut off a body part "and pass it around for everyone to take some, in order to eat it."

"I don't think that we can possibly deny the truth" of the patient's story, Connie concluded. "These are not allegations. They're descriptions of behaviors that she was forced to participate in."[21]

Though some conference attendees might have been shocked by Connie's story, it is safe to say that most were not surprised. By 1984, almost every therapist at the meeting had patients who'd recovered memories of chillingly sadistic and bizarre group crimes—or they had colleagues whose patients had these recollections.

Soon even children were telling these stories. By the mid-1980s a wave of sex-torture allegations was washing over preschools and day care centers throughout the United States. From California to Massachusetts, teachers, teacher aides, and babysitters were accused of enacting intricate, organized rapes on children barely old enough to tie their shoelaces. The charges terrified early childhood educators, driving untold numbers from the profession. Dozens of public child care facilities were shuttered.

Within a few years, thousand of adults would be investigated nationwide for crimes against the little children. Some 130 would be charged. Oddly, authorities would find no evidence. Some of the children said they had been raped with knives and gun barrels, but they never had corresponding wounds. Nor had any parents or other adults walked into these nursery schools unannounced and witnessed the abuse. Children talked of seeing their classmates assaulted, but the classmates didn't remember being hung upside down, having objects inserted in them, or being forced to chant to the Devil.

Experts came to the defendants' trials to tell the juries why so many of these children had at first denied they'd been tortured. They needed psychotherapy and repeated interrogation in order to disclose the abuse, the experts said, for the same reason that Sybil had needed her psychoanalyst for so long. Just as Sybil had been bizarrely violated as a little girl and forgot the assaults because of psychic splitting, children nowadays were being attacked, and they were protecting themselves by dissociating, or "losing time." When a child said abuse hadn't happened, the experts insisted, that was proof that it *had* happened. The "victims" were given various treatments, including drugs and hypnosis. Dozens of adults were convicted. Some got centuries of hard time.[22]

By the time of the ISSMP&D's annual conference in 1987, speakers were lecturing about "Treatment of Victims of Ritualistic Abuse" and "The Satanic Cult in Rural Mid-America." The ISSMP&D's big new idea, that cults were breaking children's minds into pieces, was invoked by people who had joined Connie in founding the organization and the multiple personality movement. More than six hundred therapists were attending ISSMP&D conferences to learn how to ferret ritual abuse memories from their patients.[23]

That same year—1987—the *DSM* appended "disorder" to "multiple personality," creating the popular acronym MPD. The 1980 *DSM* had characterized the illness as "extremely rare" and possibly caused by child abuse. The new one described it as "not nearly so rare as it has commonly been thought to be," and caused "in nearly all cases" by child abuse, often sexual. Furthermore, older requirements that alter personalities be "complex," "integrated,"[24] and mutually amnesiac for each other were dropped. Now, mere fragments of behavior, little tics that popped up for a few seconds and of which the patient was fully aware, qualified as alter personalities.

It became common for MPD sufferers to possess scores, even hundreds, of alters (one was reputed to have 4,500). Not all were human; some weren't even alive. Patients reported gorillas and lobsters, as well as unicorns, angels, and—if the alters were immobile and voiceless—trees. Supernatural-sounding claims sprang up. A person with MPD, it was said, could have one alter with blue eyes and another with brown eyes. Such a person could be diabetic but have a personality whose insulin levels were normal. Even blood types could change.

The media was all over these "facts."[25] Breathlessly, they repeated ISSMP&D speculations about MPD as a late-twentieth-century epidemic. Before *Sybil*, fewer than a hundred people over the past two centuries had been identified in Western medical literature with conditions resembling MPD. By 1984, only four years after the condition was first listed in the *DSM,* an ISSMP&D leader was suggesting that 25,000 Americans suffered from it. Another leader estimated that 3 percent of the population had MPD—over seven million people.[26]

Therapists flocked to the field, and specialized wards opened, including at Chicago's prestigious Rush-Presbyterian St. Luke's Hospital. These facilities were far more reputable than Connie's Open Hospital had been. But they used the same irregular treatments that she had: massive doses of mind-bending drugs, including barbiturates injected into veins.

Looking at the new statistics, the new wards, and the influx of therapists eager to specialize in MPD, Connie felt vindicated. Years ago, her father had called her stupid. Now she'd been recognized by the APA as a Distinguished Psychiatrist. Colleagues celebrated her for launching "a scientific revolution."[27] *Sybil*, one of them wrote, was "the most important book about a psychiatrist and patient ever written."[28] Dr. Cornelia B. Wilbur was one of the greatest physicians in America, if not the world.

At the same time Connie was receiving these accolades, Shirley got sick again. No medical records are available to reveal what her symptoms were, but when interviewed for this book, some of Connie's old colleagues in Lexington remembered hearing in the 1980s that Shirley—who most of them knew was Sybil—had entered the hospital for nonpsychiatric reasons. In 1989, at a meeting of the ISSMP&D, Connie gave a speech about her years of work identifying and treating multiple personality disorder, and her persistence even when her efforts at first were ignored. "I was raised as a pure scientist," she boasted to her audience. "I have never forgotten that if you're going to make a decision, you get as much evidence as you possibly can."[29] That is how the correct diagnosis was arrived at, she explained, no matter how many people might dispute it.

After her presentation a Q & A followed, and someone asked how Sybil was doing. Connie's answer was brief, almost throwaway. Sybil had lived for a long time without much energy, she said, because in addition to everything else that was wrong with her, she had suffered for years from a disease called pernicious anemia.

Another audience member followed with an unrelated question, and that was the end of pernicious anemia and Sybil. No one stopped to think about the bombshell Connie had just revealed.

But this was a group of psychiatrists, psychologists, and social workers, not internal medicine specialists. Few knew that pernicious anemia is a genetic disease, handed down from parent to child. Probably even fewer were aware that although the symptoms of pernicious anemia most commonly appear during middle age, they occasionally begin during early childhood or adolescence. As for Connie, she probably would not have told her audience about Shirley's pernicious anemia if she'd known that its symptoms run the gamut: from tingling and numbness in the limbs to stomach pains, fatigue, constipation, difficulty concentrating or learning, depression, social withdrawal, anxiety, irritability, headaches, insomnia, mood swings, rapid heart beat, nausea, vomiting, severe weight loss, hallucinations, muscle pains, a tendency to walk into walls, confusion about identity—and miscarriages, deadly stomach cancer, and hair gone prematurely white.[30]

The gamut encompasses Shirley's lifelong problems, and those of her mother, Mattie Mason, who no doubt passed the disease to her daughter.

When Shirley was a child, physicians such as Dr. Flores, her family practitioner, had the knowledge and technology to detect anemia by using blood tests. But doctors back then did not know that the blood of a person suffering from pernicious anemia can appear abnormal one day and normal the next, but either way it makes no difference: the disease is still there.

Not until 1948 did medical researchers discover the real cause of pernicious anemia: an inborn lack of ability in some people to process vitamin B12, which is essential for human health and life. The injections of hog liver that Shirley was prescribed as a blood thickener made her better when she was young because they happened to contain vitamin B12, though doctors didn't know that at the time. She stopped receiving the shots because the doctors mistakenly thought that when her blood looked normal, she was no longer ill.

But when her symptoms eventually returned, the doctors scrambled for an explanation. Hysteria, they decided, and Shirley and her parents had no choice but to accept the diagnosis, to embrace it, to coddle it. Soon Shirley would not know the difference between the bad feelings in her mind and the malfunctions in her body. All would combine, into a performance that eventually would became one of the most dramatic productions in the world, with help from Dr. Cornelia Wilbur and her "pure science."

How did Connie feel when she discovered she'd spent so much time unaware that Shirley suffered from pernicious anemia? Did she understand that a correct diagnosis might have saved her patient from years of drug addiction? From therapy so frequent that she became disabled during what should have been the most productive time of her life? Did Connie realize that she had pressured Shirley into blaming her symptoms on a past so riddled with fiction that it hardly qualified anymore as a meaningful life history?

There is no way to know how Shirley felt. Maybe none of it mattered anymore, especially after she developed yet another serious illness. In 1990 she was diagnosed with breast cancer and put through excruciating hospital procedures to destroy the tumors. Connie was her doctor again, arranging treatments, consulting with oncologists, comforting Shirley like a mother.[31]

Two years later the roles were reversed for the first time. Old age caught up with Connie after she turned eighty, and she had a stroke. She could no longer get out of a chair, and Shirley managed the household and hired nurses to help. Connie softened, becoming dependent and childlike. Sometimes her caretakers would gather her up and drive her to the beauty parlor. She returned with her shiny red nails and carrot hair, but getting to the beauty salon eventually became impossible.

On a Thursday in April 1992, Connie, who was eighty-three, suffered a fatal heart attack. Devastated but with a sense of duty, Shirley went downtown to the funeral home to provide the necessary data for the death certificate—date and place of birth, father's name, mother's before she was married.[32] There was a memorial service at the university, and the national press reported the passing of one of America's most famous psychiatrists. The ISSMP&D hailed Dr. Cornelia Wilbur as the person most "responsible for the current high level of interest in multiple personality disorder." Every clinician treating MPD was indebted to her. None could approach their work "without in some way being influenced by Connie."[33]

Connie's will designated her former patient Jan Morrow, who had swum laps with her every weekend in exchange for therapy, as executor.[34] The estate included her house, which was slated to be sold after everything inside was disposed of. Morrow came over to start the job and found Shirley still there, rooting compulsively through Connie's papers—papers that included thousands of pages of Shirley's own therapy records.[35]

Morrow boxed up the papers and took them to her own house, where she read them and concluded that they were not for the public to see. Over the next several days, she tore the records of America's most celebrated psychiatrist into jagged little strips, and stuffed them into bags. Then she took the bags outside and tossed them in the garbage.[36]

CHAPTER 21

CONTAINMENT

THE WAY THINGS WERE EVOLVING in the world of multiple personality disorder treatment, Connie was fortunate not to have lived past 1992. MPD was still at its apex then, a diagnosis so reputable and alluring that it had become part of the wallpaper of American culture. "This could be someone you know," proclaimed Sally Jesse Raphael as she paraded multiples on her talk show, with their stories of childhood torture. "MPD: The Syndrome of the '90s," Oprah called one of her programs.[1]

Oprah was right. By 1992 thousands of people, in every sizeable community in the United States and Canada, were in treatment for MPD. Bookstores sold memoirs by multiples: *The Flock*; *When Rabbit Howls*; *Ghost Girl* were a few titles. There were magazines, like *Many Voices*, to which multiples could contribute poems and artwork. A few courts even started allowing alter personalities to give testimony in criminal trials. In one such case, a young man was charged with raping a woman who he said agreed to have sex with him—the woman, however, argued that it was her child alter who went to bed with the man, and he should have realized she was incapable of consent. The judge swore in six of the woman's multiple personalities as witnesses. The man was convicted.[2]

There were entertainment stars who said they were multiples. Roseanne Barr appeared on talk shows to say that she had been sexually molested as a child but forgot about it until she entered therapy in her late thirties. She would later describe her twenty alter personalities. They included "Piggy," "Bambi," and "Fucker."[3]

Barr characterized having alters as an illness, but celebrity feminist Gloria Steinem published an inspirational book for women, *Revolution from Within: A Book of Self-Esteem*, which lauded multiple personalities as a gift. MPD women, Steinem wrote, could learn many foreign languages. Not only that, they could "have two or even three menstrual cycles in the same body."[4] In her acknowledgments Steinem thanked Bennett Braun, a leader of the International Society for the Study of Multiple Personality and Dissociation (ISSMP&D), for his help.

In reality, however, the disorder was becoming half Trojan Horse and half time bomb. Critics sensed that the diagnosis was about to self-destruct, along with the therapists who promoted it. The FBI since the early 1980s had been investigating the claims patients were making about ritual abuse at the hands of Satanic cults and had never found any evidence for the existence of the cults themselves. Many psychiatrists and psychologists also knew that witch hunts had wrought terrible suffering on innocent people during the Middle Ages. Some of the calmer ISSMP&D people called in an anthropologist, Dr. Sherrill Mulhern, and asked her what was going on. In analytic detail, Mulhern warned that these therapists' ignorance about patients' suggestibility, combined with their naivete about "recovered memories," had opened a Pandora's box, releasing from the collective psyche some of Western culture's most irrational (and dangerous) fears.[5]

One new group *was* paying attention to Mulhern's warning: 1992 was the founding year for the False Memory Syndrome Foundation, or FMSF. It was begun by Pamela and Peter Freyd, a Philadelphia couple whose psychology professor daughter, Jennifer, had accused her father of molesting her for years, starting when she was very young. Jennifer had only recently remembered the assaults while in therapy. She had not been diagnosed with MPD, so she was not said to have "dissociated" into different alters. Instead, she had dealt with her sexual abuse as a child by creating "repressed memories" and only later recovering them.

The notion of repressed and recovered memories was being widely promoted by many psychologists and psychiatrists by the late 1980s, as well as by a bestselling self-help book for women with emotional problems, *The Courage to Heal*. But Freyd's parents insisted their daughter's memories were bogus. They began looking for other parents claiming to be falsely accused of abuse by their grown children in therapy.

After Peter and Pamela Freyd located dozens of these parents, they decided they were dealing with a false memory epidemic. They recruited an advisory board of experts, many of them older psychiatrists who had trained and started practicing in the pre-*Sybil* generation. They had researched the pitfalls of hypnosis and memory, and they had grave reservations about recovered memories, including those elicited under treatment for MPD. The Freyds unveiled the False Memory Syndrome Foundation to the press, and reporters requested interviews with aggrieved mothers and fathers. They were increasingly easy to find, because with every news article that came out about the FMSF, the new organization heard from more people saying they, too, had been falsely accused.[6] One out of seven of these callers added that the diagnosis which had led to false memories was MPD.[7]

As skepticism about MPD spread, the FMSF began hearing from another group: women who called themselves retractors. They had been in therapy, developed chilling memories of childhood abuse, then realized the memories were false. This change of mind typically occurred after patients were terminated from therapy because their insurance had run out or when they developed a modicum of independence from their doctors. That happened to Jeanette Bartha, a former activist in NOW, the National Organization for Women, and a champion fencer in college. In the late 1980s she developed depression and visited a psychiatrist who diagnosed her with MPD. By 1992 Bartha had spent six years in and out of hospitals, almost constantly wearing pajamas and lying in bed. Then her psychiatrist took a summer vacation. While he was gone, Bartha decided to put on street clothes and start exercising every day.

"The more I exercised," Bartha would later recall, "the more I didn't need medication . . . my mind started to clear." But when she told her doctor about her improvement, "He said it was just another personality that probably wouldn't last long." Later, she told the psychiatrist, "Look, this uncle I told you had abused me wasn't even in the United States at that time. It couldn't have happened." The psychiatrist ignored her. "Oh my God," Bartha told herself. "He doesn't believe what I can prove to be true! Why?" She quit therapy. Later she filed a lawsuit.[8]

Bartha's civil complaint was settled out of court and the details were never reported on by the press. But other cases received plenty of publicity, including a massive lawsuit filed against Judith Peterson, a Texas psychologist known as an expert at using hypnosis and other methods to help clients recover hidden memories of trauma. The lawsuit against Peterson was brought by a longtime patient, Kathryn Schwiderski, whose husband was an oil-company executive in Houston. Kathryn had originally sought treatment from Peterson in 1985 because she felt depressed, but during their four years of therapy, Peterson had diagnosed her with MPD. The lawsuit claimed that Peterson and three other therapists had wrongly decided Kathryn was a longtime member of a Satanic cult who had participated in rapes, torture, electroshock, drugging, human sacrifice, cult programming, cannibalism, kidnapping, and murder. After this assessment was made, Schwiderski was placed in a dissociative disorders unit managed by Peterson.[9]

Psychologist Peterson had reported Kathryn Schwiderski and her husband to Child Protection Services because of her statements during MPD therapy that they had hurt their children. Detectives investigated, no evidence turned up, and the case was dropped. Even so, the accusations—and confessions—tore the family apart. The Schwiderskis ended up divorcing.

The state of Texas closed Peterson's dissociative disorders unit in 1993 after determining it had overused physical restraints, censored patients' mail and phone calls (supposedly to protect them from "the cult"), and, in one case, refused a request for discharge from the hospital until the patient could prove "the cult" was not a safety risk. The Schwiderskis, meanwhile, launched a lawsuit demanding $35 million in damages, and not just from Judith Peterson. They sued two dozen other people, including several MPD heroes.

The defendants all denied the charges, but the litigation received substantial press coverage. Many therapists, especially those who treated MPD, were frightened. In 1994, the American Psychiatric Association expressed doubt that hypnosis and drugs could help elicit dissociated or repressed memories, and cautioned that memories produced using these treatments were often not true.

The same year, reflecting widespread concerns that MPD had become a dangerous fad, experts working on the new edition of the APA's diagnostic manual, the *DSM-IV*, gave the condition a new name so it would sound less alluring to the public. Now it was called DID, dissociative identity disorder. The new manual suggested that DID might be "overdiagnosed in individuals who are highly suggestible," and warned about "overzealous therapists" promoting dissociation rather than curing it.[10]

Further, the *DSM-IV* commented, the high number of cases reported recently in the United States indicated DID could be a "culture-bound" syndrome—just like "falling out," the term used when African Americans in the South suddenly become paralyzed for no organic reason and cannot see, though their eyes are open; or "spell" (also Southern), when individuals "communicate" with deceased relatives or with spirits, and sometimes show changes in personality. These terms and other idioms of distress made it into the *DSM*.[11] But unlike MPD, they were shunted into a section describing the problems of marginalized people and immigrants. Some wondered if DID should be sidelined into that section, too.

Despite these reforms, the therapists were still under siege. In 1995, PBS *Frontline* aired a documentary about two other former MPD patients who were suing their therapists for misconduct similar to that which the Schwiderskis, in Texas, had described. A bemused *New York Times* TV critic compared the therapists, all of them ISSMP&D leaders, to "a coven."[12] A later *Times* article noted that as a result of her MPD therapy, one plaintiff, a woman from Iowa born in the late 1950s, had remembered having sex with President John F. Kennedy (the woman was seven years old when Kennedy was assassinated).[13]

By the late 1990s, more therapists were sued, and some were indicted on criminal charges for misdiagnosing multiple personality disorder and satanic cult involvement in order to generate huge billings and defraud insurance companies. Therapists started refusing to treat dissociative identity disorder. They abandoned the ISSMP&D, too. The organization lost half its membership.[14]

Thus MPD came to be seen as some bizarre subculture and was snickered at in the press. "Devil Doc a Crock?" the New York *Daily News* headlined an article about a therapist who performed an exorcism on a patient, complete with a fire extinguisher ("Sometimes Satan leaves a ring of fire, he explained").[15] Even Geraldo took it on the chin. He apologized for all those years of bringing multiples and therapists on his show to fuel the Satanic ritual abuse epidemic.[16]

With multiple personality disorder abolished from the *DSM*, the

ISSMP&D dropped "MP" from its name, turning itself into ISSD, the International Society for the Study of Dissociation. At the same time, the group's leaders revised their old advice to clinicians about how to treat the newly renamed condition. Previously they had urged their fellow healers to do anything necessary to help patients remember and relive their childhood trauma, no matter how much medication and hypnosis was required. New protocols were developed, specifying that no patient should be put into trance before signing a consent form which explained the risk of developing false memories. Therapists were also advised to stop glorifying alters. They were told to treat their patients as "whole persons" rather than collections of selves.[17]

Amid the withering skepticism, there remained some diehard faithful. MPD was real, they insisted. They pointed to research, initiated in the early 1970s by Dr. Cornelia Wilbur and her colleagues at the University of Kentucky, purporting to show that alters could be detected using medical tests such as EEGs. Further, MPD proponents noted, some brain imaging tests on people diagnosed with MPD showed features not visible in the brains of normal subjects.

But the studies they cited were thrown into question as investigation continued. Old research claiming that one alter personality could learn things without the other alters knowing it, was shown to be faulty. And the earlier EEG data, suggesting that alters had different brain waves, fell flat when new studies demonstrated that brain waves vary significantly even in a normal person; the differences simply show mood changes.[18]

And while it's true that MPD sufferers' brains look different from those of people without the condition, one study has found that veteran taxi drivers in England show similar differences in their brains when compared to people who haven't driven taxis. Another study indicates that professional musicians' brains appear distinct from those of amateurs. Doing the same thing, repeatedly, and for a very long time, apparently changes cerebral structures. And by the time people with MPD have shown up in labs to be tested, virtually all have spent years presenting their alters to the world, over and over and over. They seem as accustomed to behaving like multiples as the jazz maestros are to playing Coltrane, or London cabbies to navigating Fleet Street.[19]

The science no longer measured up, but there was still Sybil. Before she

227

walked into Dr. Wilbur's office, the faithful pointed out, the doctor had never heard of MPD. So how could she have suggested it to the patient? And what about the family physician, believers added, quoting from one of *Sybil* the telemovie's major plotlines. Dr. Wilbur had fact-checked the clinical history by going to the little town where Sybil grew up and finding her doctor. He had pulled out Sybil's old records containing solid evidence that she'd been battered and raped.

The problem was, no one knew if any of this had really happened, because no one knew who Sybil was. So in the late 1990s, a man known for digging up any dirt in psychiatry that he was interested in finding set his mind to learning Sybil's identity, then uncovering the facts of her psychotherapy with Dr. Cornelia B. Wilbur.

He was Peter Swales, a Welshman and a high school dropout who'd once been a manager for the Rolling Stones. A "punk historian," Swales called himself, and while researching the life of Sigmund Freud, he'd become convinced that the founder of psychoanalysis was self-serving and dishonest. Examining old archives and letters, he had concluded that Freud had carried on a love affair with his wife's sister, impregnated her, and arranged for an abortion under the guise of taking her to a health spa. Swales also uncovered the true identities of two of the women Freud had treated for hysteria, and he had demonstrated that Freud had greatly exaggerated when he claimed he cured these patients.[20]

Swales was joined in his Sybil search by Mikkel Borch-Jacobsen, a professor of comparative literature at the University of Washington. As a longtime critic of psychoanalysis, Borch-Jacobsen had interviewed Sybil's old backup psychiatrist, Dr. Herbert Spiegel, for *The New York Review of Books.* The title of the piece, published in 1997, made clear what Spiegel and Borch-Jacobsen thought of MPD. "Sybil," the article was called. "The Making of a Disease."[21]

But Swales and Borch-Jacobsen's sleuthing was stymied. Sybil was assumed to be alive somewhere, and to protect her privacy, John Jay College librarians had sealed a container in the Flora Rheta Schreiber archives marked "Box 37." It held Connie's therapy records with "Sybil" and many other materials displaying the patient's real name.

Undaunted, Swales plotted other investigative strategies. One was based on the fact that Dodge Center's family physician in the 1930s had been assigned the pseudonym "Dr. Quinoness" in *Sybil.* Of course, Swales didn't know that the real doctor was Otoniel Flores, but he correctly guessed that he had a Hispanic surname. Swales planned to check old state and county medical society records to find small, Depression-era Midwestern towns with Latino doctors. He intended to ask old-timers in these towns if a strange, artistic girl had once lived among them.[22] So famous was Swales as the Sherlock Holmes of psychoanalysis that everyone figured he would solve the mystery soon.

CHAPTER 22

DEMISE

SHIRLEY WAS PROBABLY UNAWARE THAT *Sybil*'s veracity was being questioned and that someone was tracking her down. But with Connie gone, her life was getting harder. She could barely force herself to step out onto her own front lawn, much less visit libraries to read magazines and newspapers. And though ISSMP&D conferences were a mecca for laypeople diagnosed with MPD—one regular attendee was Chris Sizemore, the real "Eve" of *The Three Faces of Eve*—Shirley had never showed her face at meetings and didn't intend to start.[1]

She had very little money to live on, much less to enjoy herself. Her royalties from *Sybil* had dropped steadily as the years passed, and by the early 1990s she was receiving only about $5,000 a year. That was virtually her only steady income, apart from Social Security payments that must have been miniscule given that during four decades after entering therapy with Connie in New York City, she had managed to work full time for only eight years. Connie had supported Shirley for most of her life, but her will gave most of her money to her nieces and to a university fund to encourage women to study medicine. To Shirley Connie bequeathed only $25,000, plus her own dwindling share of royalties.[2]

By the mid-1990s Shirley was scrambling to pay the taxes on her house and to buy the basic necessities. She kept trying to market her doll products with help from a nurse named Roberta Guy, who had cared for Connie during her final days.[3] Shirley had confided to Guy then that she was Sybil, and after Connie's death had hired Guy to be her companion.

Guy treated the dolls like an Avon business, hawking the merchandise to friends and family. Her efforts didn't go very far, so Shirley also tried to sell her artwork. Guy had a friend whose brother was an antiques dealer, and she told him she knew an elderly, indigent artist who needed help making ends meet. Wishing to be a good Samaritan, the dealer bought a few pieces and put them in his shop.[4]

After a couple of the paintings sold and Guy came back with more, the dealer and his partner threw a party where they announced that a reclusive local artist named Shirley Mason was starving—which was almost literally the case—and asked their guests to buy her paintings. Looking at them, people could see that she was trained; still, the work was uneven. Some of it was passably professional, done in a cubist style popular in the 1950s and early 1960s. But much was amateurish, especially her paintings that included people; she could barely render the human figure. A few more pieces were sold, thanks mainly to the impulse of charity.

Regardless of her artistic ability, of course, all of Shirley's paintings would have been snatched up if her dealers had known she was Sybil and advertised that connection. They didn't know, but she constantly worried that they would find out. She never went to the antiques shop and instead had Guy handle business. Guy tried to reassure her. "Don't be afraid," she said. "I'm with you and I'll never let anyone come close to you." That calmed Shirley some.

But Shirley's major comfort was her religious devotion. From Friday at sundown until Saturday twenty-four hours later, she listened to Seventh-Day Adventist inspirational tapes and read from the Bible. Sundays she enjoyed an Adventist television program, *It Is Written,* with dramatizations of Gospel stories and the lives of Christ's Apostles. For years she'd had to downplay her faith in front of the irreligious woman who had defined her life for her. Now that woman was gone. On her living room mantel she kept a large, black-and-white photograph of Connie in a buttoned-down suit jacket. But on weekends the portrait did not matter. On those days her living room was her church.

Then she discovered she was sick again. Tests revealed her cancer was back, and it had spread past her breasts into her liver and pancreas. Left untreated, she would not have long to live. What did she want, the doctors asked. Radiation? Chemo?

Neither, Shirley told them. No more of what she'd had in 1990: the hospitals, the drugs, the pain. At least Connie had helped doctor her then. That had made things bearable, but Connie was gone now, and no one could replace her. Nature would take its course this time. She was ready for death.[5]

Psychoanalysis sleuth Peter Swales never did speak with Shirley. It took him until the fall of 1998 to discover her name—which was several months too late. She died quietly in her home, surrounded by nurses, on February 26 of that year. She was seventy-five years old. It was early evening when she died.

Most of her house had always been gloomy at dusk, requiring that lamps be turned on. But the sunroom was different. Light poured in even late in the day, warming things in winter just as, seven decades earlier, it had warmed a Minnesota room built for just the same purpose. In childhood Shirley's sunroom had housed her dolls—dozens of them, bedecked in hand-stitched clothes, their hair curled and plaited, gazing into the brightness as though beckoning their owner to make up secret tales about them. Now, in 1998, the same dolls, worn and cracked with age, stared from toy cribs and high chairs in their special room in Kentucky.

After Shirley's body was taken away the nurses packed their things and left. Only the dolls remained.

EPILOGUE

I F THE STORY OF SYBIL shows us anything, it's that our collective fears and yearnings sometimes push us toward progress but impel us to reactionary behavior as well—behavior we might manage to avoid if only we knew ourselves better. The Sybil craze erupted during a fractured moment in history, when women pushed to go forward, even as the culture pulled back in fear. Sybil, with her brilliant and traumatized multiplicity, became a language of our conflict, our idiom of distress.

In some ways that idiom was silenced at the end of the twentieth century. Shirley Mason's identity and the name of her hometown had been unearthed in late 1998, after investigators Borch-Jacobsen and Swales discovered a letter to her from her childhood friend Anita that had been misfiled in the section of Flora's archive that was open to the public.[1] It was too late then to talk to Shirley, but the media found plenty of debunkers from Minnesota who dismissed her claims that Mattie had abused her, and skepticism reached as far as *Newsweek* and *The New York Times.*[2] Shirley's diagnosis was generally dismissed, and Connie's and Flora's names were besmirched.

The idea of multiple personalities went into hibernation, at least among psychiatrists. One of them, a professor at Harvard University's school of medicine, surveyed a sample of his American colleagues in 1999, asking what they thought of dissociative identity disorder. Most responded that there was insufficient scientific evidence to justify listing it in the *DSM*, and many suggested that it be deleted.[3] The controversy persists today, even as *Sybil* remains in print. In fact, a new edition came out in 2009 with a

233

three-page advisory for readers; it warns that questions exist about Shirley Mason's diagnosis and the truthfulness of her life story.[4]

Nonetheless, *Sybil* still has readers, many of them high school students assigned the book in their English and psychology classes. The first thing they see is the cover, still blaring in bright letters that the following pages tell "The Classic True Story of a Woman Possessed by Sixteen Personalities."[5] After that they hit the caveat. The takeaway message is that Sybil is beautiful and spooky in the same way that angels and ESP are beautiful and spooky. When it comes to science, she is not to be taken seriously. Still, the takeaway continues, maybe we *could* take her seriously if the scientists would only come up with better research.

New books and films for the lay public have also appeared with a similar message, featuring multiple-personality-disordered women, and men, too.[6] There is a television remake of *Sybil*, with Jessica Lange as Dr. Wilbur, and featuring a warning similar to the book's. The series *United States of Tara*—which was billed as a comedy about MPD—won Emmy awards. A 2010 Hollywood film, *Frankie and Alice*, starred Halle Berry as a dancer split into two alter personalities: an African American and a white racist. Berry was helped to prepare for her roles by a psychiatrist who early on worked with Connie Wilbur to get MPD recognized by psychiatry. And scriptwriters for *United States of Tara* were advised by Dr. Richard Kluft, another pioneer and a founder of what is today the ISSTD, or International Society for the Study of Trauma and Dissociation.[7]

I attended the ISSTD's 2009 annual convention and spoke with leaders a few minutes after they had wrapped up their luncheon to recognize outstanding researchers and clinicians in the field of dissociation. Plaques had been presented to people who were still trying to objectively prove that DID/MPD exists. Others were diagnosing new cases, including in distant countries which had barely heard of these disorders until the ISSTD doctors set up shop. One woman I talked with had just received the Cornelia B. Wilbur Award.

I told her and the others about the extensive evidence of Connie's ignorance, arrogance, and ethical misconduct that I had discovered during my research for this book. Her work with the patient who became Sybil might have started out as well intentioned, I pointed out. But its end product was largely a performance based on fiction.

"So what?" replied psychotherapist and ISSTD president Kathy Steele. "I don't know what difference it makes." She urged me to look at recent studies conducted to scientifically demonstrate the existence of dissociative identity disorder and its relationship to child abuse. That research, Steele insisted, "has got nothing to do with Sybil." I looked at the studies and they turned out to suffer from the same limitations as the older work.

Down the hall from my meeting with ISSTD's directors, Dr. Kluft was conducting a very stale workshop about Margaret, a patient he'd been seeing for years. Margaret's parents, Kluft said, were secret Ku Klux Klan members who routinely slaughtered infants and delivered electric shocks to Margaret's vagina until she escaped by joining the U.S. military, but then she got kidnapped and tortured by high-ranking generals and she only remembered all this during years of therapy for multiple personality disorder. Kluft expressed no doubt that her story was true. Not a hint of audience skepticism surfaced during the question and answer period.

Perhaps no one had questions because Margaret was described as being as pretty as the late Grace Kelly and just as rich—implying that she was paying out of her own pocket for Kluft's work on her. During the rise of managed health care in the 1990s, insurance companies stopped reimbursing therapists for the years, even decades, of treatment deemed necessary to cure a multiple. That policy change relegated MPD and DID to the medical sidelines, along with stem-cell facelifts and high colonics. As a result, the ISSTD had become so marginalized that its members could say anything they wanted to and few outside the organization would care, because few were listening anymore. In the desiccated little world of dissociation studies and treatment, Sybil was a dead issue.

But beyond that world she survives, at least in spirit.

As psychologist Antonio Martinez-Taboas has noted, people in modern Western culture are socialized to nurture complex selves, rich interior lives, and individualistic experiences apart from their communities. In times of crisis, Martinez-Taboas speculates, the idea of having multiple selves, complete with lavish role playing and feelings of separation from the world—dissociation—may be the perfect psychic container for people's troubles.[8]

And they do have troubles, the vast majority of which are not invented but sincerely experienced—in ways strictly predetermined by culture. Shirley's vitamin B12 deficiency made her sick in the 1930s and early 1940s, with very real neurological and physical symptoms. Sadly, medical ignorance was also very real; doctors knew little about vitamins. But they did know about Freud, and they gave a name to Shirley's aches, numbness, lurching, weight loss, sadness, moodiness, and faints: hysteria. And later another, more heroic name, MPD.

With each new diagnosis came rules about how to feel and speak her suffering. She did as she was told and then some—and within a few years, a girl who'd started out with low blood counts became a woman with countless selves. It was Dr. Wilbur's fault that this happened, and it was not her fault. All of her professional life she had made extraordinary efforts to assist women in healing and fulfilling their dreams. She wanted to help and she did the best she knew how, all the while lauding her work as "pure science."

Being MPD made Shirley Mason an invalid and a recluse, but it also made her feel important. University of Pennsylvania social work professor Lina Hartocollis has thought about what a person like Shirley could gain from adopting and enacting MPD. For some people in our modern, secular culture, Hartocollis speculates, forgetting one's identity and playing with another may replace religious experience as an escape from the problems of everyday life.[9] If that's how it was for Shirley, perhaps she really did have the happy ending that Flora wanted for her, and which we can assume Connie did, too, if we give her even the slightest benefit of the doubt.

Still, Shirley's happy ending came freighted with terrible contradictions, and not just for her. The book that resulted from her having been diagnosed with MPD tapped into the public's fears of danger, threat, and insidiousness under the surface of American life. The millions and millions of Sybil fans who came to think of themselves as empowered to do great things also felt so damaged by the cruelties of traditional family life that they could not trust their own mothers, much less their memories. As in the case of Jeanette Bartha, the college athlete and activist who ended up in bed all day, women and their social struggles were reduced to a bizarre illness. The cure was not critical inquiry or protest marches or efforts at the polls. Instead, the cure was drugs, hypnosis, and pajamas.

Could a mistake like this happen again? If so, it might voice itself through a new psychological idiom of distress, something more attuned to the times than multiple personality disorder, yet equally garbled and unable to clearly express people's true needs. That would be a tragic replay, but perhaps it could be avoided. Connie Wilbur called herself a scientist, but science warns against professing certainty, especially about something as subjective as the study of human behavior. If Sybil teaches us anything, it is that we should never accept easy answers or quick explanations. Knowledge in medicine changes constantly, and anyone unprepared to welcome the changes and test them is not to be trusted.

Psychotherapy can do enormous good when it is cautious about delving into the mind, skeptical of anyone offering definitive answers, wary of the overly confident, critical about the political and social milieu in which it operates, and accepting of the enormity of what we do not know. When healers and the public ignore these tenets, however, what emerges—on the couch and in the culture—can be as powerful yet pernicious as Sybil unexposed.

ACKNOWLEDGMENTS

D OZENS OF PEOPLE HELPED ME to create this book, but without the pioneering efforts of two of them, I could never have started my work.

Beginning in the early 1990s, scholar Mikkel Borch-Jacobsen and historian Peter Swales spent years trying to uncover the identity of the woman with the pseudonym "Sybil." During the time this sleuthing was going on, records of Shirley Mason's life languished in a library archive, tightly sealed from researchers. Mikkel and Peter eventually were successful in naming Shirley, and as a result, the archives were opened to people like me.

When I got hold of Mikkel and told him that I, too, was investigating Shirley's life, he shared a trove of knowledge and even mailed me an audiotape. It was a long interview that he and Peter had done years earlier with Virginia Flores Cravens, a childhood neighbor of Shirley's. Cravens possessed firsthand knowledge of Shirley's early emotional problems, but by the time I started my research she was suffering from dementia and could no longer remember or talk. Mikkel's generosity resurrected Craven's memories.

Mikkel and Peter also led me to David Eichman, a grandson of Shirley's stepmother, Florence Eichman Mason. David had inherited and saved piles of old correspondence between Shirley and her father and Shirley and Florence, as well as many pieces of Shirley's artwork, and photographs of her as a young woman. David and his wife, Bonnie, made this material available, and helped me to organize and interpret it.

I also found Dan Houlihan. A psychology professor at the University of Minnesota at Mankato—the same school Shirley attended as an undergraduate—Dan

239

had heard the local gossip for years, so he knew who she really was even back in the 1970s. He, himself, was a student at Mankato then, and spent his spare time poking around to learn more. Dan was unstintingly helpful to me, donating old correspondence he'd collected between Shirley and her former teachers, legal documents about her father's business affairs, old college yearbooks and registrar's office material, and even the names and whereabouts of Shirley's dorm mates from the 1940s.

Dan directed me to Muriel Odden Coulter, the daughter of one of those dorm mates. Muriel, too, shared an enormous collection of letters that Shirley had written to her mother and her when she was a child.

Stanley Giesel, Vadah Purtell, Frank Weeks, Vivian Beaver, Roy Langworthy, and Joan Larson grew up in or around Dodge Center, Shirley's little hometown in Minnesota. Most knew Shirley, and they supplied me with reminiscences and photographs. Dennae Ness Wilson was living in the Mason's old house when I knocked on her door in in 2009 and asked for a tour. She graciously waved me in.

Janet Kolstadt Johnson, Roger Langworthy, and Melanie Wheeler Langworthy spoke to me by phone about growing up in Dodge Center decades ago. Miranda Marland, daughter of Shirley's best childhood friend, Robert Moulton, recalled what Robert had told his own children about his pal. Shirley's cousins Patricia Alcott, Lorna Gilbert, Arlene Christensen, and Marcia Schmidt sorted through family keepsakes and found beautiful pictures of their relative, some of which you see in this book.

Shirley's life-long experience as a Seventh-Day Adventist was crucial to making her the person she was, and I want to thank several people for helping me to understand this fascinating American religion. In Dodge Center, Adventist church pastor Thomas Bentley and his wife, Julie, welcomed me to Sabbath services when I visited in 2009, then showed me yellowing, leather-bound church records from the late nineteenth and early twentieth centuries. I got goose bumps viewing Shirley's parents' handwriting on the fragile pages, and the penciled-in baptism date of their daughter.

I also got help from Dr. Ronald Numbers, a historian at the University of Wisconsin and an expert on Seventh-Day Adventism who, himself, was raised in the faith. Ron introduced me to fellow scholar T. Joe Willey. T. Joe also had an Adventist childhood, like Shirley's in the rural Midwest, and he plied me with conversation and his own writings.

Jean Lane also comes from Adventist stock. She was Shirley's best friend during college, and I first visited her in 2008 she was in her late eighties, still producing beautiful art and possessed of a fine memory for events from seven decades earlier. Jean has since chatted with me for hours and always responded quickly when I've written or called with more questions about her old friend. Her energy and intelligence are inspiring.

Robert Rieber, an emeritus psychology professor at John Jay College in New York City, taught at John Jay along with Flora Schreiber. He once received a gift from her: a set of audiotapes that—as he discovered years later when he finally listened to them—included one of Shirley undergoing a therapy session with her psychoanalyst. Professor Rieber donated this material to the college's library, where I was able to listen to it as part of my research. In addition, he introduced me to Dr. Herbert Spiegel, a preeminent psychiatrist and hypnotherapist who briefly worked with Shirley in the late 1950s and early 1960s.

When I met Herb Spiegel, in 2008, he was ninety-four years old and still walking to his office every day to see patients. I interviewed him several times; he was unfailingly enthusiastic, patient, and thorough in explaining his treatment of Shirley and his views about the nature of her problems. His wife, the psychologist Marcia Greenleaf, assisted with the interviews. Herb died in his sleep in 2009. I feel very lucky to have been able to work with him and Marcia, and to have seen his treatment records of Shirley.

Other elderly New Yorkers or former New Yorkers—many of them psychiatrists and most still working—spoke with me about what it was like to be a therapist or mental health researcher in Manhattan in the 1950s and 1960s, when Sybil's full-time psychoanalyst, Dr. Connie Wilbur, was working there. Thanks to Dr. Ann Ruth Turkel, Dr. Sylvia Brecher Marer in Rhode Island, Dr. Nathaniel Lehrman, and Dr. Arthur Zitrin for their reminiscences.

Several people helped me trace Connie Wilbur's life to her formative years. Her cousin on her mother's side, Robert Schade, recounted family lore and sent me a photograph of Connie and her brother. Deborah Brown Kovac, a niece of Connie's second husband, reminisced about her aunt's and Shirley's family visits in the 1960s and 1970s. In Canada, Connie's nephew Neil Burwell and her great-nephews Warner and Douglas Burwell provided photographs and rich anecdotes, as did great-niece Brenda Burwell Canning, who lived with Connie in the 1970s. A cousin well into her nineties, Ruth Barstow Dixon, also shared memories and hand-me-down family stories, some dating to the 1800s.

I was especially fortunate to find Dr. Richard Dieterle in Ann Arbor, Michigan, and his sister, Caroline Dieterle, in Iowa City. Their psychiatrist father, Dr. Robert Dieterle, was Connie's professor and mentor when she was in medical school in the 1930s. Richard was kind enough to root around in a cold, drafty barn, where he dug out an extraordinary film about multiple personalities that his father made during the years he was teaching Connie. Until Richard found the film for me, no one had laid eyes on it for almost seventy years.

My brilliant assistant Annie Slemrod helped locate and digitize the Dieterle film, and she ferreted out records about Connie in Michigan that I never imagined existed. Other young people also made my work easier. Michael Galvin helped with translation. Merryl Reichbach did records gathering in New York City. My daughter, Sophy Naess, helped organize my files as they burgeoned out of control.

Documentary filmmaker Deborah S. Esquinazi taught me how to make quality audio and video recording of my interviews. Suzan Kern, in Silver Spring, Maryland, hosted me at her home when I came to that area to do research. Kathy Eubanks helped in Texas. My sister Miriam Lerner and cousin Annette Pinder traveled to Canada with me to see Connie's family.

Exposing Sybil became even more of a family affair as my husband, Morten Naess, explored rural Minnesota with me while I did interviews there. Morten is a physician, and he also helped interpret medical records pertaining to Shirley and her kin. My son Willy Naess, who was in college in Minnesota majoring in history, helped with archival research at the State Historical Society in St. Paul. My father-in-law, Harald Naess, did similar work years ago in the Upper Midwest as a historian of Scandinavian immigration, and he was a constant inspiration as I studied the same population. Willy accompanied me on a road trip to West Virginia and Lexington, Kentucky, to research Shirley's and Connie Wilbur's longtime tenure in that region.

Many people with ties to that area gave me invaluable assistance.

Dr. Arnold Ludwig, now living in Rhode Island, described his work with Connie when he was chairman of the University of Kentucky medical school's psychiatry department in the early 1970s. Dr. Lon Hays, who held the same position when I was working on this book, organized a meeting between me and several psychiatrists who once worked with Connie or studied under her. One, Dr. Robert Aug, hosted me for lunch at his country house, and psychologist Billie Ables not only had me over, she followed up with phone calls and letters. Dr. Rosa K. Riggs told me about working with Connie at her short-lived private hospital.

Dr. German Gutierrez described being a resident and learning from her how to use hypnosis to evoke multiple personalities.

Others gave me time in person and on the phone. John and Gerry McGee, and Patsy Gibson, who live on the same street that Connie did, recalled what she was like as a neighbor. Home-care nurse Roberta Guy spoke about caring for Connie and Shirley when each was terminally ill. Mark Boultinghouse recounted what it was like to serve as Shirley's art dealer without having any idea she was Sybil. And Dianne Morrow, whose mother was Connie's psychiatric patient and her friend, was stunningly generous with memories, thoughtful musings, and photographs.

Flora's last surviving first cousin, Dr. Stanley Aronson, the former president of Brown University's medical school, invited me to his home in Providence to share memories and his trenchant observations about the world in general—while his wife, Gale, made me and my husband feel at home with a delicious Sunday brunch. Georgiana Peacher and Mildred Rumack told about working in academia with Flora during the World War II era and beyond. Mary Anne Guitar, Norman Lobsenz, Harriet LaBarre, and Harrison Kinney reminisced about freelance magazine writing and editing in New York City in the 1950s and 1960s.

Flora's housekeeper during the 1970s and 1980s, Flossie Simmons, spoke about her boss, and Flossie's daughter, Inez, added details. Ben Termine, Emma Long (since deceased), Tom Davis, Charlotte Gray, Christina Winsey-Rudd, Dominick Abel, James McClain, Monty Norris, and Jeff Long filled in many blanks about Flora's life. Al Paris gave me the back story about a lawsuit his parents filed against her and her collaborators on the book *Sybil*.

And course there were librarians. At the New York Academy of Medicine, on Manhattan's Upper East Side, staff were always ready to find old medical journal articles for me and to make copies. Nearby, Alexandra Owens, director of the American Society for Journalists and Authors, made available that organization's archives from back when it was called the Society for Magazine Writers and Flora was active with the group.

Farther afield, staff at the University of Iowa Library's special collections department hosted me for a week in 2009 as I examined screenwriter Stewart Stern's papers about the making of the telemovie *Sybil*. In Dodge County, Minnesota, Earlene King, then director of the local historical society, schmoozed with area old timers to find some I could interview. In western New York, Dr. Joseph Bieron, a chemist and archivist of historical records pertaining to that occupation, found information about Connie Wilbur's tenure in Niagara Falls as a young chemist during the Great Depression. Bert Haloviak, librarian for the Seventh-Day Adventist Church's General Conference, in Maryland, taught me how to do research with the church's extensive, digitized records. Staff at the National Library of Medicine, also in Maryland, helped me locate, view, and copy teaching films from the 1940s that featured Connie.

The admirable cheer and industry of these librarians only highlighted the extraordinary enthusiasm of another group of archivists, on Manhattan's far west side. Beginning on a cold, February day in 2008 and continuing for the next three years, I spent hundreds of hours looking at the Flora Rheta Schreiber papers, in the Special Collections Department of the library at John Jay College. I started feeling as though I'd moved in, and head archivist Ellen Belcher—my "roommate"—always bent over backwards to make my tenure productive and pleasant. Assistant archivist Tania Colmant-Donabedian did the same when she filled in for Ellen. Larry Sullivan, the library's director, made himself available when I needed administrative assistance.

One of my most exciting days working at John Jay occurred after I started to suspect that Shirley's high school and college diaries were hoaxes. I needed what's known as a "questioned document examiner," but I couldn't afford to pay the thousands of dollars that these experts charge for their work. My problem was solved when Peter Tytell, one of the field's most respected members, agreed to look at the diaries for free. I am infinitely grateful to Peter, and also to Gerry LaPorte, an equally prominent examiner, who donated a follow-up analysis after archivist Belcher offered up her fancy, digital camera-microscope to photograph diary samples and email them to Gerry.

Several scholars, writers, activists, and ex–psychiatric patients shared with me research, primary documents, theories, and experiences regarding multiple personality disorder and the politics of mental health diagnosis and treatment. Special thanks to Sherrill Mulhern; Harold Mersky; Evan Harrington; Pamela Freyd; Mark Pendergrast; Ben Harris; Jan Haaken; Jeanette Bartha; Bill Dobbs; John Bloise; two people whom Connie once treated, and the family of another of her patients who later died. You in the last group have asked me for anonymity, but know that your information and insights were invaluable.

Former Hollywood celebrities talked with me as well: Stewart Stern, the screenwriter for the *Sybil* telemovie; and Diana Serra Cary, who was known as "Baby Peggy" when she worked as a child star in silent movies in the 1920s and had a doll named after her.

Kathy Steele, former director of the International Society for the Study of Trauma and Dissociation (ISSTD), arranged my attendance at the group's 2009 conference in Washington, D.C., and organized an interview between me and ISSTD's officers. I am grateful, as well, to Dr. Richard Kluft. He declined to discuss his working and personal relationship with Connie Wilbur, but he did allow me to sit in on a presentation he gave at the conference. Psychologist and ISSTD long-timer Barry Cohen gave me key information about Connie Wilbur. Dr. Vedat Sar directed me to recent medical studies regarding dissociation and dissociative identity disorder.

I also want to thank Dr. Leah Dickstein for a fascinating, though off-the-record, morning and afternoon spent at the Schreiber archives at John Jay College. Dr. Dickstein holds several files of papers which belonged to Connie Wilbur. She has cited this material in her own research but will not share it with others. I hope she eventually releases it.

Jan Haaken, Mike Snedeker, Miriam Lieberstein, and Miriam Lerner read *Sybil Exposed* when it was still a work in progress. Their critiques buoyed me through a long process that seemed especially lonely because I was thinking and writing about an earlier time and about people who, in the main, were dead. It helped to have feedback from the here and now.

It's customary when writing acknowledgments to wait till the end to thank one's agent. Though I'm following that rule on paper, Jennifer Carlson holds top billing on the list inside my head. I cannot imagine a smarter, more enthusiastic and harder working agent than Jen—or one as out-and-out classy.

With Jen's work and guidance I ended up with my editors—first, Wylie O'Sullivan, then Leah Miller when Wylie moved on. Both have been a joy to work with: Not only do they know how to sprinkle fairy dust on a manuscript, they've conveyed deep interest in the same fascinating and troubling things about the Sybil tale that grabbed me when I first learned of it, years ago. A generation divides the present, when Sybil is a piece of history, from the near past, when she was a craze. My editors have been passionate about that evolution—and about the dilemmas of women and medicine in general. I'm grateful.

I'm thankful, also, that Flora Rheta Schreiber left her papers to posterity. Would she have been satisfied to see how I've read her life? I like to think so, and that Connie and Shirley would be happy, too—or, at least, respectful of my efforts.

NOTES

DE: David Eichman private collection, Roseburg, Oregon

FM: Florence Mason (Florence Eichman before her 1958 marriage to Walter Mason)

FRS: Flora Rheta Schreiber, and Flora Rheta Schreiber Archives at John Jay College Library Special Collections, New York City

MC: Muriel Coulter private collection, Tracy, Minnesota

SAM: Shirley Ardell Mason

STERN: Stewart Stern Papers, University of Iowa Libraries Special Collections, Iowa City

WM: Walter Mason

INTRODUCTION

1. FRS Box 37, File 1093, Tape 66.

CHAPTER 1

1. (Seventh-Day Adventist) *Review and Herald*, 6 July 1933, at <www.adventist archives.org/documents.asp?CatID=27++&SortBy=0&ShowDateOrder= True&offset=4000>. Last viewed April 2011. Copy in author's possession.

2. Ronald L. Numbers and Jonathan M. Butler (eds.), *The Disappointed: Millerism and Millenarianism in the Nineteenth Century* (Knoxville: University of Tennessee Press, 1993); Ronald L. Numbers, *Prophetess of Health: A Study of Ellen G. White*, 3rd ed. (Grand Rapids, MI: Eerdmans, 2008).

3. FRS Box 37, File 1087.

4. Nineteenth- and early twentieth-century church records of the Seventh-Day Adventist Church in Dodge Center, MN, examined by the author in October 2009. The example of testimony by rural Midwestern Adventists in the 1920s and 1930s was provided to the author by T. Joe Willey, a historian of Seventh-Day Adventism whose family was Adventist and whose father was a minister in the church.

5. Martha Atkinson Mason's background was supplied by her third cousins Arlene Christensen, in Ojai, CA; Marcia Schmidt, in Palmdale, CA; and cousin by marriage Lorna Gilbert, in Houston. Author phone conversations in January 2011. Also FRS Box 37, File 1091, Tape 32. Martha Atkinson Mason's health records from the Mayo Clinic are in FRS Box 37, File 1078. For WM's history with the Seventh-Day Adventist Church, see FRS Box 37, Files 1095, 1097.

6. Shirley Mason birth records are in FRS Box 37, File 1078.

7. Seventh-Day Adventist Church records, Dodge Center, MN.

8. *Bible Readings for the Home Circle* (Washington, DC: Review and Herald Publishing, 1919 and 1923), p. 268; Arthur S. Maxwell, *Uncle Arthur's Bedtime Stories*, Vols. 1–4 (Takoma Park, MD and Washington, DC: Review and Herald Publishing, 1919).

9. FRS Box 37, File 1086.

10. FRS Box 37, Files 1084, 1086, 1087; for information on Adventist prohibitions against masturbation and fiction reading, see Numbers, *Prophetess of Health*, p. 208; and E. G. White, *Messages to the Youth* (Takoma, MD and Washington, DC: 1930, reprinted 2008), pp. 76–77, 290. For fighting in church, see SAM to FM, 25 December 1962, DE.

11. FRS Box 37, File 1096.

12. FRS Box 37, File 1089, Tape 12; File 1094, Tape 11; telephone interviews with Marcia Schmidt and Arlene Christensen, January 2011. For *Good Housekeeping* articles, see that magazine, April and November 1933.

13. For founding of Adventist school in Dodge Center, see *Advent Review and Sabbath Herald*, 1 October 1901, p. 641; 14 October 1902, p. 19. At <www .adventistarchives.org/documents.asp?CatID=27++&SortBy=0&ShowDate Order=True&offset=2500>. For theology about schooling and the Dodge Center school in the Depression era, see W. J. Smith, "Christian Education," *Adventist Review and Sabbath Herald*, 6 July 1933, pp. 17 and 18, at <www .adventistarchives.org/documents.asp?CatID=27++&SortBy=0&ShowDate

Order=True&offset=4000>. All last viewed April 2011. Copies in author's possession.

14. White, *Messages*, pp. 281–282, 290.
15. FRS Box 37, File 1086.
16. FRS Box 37, Files 1083, 1084.
17. Pearl Lohrbach Book Club Report, 1975, copy at Dodge Center, MN, public library and in author's possession; Monty Norris, "Sybil: A shocked Dodge Center thinks she grew up there," Minneapolis *Star-Tribune*, 27 August 1975.
18. FRS Box 37, File 1095, Tape 117; File 1080.
19. For Bobby Moulton see FRS Box 37, Files 1084, 1085. Information also obtained from author telephone interview with Bobby's daughter, Miranda Marland, of Falmouth, Maine, in December 2010. Anita Weeks material from author interview in Mantorville, Minnesota, with Frank Weeks, a cousin of Anita, in October 2009. See also records of the Seventh-Day Adventist Church for 1920s and 1930s in Dodge Center, Minnesota.
20. For economic crisis in the Mason family see FRS Box 37, Files 1084, 1095, 1096.
21. For Shirley's childhood problems with depression and isolation see FRS Box 37, Files 1079, 1080, 1085, 1095, Tape 117.
22. FRS Box 37, File 1095, Tape 117.
23. For Shirley's phobias, see FRS Box 37, Files 1084, 1085. *Fortune* magazine reading: "The Nervous Breakdown," *Fortune*, April 1935, pp. 84–88 and 167–202.
24. FRS Box 37, Files 1084, 1085.
25. FRS Box 37, File 1095.
26. FRS Box 37, File 1095, Tape 117.
27. 1998 interview of Dr. Virginia Flores Cravens, at her home in Nacogdoches, Texas, by Mikkel Borch-Jacobsen and Peter Swales. Copy of audiotape of interview provided to the author by Borch-Jacobsen.

CHAPTER 2

1. Richard P. Kluft and Catherine G. Fine, *Clinical Perspectives on Multiple Personality Disorder* (Washington, DC: American Psychiatric Publishing, 1993); M. Sara Rosenthal, *The Thyroid Sourcebook* (Los Angeles: Lowell House, 1993); Stephen Lock et al., *The Oxford Illustrated Companion to Medicine* (New York: Oxford University Press, 2001).

2. Leah J. Dickstein and Carol Nadelson (eds.), *Women Physicians in Leadership Roles* (Washington, DC: American Psychiatric Press, 1986); Craig Thompson, *Since Spindletop* (Houston: Gulf Oil Co., 1950).

3. John T. Horton, *History of Northwestern New York: Erie, Niagara, Wyoming, Genesee and Orleans Counties* (New York: Lewis Historical Publishing Co., 1947), see entry on Arthur W. Burwell; *Who Was Who in America*, Vol. 2 (Chicago: Marquis, 1950); *Lubrication Engineering*, "Necrology" for Dr. A. W. Burwell, September 1946, p. 122; United States Patent Office, C. E. Baker and A. W. Burwell, "Process of Treating Ores," patented October 13, 1903, Patent No. 741,439; "Has a new process for ore treatment," *Anaconda (MT) Standard*, 3 July 1908; "New electrolytic plant proposed," *Anaconda (MT) Standard*, 24 December 1909; Thomas Parke Hughes, *Elmer Sperry: Inventor and Engineer* (Baltimore: Johns Hopkins Press, 1971); *The World 1909 Almanac and Encyclopedia* (Press Pub. Company: The New York World, 1909); *The World Almanac and Book of Facts* (Chicago: Newspaper Enterprise Association, 1909).

4. Homestead land grant title for Arthur W. Burwell: United States of America Kalispell 03945 (Kalispell, MT) #715933, dated 30 October 1919. Copy in author's possession; Cornelia Wilbur's description of hunting with her father is in STERN.

5. "More than $7,000,000 in worthless stocks," *New York Times*, 19 July 1916; "School pupils to graduate Thursday," *Poughkeepsie Eagle-News*, 26 June 1922; "Girl Scout entertainment," *Poughkeepsie Eagle-News*, 26 April 1922; "Scouts awarded badges at court," *Poughkeepsie Eagle-News*, 9 December 1922; Poughkeepsie Public Library (information on family address in 1922).

6. Cornelia Wilbur to Flora Schreiber, 26 July 1965. FRS Box 37, File 1102; Dickstein and Nadelson, *Women Physicians*.

7. Student records for Cornelia Burwell on file at Hobart and William Smith Colleges, Geneva, NY; and in registrar's office of the University of Michigan, Ann Arbor, copy in author's possession; University of Michigan student records available in registrar's office; *College & Private School Directory of the United States*, Vol. 22 (Chicago: Educational Aid Society, 1936); Porter Sargent, *A Handbook of Private Schools for American Boys and Girls* (Boston: Porter Sargent, 1934); information on Bertha Burwell's conversion to Christian Science in SAM letters to FM, 22 June 1962 and 25 December 1962, DE.

8. Mary Baker Eddy, *Science and Health* (Boston: First Church of Christ, Scientist, 1875/1994), pp. 390, 392–393, 150–151.

9. Cornelia Wilbur student records, University of Michigan registrar's office, copies in author's possession; John Kraus, *Big Ear Two* (Powell, OH: Cygnus-Quasar Books, 1995).

10. Bureau of Vocational Information, *Women in Chemistry: A Study of Professional Opportunities* (New York: Select Printing Co., 1922), pp. 80, 87; "Scientific careers for women," *New York Times*, 4 June 1921, cited in Margaret W. Rossiter, *Women Scientists in America* (Baltimore: Johns Hopkins Press, 1982/1992), p. 12.

11. *Double Bond* (newsletter of the Western New York Section, American Chemical Society) 4:4 (1931), p. 11, and various issues, 1931, 1932, available in Special Collections, SUNY Buffalo Library, copies in author's possession; Committee on History and Records, *Western New York Section American Chemical Society, Fifty Year History and History of Its Precursors: 1905–1955* (Niagara Falls, NY, n.d.); Robert Burns McMillan, "Our History: ACS of Western New York." Viewed in April 2009 at <http://membership.acs.org/w/wny/history.html>

12. Benjamin Atlas, "Discover new soap to cure skin disease," *Syracuse (NY) Herald*, 26 June 1932; "Chemists at Washington," *Time Magazine*, 10 April 1933; "Chimpanzee shows kinship to mankind in weight of body," *Washington Post*, 29 March 1933; "Dr. Langmuir asks shorter work day as chemists meet," *Washington Post*, 30 March 1933; *Industrial and Engineering Chemistry* News Edition, 11: 7 (10 April 1933): 101; United States Patent Office, "Insecticidal, Fungicidal and Bactericidal Compositions," A. W. Burwell, patent applied for 8 May 1933, patent granted 17 April 1934, Patent No. 1,955,052.

13. "Germicidal and Fungicidal Composition," Cornelia Burwell, patent applied for 17 March 1934, patent granted 30 November 1937, Patent No. 2,100,469.

14. Kluft and Fine, *Clinical Perspectives*, p. xxvi.

15. University of Michigan records for Henry Wilbur, in registrar's office, copies in author's possession; Neil Burwell, Warner O. Burwell, and Brenda Burwell Canning (great-nephews and great-niece of Cornelia Burwell), author interviews April 2009 in Ancaster, Ontario (Canada); FRS Box 37, File 1096.

16. Quoted in Franz Alexander, *Psychosomatic Medicine* (New York: Norton, 1950), p. 176; FRS Box 37, File 1089, Tape 13.

CHAPTER 3

1. Information about the Schreiber home was provided in 2010 by her cousin, Dr. Stanley Aronson, of Providence, RI. For Willy Schreiber's contribution to the Emily Post book, see FRS Box 34, File 1052.
2. FRS Box 33, Files 1033, 1034, 1047.
3. FRS Box 34, File 1052.
4. Author interviews with with Dr. Stanley Aronson, January 2010, May 2010.
5. Flora Schreiber to Willy and Esther Schreiber, "Notes on Going to Church," 17 June 1935, in FRS Box 33, File 1039; and see File 1043.
6. Anna Lee, Maureen O'Hara, Barbara Rojisman, *Anna Lee: Memoir of a Career on General Hospital and in Film* (Jefferson, NC: McFarland, 2007), p. 47.
7. Ibid., p. 48.
8. FRS Box 6, File 149.
9. Flora Schreiber to "Bob," 23 August 1941, FRS Box 34, File 1075.

CHAPTER 4

1. Author telephone interview with Richard Dieterle, son of Dr. Robert Dieterle, Ann Arbor, MI, December 2008; author interview with Caroline Dieterle, daughter of Dr. Robert Dieterle, Iowa City, IA, October 2008; *Biographical Directory of Fellows and Members of the American Psychiatric Association* (New York: The American Psychiatric Association, 1950), viewed online March 2011 at www.archive.org/details/biographicaldire007514mbp; records of the University of Michigan Medical School, at the Bentley Historical Library, University of Michigan.
2. C. G. Goetz et al., *Constructing Neurology* (Oxford: Oxford University Press, 1995); C. G. Goetz, *Charcot, the Clinician. The Tuesday Lessons* (New York: Raven Press, 1987); D. M. Bourneville and P. Regnard, *Iconographie photographique de la Salpêtrière, Service de M. Charcot* (Paris: Bureau du Progres Medical, V. Adrien Delahay et. Cie, 1877).
3. Dieterle's paper was published as Robert R. Dieterle and Edward J. Koch, "Experimental induction of infantile behavior in major hysteria," *Journal of Nervous & Mental Disease* 86(6) (December 1937): 688–710. The film made to accompany the paper is now owned by Dr. Richard Dieterle.
4. Dieterle and Koch, "Experimental induction," p. 710.
5. Cornelia Burwell Wilbur academic transcript, University of Michigan Medical School registrar, copy on file with author.

6. Dickstein and Nadelson, *Women Physicians; Michiganensian* (yearbook of the University of Michigan, 1939).

7. *Report of the Board of Trustees, 1889–90, Michigan Asylum for the Insane*, on file at the Michigan University Archives and Regional History Collections in Kalamazoo, and cited in Rory J. Becker and Michael S. Nassaney, "An Assessment of the Asylum Lake/Colony Farm Orchard Property in Kalamazoo, Michigan" (viewed by author in March 2011 at <www.wmich.edu/asylum lake/social/Archeological%20Assessment/Archeological%20Assessment%20 Frameset.htm>

8. STERN.

9. Ibid.; and Denis Brian, *The Voice of Genius* (Cambridge, MA: Perseus, 1995), p. 339.

10. Edward Shorter, *A History of Psychiatry* (New York: Wiley, 1997), p. 216.

11. J. B. Craig and M. E. Schilling, "A comparison of the results of metrazol therapy with a group of matched controlled cases," *American Journal of Psychiatry* 98:2 (1941): 180–184.

12. David Herman and Jim Green, *Madness: A Study Guide* (London: BBC Education, 1991).

13. Author telephone conversation with Dr. Richard Dieterle.

14. "Rushton takes hand in state investigation of hospital death," *Adrian (MI) Daily Telegram*, 14 June 1943; "Asks quiz of state asylum," *St. Joseph (MI) Herald Press*, 27 February 1945; James A. O. Crowe, "Ask probe into Pontiac State Hospital," *Ludington (MI) Daily News*, 12 July 1947; "Michigan probe says orderlies choked inmates," *Chicago Daily Tribune*, 13 July 1947.

15. Peter A. Martin, "Convulsive therapies: Review of 511 cases at Pontiac State Hospital," *Journal of Nervous and Mental Disease* 109:2 (1949): 142–157.

16. E. Lindemann, "Psychological changes in normal and abnormal individuals under the influence of sodium amytal," *American Journal of Psychiatry* 88 (1932): 1083–1091.

17. J. Stephen Horsley, *Narco-Analysis: A New Technique in Short-Cut Psychotherapy* (London: Oxford University Press, 1943), p. 2; Horsley, "Narco-Analysis," *The Lancet* 1:55 (4 January 1936); "Pentothal sodium in mental hospital practice," *The British Medical Journal*, 9 May 1936, pp. 938–939.

18. C. B. Wilbur, "The use of intravenous barbituates in determining the prognosis in metrazol therapy," *Diseases of the Nervous System*, Vol. 4 (December 1943): 369–372.

19. "Medicine: Psychosurgery," *Time Magazine*, 22 November 1942. Viewed online in August 2010 at <www.time.com/time/magazine/article/0,9171,766670-1,00.html?artId=766670?contType=article?chn=us>; J. L. Hoffman, "Clinical observations concerning schizophrenic patients treated by prefrontal leukotomy," *New England Journal of Medicine* 241 (1949): 233–236; Jack D. Pressman, *Last Resort: Psychosurgery and the Limits of Medicine* (Cambridge: Cambridge University Press, 1998), p. 328; "Personality shift is laid to surgery," *New York Times*, 14 December 1947.

20. A. E. Bennett, "Curare: A preventive of traumatic complications in convulsive shock therapy," *American Journal of Psychiatry* 97 (March 1941): 1040–1060.

21. "Books: Precious poison," *Time Magazine*, 22 July 1940; "Medicine: Useful poison," *Time Magazine*, 21 February 1944.

22. Shorter, *History of Psychiatry*, p. 223.

23. "Notes on science: Operations on the brain for insanity—'Cat Cracker,'" *New York Times*, 5 December 1943; Abram Elting Bennett, *Prefrontal Lobotomy in Chronic Schizophrenia* [motion picture] (Omaha: Bishop Clarkson Memorial Hospital, circa 1944), available at the National Library of Medicine, Bethesda, MD.

24. William Sargant, *The Unquiet Mind: The Autobiography of a Physician in Psychological Medicine* (Boston: Little Brown, 1967), p. 87; Roy Grinker and John Spiegel, *War Neurosis in North Africa: The Tunisian Campaign (January–May 1943)* (New York: Josiah Macy, Jr., Foundation, 1943; republished as *War Neurosis* [Philadelphia: Blakiston, 1945]), p. 80.

25. W. Sargant and E. Slater, *Physical Methods of Treatment in Psychiatry* (Edinburgh, Scotland: E. & L. Livingstone, 1944); Ben Shepard, *A War of Nerves: Soldiers and Psychiatrists in the Twentieth Century* (London: Jonathan Cape, 2001), pp. 208–209; S. Brandon, J. Boakes, et al., "Recovered memories of childhood sexual abuse: Implications for clinical practice," *British Journal of Psychiatry* 172 (1998): 296–307; Alison Winter, "Film and the construction of memory in psychoanalysis, 1940–1960," *Science in Context* 19: 1 (2006): 111–136.

26. Bishop Clarkson Memorial Hospital Department of Psychiatry, *Narcosynthesis* (film), 1944, currently held at the National Library of Medicine, Historical Audiovisuals Collection, Rockville, MD.

27. Cornelia Wilbur resume in FRS Box 13, File 315.

28. FRS Box 37, File 1095, Tape 130, and File 1096, Tape 29; STERN.

CHAPTER 5

1. FRS Box 37, File 1096, Tape 134.
2. FRS Box 37, File 1084.
3. "Former Centerite shot at Kasson," *Dodge Center Star-Record*, 29 August 1940, p. 1 Available at the Minnesota State Historical Society, St. Paul, MN.
4. FRS Box 37, File 1084.
5. Shirley Mason, "Pen name of Samuel Clemens immortalizes river boat pilot," *The Reporter* (Mankato State Teachers College), 18 April 1943, p. 4.
6. *1940 Katonian* (yearbook of Mankato State Teachers College), 1940, pp. 15–18.
7. Linda Mack Schloff, "Overcoming Geography: Jewish Religious Life in Four Market Towns," *Minnesota History*, Spring 1988, pp. 2–14.
8. Wanda Gäg, *Growing Pains: Diaries and Drawings from the Years 1908–17* (St. Paul: Minnesota Historical Society Press, 1984).
9. Josef Breuer et al., *Studies in Hysteria* (New York: Nervous and Mental Disease, 1936).
10. FRS Box 37, File 1078, File 1094, Tape 14, File 1097.
11. FRS Box 37, File 1095, Tape 115.
12. Merlaine Nelson Samuelson letter to Daniel Houlihan, 9 February 1999, in Daniel Houlihan Collection, Mankato, MN, copy in author's possession; SAM to Wylene Frederickson, 14 December 1943, in Daniel Houlihan collection; Author interview of Jean Lane.
13. Merlaine Nelson Samuelson, ibid.
14. FRS Box 37, File 1095, Tape 115.
15. Mayo Clinic letter to Dr. Wilbur, 22 July 1964, FRS Box 37, File 1078, File 1095, Tape 115, File 1097; Dr. H. W. Woltman to Dr. H. B. Troost, 1 April 1942, in FRS Box 37, File 1078.
16. FRS Box 37, File 1095, Tape 115.
17. SAM to Wylene Frederickson, 14 December 1943; SAM to Louella Warnke (Odden), n.d. postmarked 16 January 1944. MC; Robert Rieber donation to FRS, Tape 1.
18. FRS Box 37, File 1095, Tape 115; Tape 2 in Robert Reiber donation to FRS.
19. FRS Box 37, File 1086.
20. FRS Box 37, File 1095, tape dated 12/13 August 1970.
21. FRS Box 37, Files 1079, 1081, 1095.

22. FRS Box 37, File 1095, Tape 130, 12 or 13 August 1970.

23. FRS Box 37, File 1095, Tape dated 13 August 1970, and File 1096, Tape 129.

24. FRS Box 37, File 1083; STERN.

25. Sidney Howard, *The Silver Cord* (Hollywood, CA: Samuel French, 1928); Morton Prince, *The Dissociation of a Personality* (New York: Longmans, Green, 1905, First Edition).

26. Tape 2, Robert Rieber donation to FRS.

CHAPTER 6

1. Michele Hilmes, *Radio Voices: American Broadcasting, 1922–1952* (Minneapolis: University of Minnesota Press, 1997).

2. Flora left no evidence in her archive that she had ever volunteered at WNYC. But definitive records in Germany attest that, in the late 1930s and early 1940s, she was assisting the Marxist philosopher Theodor Adorno when he was a refugee from Naziism in New York City and was writing scripts for shows for WNYC. See Stefan Müller-Doohm, *Adorno: A Biography* (Cambridge, England: Polity, 2004), p. 253; Theodor Adorno, *Current of Music*, ed. Robert Hullot-Kentor (Cambridge, England: Polity, 2009).

3. Hilmes, *Radio Voices*; for George Kondolf, see Douglas McGill, "George Kondolf is dead at 85: Theater and radio producer," *New York Times*, 26 December 1985, viewed online March 2011 at www.nytimes.com/1985/12/26/arts/george-kondolf-is-dead-at-85-theater-and-radio-producer.html>; Irving Foulds Luscombe, "WNYC: 1922–1940—The Early History of a Twentieth-Century Urban Service" (Ph.D. dissertation, Ann Arbor, MI: University Microfilms, 1968).

4. *Haym [sic] Solomon* and *Metamorphosis* typescripts in FRS Box 27, File 724.

5. FRS Resume; Flora Rheta Schreiber, "Battle of the Soap Opera," *Film and Radio Discussion Guide* 10:7 (April 1944): 16, copy in FRS Box 6, File 125.

6. Flora Rheta Schreiber, "Television: A New Idiom," *Hollywood Quarterly*, Winter 1949; FRS Box 6, Files 136 and 137.

7. Author telephone interview in February 2010 with Flora's Brooklyn College colleague Georgiana Peacher, of Brunswick, ME.

8. FRS Box 31, File 1006.

9. FRS Box 31, File 1003.

10. "Popularity of the soap opera analyzed by Eugene O'Neill, Jr.," *Lewiston (ME) Daily Sun*, 17 February 1950. Information about O'Neill Jr.'s life and death is

from Croswell Bowen, *The Curse of the Misbegotten* (New York: McGraw-Hill, 1959); Arthur and Barbara Gelb, *O'Neill* (New York: Harper & Row, 1960; subsequent editions 1962, 1973); Louis Sheaffer, *O'Neill: Son and Artist* (New York: Little Brown, 1973).

11. FRS Box 34, File 1051.
12. Ibid.
13. See, e.g., "O'Neill suicide has tragic note," *(Bend, OR) Bulletin*, 26 September 1950.
14. FRS Box 34, Files 1054, 1056.

CHAPTER 7

1. FRS Box 37, File 1095, Tape 116.
2. SAM to Luella Warnke, postmarked 16 January 1944, MC.
3. Author interview with Jean Lane, May 2008, in Portland Oregon; SAM to Miss Frederickson, 14 December 1948, DE; SAM to Luella Warnke, n.d., MC.
4. FRS Box 37, File 1095.
5. Author interview with David Eichman, of Rosenburg, OR, May 2008; SAM to Luella Odden, MC.
6. "Annual Commencement Art Exhibit" (invitation), Mankato State Teachers College, 27 May–3 June 1949, DE.
7. Shirley Mason resume in FRS Box 37, File 1078; DE op. cit.; FRS Box 37, File 1080; SAM to Miss Frederickson, 14 December 1948 and 5 December 1950, Daniel Houlihan Collection, Mankato, MN, copies in author's possession.
8. Shirley Mason resume; SAM to FM, postmarked 4 October 1952, DE.
9. SAM to FM, ibid.; SAM to FM postmarked 4 January 1954; SAM to 15 April 1954, all in DE.
10. FRS Box 37, File 1095.
11. Mabel Curry, "Memphis artist wins recognition with paintings," *Port Huron (MI) Times-Herald*, 30 November 1952; author interview with Earlene King, director, Dodge County, MN Historical Society; Dodge County Sesquicentennial, *150 Dodge County Fairs: 1857–2007* (available at the Dodge County Historical Society, Mantorville, MN).
12. Author interview with Jean Lane in Portland, OR, May 2008.
13. SAM to FM, n.d. but by context early 1954; SAM to FM, 10 November 1954. Both in DE.

14. SAM to FM postmarked 6 October 1954; SAM to FM, n.d. but letter appears to have been written October 1954. Both in DE.

15. "Cornelia Wilbur" entry in *Biographical Directory of Fellows and Members of the American Psychiatric Association* (New York: American Psychiatric Association, 1950); M. J. Tissenbaum and H. M. Harter, "Survey of a mental hygiene clinic—21 months of operation," *Psychiatric Quarterly* 24:4 (1950): 677–705.

16. Stephen Farber and Marc Green, *Hollywood on the Couch* (New York: Morrow, 1993).

17. James Strachey and Anna Freud (eds.), *The Standard Edition of the Complete Psychological Works of Sigmund Freud* (London: Hogarth Press, 1966), Vol. 23, p. 228.

18. "Medicine for the psyche," *Time Magazine*, 2 September 1946, accessed in 2010 at www.time.com/time/magazine/article/0,9171,803953,00.html

19. Farber and Green, *Hollywood on the Couch.*

20. For neo-Freudian ideas, see Nathan G. Hale, Jr., *The Rise and Crisis of Psychoanalysis in the United States* (New York: Oxford, 1995), and Joel Kovel, *A Complete Guide to Therapy* (New York: Pantheon, 1975). For Frieda Fromm-Reichmann's ideas, see Edward Dolnick, *Madness on the Couch* (New York: Simon & Schuster, 1998), p. 99, quoting from Jeanne Block et al., "A study of the parents of schizophrenic and neurotic children," *Psychiatry: Journal for the Study of Interpersonal Processes* 21 (1958): 387–397.

21. William V. Silverberg, *Childhood Experience and Personal Destiny: A Psychoanalytic Study of Neurosis* (New York: Springer, 1952), p. 254.

22. *Biographical Directory of Fellows and Members of the APA.*

23. Ibid.

24. STERN.

25. *Biographical Directory of Fellows and Members of the APA.*

26. Author telephone interview with Keith Brown's niece Deborah Brown Kovac, of Bushnell, IL, November 2008.

27. *The Michigan Alumnus* 60 (October 3, 1953 to August 7, 1954): 148.

28. FRS Box 37, File 1102.

29. See Connie's contributions in Alfred H. Rifkin (ed.), *Schizophrenia in Psychoanalytic Office Practice* (New York: Grune & Stratton, 1957).

30. STERN.

31. Author telephone interview with Dr. Arthur Zitrin, New York City, October 2009.

32. C. H. Thigpen and H. Cleckley, "A case of multiple personality," *Journal of Ab-normal and Social Psychology* 49(1954):135–151. Quotes from pp. 137, 141–142, 145. A later version of the film shown at the meeting is available as *A Case Study in Multiple Personality: The Three Faces of Eve*, Corbett H. Thigpen and Hervey M Cleckley (University Park, PA: Penn State Media Sales, and New York: Insight Media, 2006/1954).

33. "Medicine: Order in Disorder?" *Time*, 18 May 1953, retrieved December 2009 at <http://www.time.com/time/magazine/article/0,9171,818495,00.html>

34. Thigpen and Cleckley, "A case of multiple personality," p. 148.

35. Rennie Taylor, Associated Press: "Demure brunette, 'devilish creature' puzzles doctors," *Eugene (OR) Register-Guard*, 9 May 1953. Retrieved December 2009 at http://news.google.com/newspapers?id=4IcRAAAAIBAJ&sjid=ueIDAA AAIBAJ&pg=6353,1318497&dq=eve+black&hl=en

36. For Rennie Taylor's background as an Associated Press science writer, see "Science: Skeptic's Prize," *Time* 3 July 1978, retrieved December 2009 at <http://www.time.com/time/magazine/article/0,9171,946008,00.html>; Thigpen and Cleckley, "A case of multiple personality."

CHAPTER 8

1. SAM to WM, n.d. but from context, September or October 1954. DE.

2. Ibid.

3. FRS Box 37, File 1095, Tape 116.

4. Edward Shorter, *Before Prozac: The Troubled History of Mood Disorders in Psychiatry* (New York: Oxford University Press, 2009).

5. For Shirley Mason's Seconal dosage see FRS Box 37, Files 1081, 1084. For her Demerol consumption, see FRS Box 37, File 1086. For Edrisal and Daprisal dosages, see FRS Box 37, File 1083. For side effects of Seconal, Demerol, and amphetamines, see H. Winter Griffith et al., *Complete Guide to Prescription and Non-Prescription Drugs 2011* (New York: Penguin, 2010).

6. SAM to Miss Weblemoe, 26 May 1958, FRS Box 37, File 1099; Robert Rieber donation to FRS, Tape 1.

7. SAM treatment diary in FRS Box 37, File 1081 (21 February 1956).

8. Robert Reiber donation to FRS, Tape 1.

9. STERN; Connie Wilbur to FRS, 26 July 1965, FRS Box 37, File 1102.

10. Ibid.

11. Record of therapy, FRS Box 37, File 1098; SAM to Miss Weblemoe, 26 May 1958, FRS Box 37, File 1099.

12. Robert Rieber donation to FRS, Tape 1; FRS Box 37, Files 1081, 1097, 1099 (therapy diary, 26 May 1958), 1102.

13. FRS Box 37, File 1089, "Tape 5/6."

14. Robert Rieber donation to FRS, Tape 1.

15. FRS Box 37, Files 1081 (Analysis Diary 9 January 1956, 13 June 1956, 15 November 1956), 1082, 1083; Rieber addition to FRS, Tape 1.

16. FRS Box 37, File 1089, Tape 5/6; Flora Rheta Schreiber, *Sybil*, 1st ed. (Chicago: Regnery, 1973).

17. "John Greenwald dies from gun accident," *Dodge County Republican*, 29 August 1940, available at the Minnesota Historical Society archives, Minneapolis. Online death record viewed December 2011 at <http://people.mnhs.org/dci/>

18. FRS Box 37, File 1089, "Tape 5/6" transcription.

19. FRS Box 37, File 1085 (11 October 1958).

20. FRS Box 37, File 1090.

21. FRS Box 37, File 1084; SAM to FM, 3 February 1955, DE, copy in author's possession.

22. FRS Box 37, Files 1082, 1097, Tape 124.

23. FRS Box 37, File 1103.

24. FRS Box 37, Files 1087, 1101, 1103.

25. FRS Box 37, File 1081 (Shirley Mason treatment diary, 17 January 1956); SAM to Miss Weblemoe, 26 May 1958, FRS Box 37, File 1099.

26. FRS Box 37, File 1081, treatment diary, 20 December 1955.

27. Ibid., treatment diary, 4 November 1955, 18 November 1955.

28. Ibid., treatment diary, 25 November 1955.

29. Ibid., treatment diary, 14 December 1955; SAM to Luella Warnke Odden, 1956, in MC.

30. FRS Box 37, File 1081, treatment diary, 15 December 1955 and 9 January 1956.

31. FRS Box 37, File 1081, treatment diary, 9 and 12 January 1956. For Lorand's biography see Franz Alexander et al. (eds.), *Psychoanalytic Pioneers* (New York: Basic Books, 1966).

32. SAM to Florence Eichman, 4 May 1963, DE.

33. FRS Box 37, Files 1081, 1983, 1090, 1094; SAM to Miss Weblemoe, 26 May 1958 in FRS Box 37, File 1099.

34. FRS Box 37, File 1081.
35. FRS Box 37, File 1081. For media claims and for side effects of Miltown and related new drugs of the 1950s see Jonathan Metzl, *Prozac on the Couch* (Durham, NC: Duke University Press, 2005); and Shorter, *Before Prozac.*
36. FRS Box 37, File 1081. For side effects, see Metzl, *Prozac*, and Shorter, *Before Prozac.*
37. FRS Box 37, File 1081.
38. FRS Box 37, Files 1081, 1097, Tape 124.
39. FRS Box 37, File 1081, treatment diary, fall 1955 to early winter 1956.
40. FRS Box 37, File 1081, treatment diary, January to February 1956.

CHAPTER 9

1. FRS Box 37, Files 1081 (June 1956 and 13 October 1956), 1082, 1083, 1090, 1097.
2. FRS Box 37, File 1084, therapy diary, 26 May 1957.
3. FRS Box 37, Files 1080 (therapy diary, 13 June 1956), 1081 (June 1956), 1083, 1088.
4. FRS Box 37, File 1083 and File 1089, Tape 12 (November 1958); STERN.
5. FRS Box 37, Files 1082 and 1089.
6. FRS Box 37, File 1083.
7. FRS Box 13, File 316.
8. FRS Box 37, File 1089, Tape 15; File 1102.
9. Author interviews with Jean Lane at her home in Portland, OR, May 2008; and Sag Harbor, NY, July 2009.
10. Shirley's concern with homosexuality is reflected in notes that she took and saved from an article she obviously read, probably at the New York Academy of Medicine Library, where Connie often sent her to do research. The article is Eric P. Mosse, "Psychological mechanisms in art production," *Psychoanalytic Review* 38 (1951): 66–74. See Shirley's handwritten notes in FRS Box 37, File 1088. For passage about Willie Price in Shirley's bed, see FRS Box 37, File 1102, and Schreiber, *Sybil* (1st ed.), pp. 264–265.
11. Cornelia Wilbur, "Clinical Aspects of Female Homosexuality," in Judd Marmor (ed.), *Sexual Inversion: The Multiple Roots of Homosexuality* (New York: Basic Books, 1965).
12. SAM to Dr. Cornelia Wilbur, FRS Box 37, File 1099, 26 May 1958.
13. STERN.

14. Ibid.; FRS Box 37, File 1081; SAM to Miss Weblemoe, 26 May 1958, FRS Box 37, File 1089.
15. FRS Box 37, File 1089, Tape 15.
16. SAM therapy diary in FRS Box 37, File 1085, 6 July 1958.
17. Schreiber, *Sybil* (first edition); FRS Box 3, File 1089; STERN.
18. FRS Box 37, File 1089, Tape 13.
19. STERN; FRS Box 37, File 1089.
20. FRS Box 37, File 1097, Tape 24.
21. FRS Box 37, Files 1081, 1089.
22. STERN.

CHAPTER 10

1. Flora Rheta Schreiber, "Vitamins Can Help You Live Longer," *Pageant*, April 1959, pp. 86–88, copy in FRS Box 6, File 145.
2. FRS to Vice-President Richard Nixon's Special Assistant Herbert G. Klein, 17 August 1959 and 2 September 1959, FRS Box 28, File 840; "Getting Around at GH," *Good Housekeeping*, June 1960, p. 14.
3. Flora Rheta Schreiber, "The woman who, by a year, missed seeing her son become president," *Spartanburg (S.C.) Herald-Journal*, 19 January 1969; Flora Rheta Schreiber, "Richard Nixon: A Mother's Story," *Good Housekeeping*, June 1960, pp. 55–57, 207–208, 212–213.
4. "Getting Around at GH."
5. Shaun Casey, *The Making of a Catholic President* (New York: Oxford University Press, 2009), p. 98.
6. For Lady Bird Johnson as a vice-presidential wife, see *Family Weekly*, October 1960, copy in FRS Box 5, File 124. For Jackie Kennedy, *Good Housekeeping*, October 1962. For Lady Bird as first lady, *Cosmopolitan*, February 1964, copy in FRS Box 5, File 119. For Lady Bird as hostess, *Accent*, Summer 1965, copy in FRS Box 5, File 109.
7. Curtis Mitchell to FRS, 6 May 1963, FRS Box 26, File 714.
8. List of freelance rates, by magazine, *Society of Magazine Writers Newsletter*, November 1961, pp. 13–16, and Summer 1960. Archived at the offices of the American Society for Authors and Journalists (successor organization to the Society of Magazine Writers), in New York City.
9. Author interview with 1950s-and-60s-era magazine freelancer and editor Mary Anne Guitar at her home in West Redding, CT, February 2010; author

telephone interview with former women's magazine editor Harrison Kinney, of Lexington, VA, March 2010.

10. Evan McLeod Wylie, "A Day in the Life of an Obstetrician," *Good Housekeeping*, January 1963, p. 126.

11. FRS to Jack (Schreiber), n.d. FRS Box 33, File 104; FRS to Marion, n.d., Box 33, File 1033.

12. *Society of Magazine Writers Newsletter*, November 1961, p. 5.

13. Ibid.

14. Ibid, p. 6.

15. Ibid., p. 7.

16. Terry Morris (ed.), *Prose by Professionals* (New York: Doubleday, 1961); Terry Morris, *Confessions of a Freelance Writer* (San Jose, CA: ASJA Press, 2001).

17. Morris, *Prose by Professionals*, p. 164.

18. Morris, *Confessions*, p. 108.

19. Morris, *Prose by Professionals*, p. 47.

20. *Society of Magazine Writers Newsletter*, 9 May 1962.

21. For Herman's background see Lucy Freeman and Martin Theodores (eds.), *The Why Report* (New York: Pocket Books, 1964). For names of private hospitals, see J. Martin Meyers et al., "Report on Five Concurrent Section Meetings," *Mental Hospitals*, June 1964, pp. 340–343; Melvin Herman to Perry C. Talkington, 26 February 1963, FRS Box 31, File 971.

22. Flora Rheta Schreiber, "I Committed My Daughter," *Cosmopolitan*, May 1962, pp. 57–63 (copy in FRS Box 5, File 117); notes and correspondence related to the article in FRS Box 30, Files 952, 958, 963.

23. Flora Rheta Schreiber, "Family Therapy," *Cosmopolitan*, February 1961, FRS Box 5, File 117.

24. "Family Therapy" work materials in FRS Box 30, Files 953 and 958.

25. Herman to Talkington, 26 February 1963.

26. "An Interview with Cornelia B. Wilbur, MD," in Dickstein and Nadelson, *Women Physicians*.

27. Author telephone interview with Dr. Harriette Kaley, New York City, June 2008; author personal interview with Brenda Burwell Canning, Ancaster, Ontario, Canada, April 2009; Patrick Suraci self-published manuscript, *Sybil in Her Own Words*. Suraci lives in New York City.

28. Irving Bieber et al., *Homosexuality: A Psychoanalytic Study* (New York: Basic Books, 1962).

29. For an extensive critique of *Homosexuality: A Psychoanalytic Study*, see Kenneth Lewes, *The Psychoanalytic Theory of Male Homosexuality* (New York: Meridian), 1988. For the former APA president's comment, see Michael Blumenfield, "An Interview with Alfred M. Freedman, MD," *Journal of Gay & Lesbian Mental Health*, 13:1 (2009), p. 65.

30. For McDowall's life, see Kenneth T. Jackson et al., *The Scribner Encyclopedia of American Lives*, Vol. 5. For his homosexuality, discussed after his death, see Robert Hofler, "Secrets and Bios," *The Advocate*, 11 October 2005, pp. 74–81; Joann Malloy, "Lies and suffering lurked behind Taylor's glamour," New York *Daily News*, 24 March 2011, last viewed on 25 April 2011 at http://articles.nydailynews.com/2011-03-24/gossip/29355378_1_elizabeth-taylor-child-stars-roddy-mcdowall; for the description of "Case 29," see *Homosexuality: A Psychoanalytic Study*, op. cit, pp. 54–58.

31. FRS Box 29, File 866.

32. Ibid.

33. Ibid.

34. Melvin Herman to FRS, 2 December 1962; FRS to Melvin (Herman), 4 December 1962. Both in FRS Box 31, File 972.

35. Flora Rheta Schreiber, "I Was Raising a Homosexual Child," *Cosmopolitan*, January 1963, pp. 60–64.

36. Dickstein and Nadelson, *Women Physicians*, p. 16; Cornelia B. Wilbur, with Moshe Torem, "A Memorial for Cornelia B. Wilbur, M.D., in Her Own Words: Excerpts from Interviews and an Autobiographical Reflection," *Clinical Perspectives on Multiple Personality Disorder*, edited by Richard P. Kluft and Catherine G. Fine (Washington, D.C., American Psychiatric Press, 1993), p. xxix.

37. SAM to FM, postmarked 7 September 1962, DE; Dickstein and Nadelson, *Women Physicians*.

38. SAM to FM, 23 April 1962 and 4 May 1963; SAM to "Florence and Dad," n.d. but by content 1962 and marked "2nd day of spring." All in DE.

39. STERN.

40. See for example SAM to WM and FM, 1 February 1962, and FRS Box 37, File 1087; SAM to WM and FM, postmarked 8 March 1962; SAM to WM and FM, n.d. but by content 1962 and marked "2nd day of spring." Both in DE. SAM to WM and FM, 5 February 1962, DE.

41. SAM to WM and FM, 21 February 1962, DE.

42. Maxwell, *Uncle Arthur's Bedtime Stories*, p. 51; STERN; Rieber addition to FRS, Tape 1.

CHAPTER 11

1. List of therapy hours and charges 1954–1965, FRS Box 37, File 1089; 1098.
2. *American Psychiatric Press Review of Psychiatry*, Vol. 13. Edited by J. M. Oldham and M. B. Riba (Washington, DC: American Psychiatric Press, 1994); Glen O. Gabbard and Eva P. Lester, *Boundaries and Boundary Violations* (Washington, DC: American Psychiatric Publishing, 2003).
3. SAM to WM and FM, 1 October 1962, DE.
4. SAM to WM and FM, 1 February 1962 and SAM to FM, 1 October 1962, DE.
5. STERN.
6. SAM to WM and FM, 2 February 1962, DE.
7. FRS Box 37, Files 1086, 1090, Tape 28.
8. SAM to FM, 6 August 1962, DE.
9. SAM to FM 26 July 1962, SAM to FM, 3 September 1962, both in DE.
10. FRS Box 37 File 1090, Tape 27.
11. FRS Box 37, File 1092 ("Late March-Early April 1960").
12. Therese Benedek and Franz Alexander, *Psychosomatic Medicine, Its Principles and Applications* (New York: Norton, 1950); Franz Alexander and Thomas M. French, *Psychoanalytic Therapy: Principles and Application* (New York: Ronald Press, 1946). For Connie's embrace of "corrective emotional experience" theory, see Tape 2 (4 April 1971) of Rieber donation to FRS.
13. FRS Box 37, File 1090, Tape 35.
14. SAM to WM and FM, 8 April 1962, DE.
15. SAM to WM and FM, 25 December 1962, DE.
16. SAM to FM, 25 November 1962, DE.
17. Columbia University registar's office, verification of pre-medicine studies for Shirley Ardell Mason, 1960–61. Available from <www.studentclearinghouse.org>
18. Letter from Arthur Brown, Columbia University Dean of Students, to Cornelia Wilbur 23 June 1961, FRS Box 37, File 1103.
19. SAM to WM and FM, 22 February 1961; 27 November 1962, DE.
20. Ibid.
21. SAM to Wyelene Frederickson, 7 December 1964, Daniel Houlihan collection, Mankato, MN, copy in author's possession.

22. STERN.
23. SAM to Luella Warnke Odden, n.d. but content indciates late November 1962, MC.
24. SAM to FM, postmarked 10 October 1962 and 25 November 1962, DE.
25. Ibid.
26. SAM to FM, 31 October 1962, DE.
27. SAM to FM, n.d. but by content June 1963, DE.
28. SAM to FM, 20 January 1963, DE.
29. SAM to FM, n.d. but by content March 1963, DE.
30. FM to SAM, 14 March 1963, DE.
31. SAM to FM, 12 December 1962, DE.
32. SAM to FM, 16 May 1963, DE.
33. SAM to WM and FM, 16 March 1961 and 25 January 1962; SAM to WM and FM, postmarked 12 January 1962, all in DE.
34. Donald S. Connery, *The Inner Source: Exploring Hypnosis* (New York: Helios Press, 2003); Herbert Spiegel, "The Grade 5 syndrome: The highly hypnotizable person," *International Journal of Clinical and Experimental Hypnosis* 23:4 (1973): 303–319; Herbert Spiegel, "Memory & Hypnosis: Facts & Fictions," unpublished paper delivered to the American Psychiatric Association, May 2002, copy in author's possession.
35. Mikkel Borch-Jacobsen, "Sybil—The Making of a Disease: An Interview with Dr. Herbert Spiegel, *New York Review of Books*, 24 April 1997.
36. Dr. Herbert Spiegel, clinical notes for patient Shirley A. Mason, 20 June 1959 to 27 May 1963. Copy in author's possession.
37. FRS Box 37, File 1091, Tape 40, dated 14 March 1960; Tape 44.
38. Transcript of Tape 18, "Hypnotic Session Feb. 8, 1960," in FRS Box 37, File 1090; and File 1091, Tape 44.
39. FRS Box 37, File 1090, Tape 28; and File 1093.
40. Tape 2, 4 April 1971, Robert Rieber addition to FRS.
41. FRS Box 37, File 1087, n.d.
42. Author visit in 2010 to Shirley Mason's apartment building from 1960 to 1965, at 414 E. 78th Street, New York, NY.
43. See, for example, SAM to Wyelene Frederickson, 7 December 1964, Daniel Houlihan collection, Mankato, MN, copy in author's possession; SAM to Luella and Muriel Odden, in MC.
44. SAM to FM, 28 May 1963, DE; Dr. Herbert Spiegel clinical records for SAM;

SAM to Dr. Cornelia Wilbur n.d., FRS Box 37; see also SAM to FM, postmarked 22 October 1962, DE.

45. SAM to FM, 29 May 1963, DE; "My Friends, Sybil Dorsett," FRS Box 26, File 702; Lee Moss, "Putting 'Sybil' together," *Ithaca (N.Y.) Journal*, 18 February 1977, copy in FRS Box 34, File 1072; FRS Box 37, File 1094, Tape 14.

CHAPTER 12

1. FRS Box 12, File 294, Robert D. Moulton to Cornelia Wilbur, 27 September 1973, and Box 37, Files 1084, 1085; SAM to Wyelene Frederickson, n.d. but by content December 1964, DE; author telephone interview with Robert Moulton's daughter, Miranda Marland, of Falmouth, ME, December 2010.

2. FRS Box 37, File 1094, Tape 11, and File 1103.

3. FRS Box 37, File 1096.

4. SAM to FM, marked as received 15 August 1963; 16 August 1963; received 10 September 1963, all in DE.

5. Ibid.

6. SAM to FM, received 10 September 1963, DE.

7. STERN.

8. Ibid.

9. Stratton L. Douthat, "Weston—Besieged by overpopulation," *Charleston (WV) Gazette*, 20 December 1965; N. S. Ludington, "Weston Hospital not like Lakin," *Beckley (WV) Register*, 11 November 1965.

10. FRS Box 37, File 1095, Tape 130, 12 or 13 August 1970; File 1086.

11. Ibid.

12. Ludington, "Weston Hospital"; author telephone interview with Dr. Mildred Bateman, Charleston, WV, December 2009.

13. STERN; FRS Box 37, File 1096, Tape 12.

14. As recounted in Schreiber, *Sybil*, 1st ed., p. 400.

15. Author interview with Brenda Burwell Canning, Cornelia Wilbur's niece, in Ancaster, Ontario, Canada, April 2009. See also photograph of Dr. Cornelia Wilbur in *Pylon* (1967), yearbook of the medical college at West Virginia University.

CHAPTER 13

1. FRS to Cornelia Wilbur, 23 July 1965; FRS Box 37, File 1102, August 1965; Box 37, File 1102.

2. Ibid.; FRS Box 37, File 1095, Tape 128.
3. Cornelia Wilbur to FRS, FRS Box 37, File 1102, 4 August 1965.
4. Truman Capote, "In Cold Blood," *The New Yorker*, 25 September, 2 October, 9 October, and 16 October 1965.
5. George Plimpton, "The Story Behind a Nonfiction Novel," *New York Times*, Book Review, 16 January 1966, p. 2.
6. Gerald Clarke, *Capote: A Biography* (New York: Carroll & Graf, 1988).
7. Liz Meegan, "Sybil: Not an ordinary girl," *Moline (IL) Daily Dispatch*, 2 August 1973; and *Peoria Journal Star*, 2 August 1973. Both articles as clippings in FRS Box 1, File 4.
8. FRS Box 33, Files 1035–1038; FRS, "The Johnson Girls: A Study in Contrasts," *Family Weekly*, 1 May 1966.
9. SAM to Luella Odden, December 1966, MC; SAM to FRS, n.d., FRS Box 34, File 10.
10. Shelby Young, "Sybil unrest: How a shattered woman who became a media sensation found a new beginning in the Mountain State," *Charleston (WV) Gazette–Mail Putnam Edition*, 19 April 2006. Additional information about Shirley's tenure at the Lakin hospital from author telephone interview with Mildred Bateman, of Charleston, WV, former head of West Virginia's Department of Mental Health, December 2009; and SAM to unknown recipient, December 1966, DE.
11. SAM to Cornelia Wilbur, 4 July 1966, FRS Box 37, File 1102.
12. FRS to Cornelia Wilbur, 15 August 1966, FRS Box 23, File 624; and Box 37, File 1103.
13. Information about problems at Weston Hospital from "Situation at Weston has been studied," *Charleston (WV) Daily Mail*, 7 December 1967; "Director of Weston State Hospital quits," *Weirton (WV) Daily Times*, 31 August 1967; "Smith might want Dr. Bateman out," *Charleston (WV) Gazette*, 24 December 1965; Cornelia Wilbur to FRS, 31 January 1966, FRS Box 37, File 1102.
14. Author interviews with University of Kentucky Psychiatry Department current and former faculty and staff: Dr. Billie Ables, Dr. Robert Aug, Dr. Lon Hays, Dr. Otto Kaak, Dr. Robert Kraus, Cathy Martin, Dr. Daniel Nahum, Dr. Jim Norton, Richard Welsh, in Lexington, KY, August 2010.
15. Ibid.
16. Ibid.

17. Ibid.

18. Author telephone interview with Dr. German Gutierrez, of Lexington, KY, April 2010. See also STERN. For mirror gazing research, see Giovanni B. Caputo, "Strange-face-in-the-mirror illusion," *Perception* 39 (2010): 1007–1008.

19. Cornelia Wilbur, "Symposium 44: Recent advances in psychotherapeutic techniques," reprinted from *Excerpta Medica International Congress,* Series No. 274, Psychiatry (Part II). *Proceedings of the V World Congress of Psychiatry,* Mexico, D.F., 25 November–4 December 1971. Copy archived in STERN; and Cornelia Wilbur, "Dual and Multiple Personalities," read at the Annual Meeting of the Southern Psychiatric Association, Charleston, SC, 4 October 1971, copy archived in STERN.

20. Author interviews with University of Kentucky doctors and staff (see n. 14). See also Arnold M. Ludwig et al, "The control of violent behavior through faradic shock: A case study," *Journal of Nervous and Mental Disease* 48:6 (1969): 624–637; Nancy D. Campbell et al., *The Narcotic Farm: The Rise and Fall of America's First Prison for Drug Addicts* (New York: Abrams, 2008); Arnold M. Ludwig et al., *LSD and Alcoholism: A Clinical Study of Treatment Efficacy* (Springfield, IL: Thomas, 1970); James Galvin and Arnold Ludwig, "A case of witchcraft," *Journal of Nervous and Mental Disease* 133 (1961): 161–168; Arnold Ludwig and Jerome Levine, "A controlled comparison of five brief treatment techniques employing LSD, hypnosis, and psychotherapy," *American Journal of Psychotherapy* 19 (1965): 417–435.

21. Arnold M. Ludwig et al., "The objective study of a multiple personality. Or, are four heads better than one?" *Archives of General Psychiatry* 26:4 (1972): 298–310.

22. Ibid.

23. Author telephone interview with Prof. Ray Matura, University of Rio Grande & Rio Grande Community College, Rio Grande, OH, February 2010.

24. Information about Flora Schreiber's affair with Leonard Reisman from author telephone interview with Ben Termine, 23 February 2010. Termine lives in Clearwater, FL. For more on Reisman, see Gerald Markowitz, *Educating for Justice: A History of John Jay College of Criminal Justice* (New York: John Jay Press, 2004); and Ruth Lonsdale audiotaped interview with Flora Rheta Schreiber, 2 August 1984, John Jay College Library Special Collections.

25. Ruth Lonsdale interview, op. cit.; SAM to FRS, 10 January 1968, FRS Box 37, File 1102.
26. SAM to FRS, 10 January 1968, FRS Box 37, File 1102.
27. FRS Box 32, File 1023.
28. FRS Box 9, File 249; Box 23, Files 626–628; Box 24, Files 681–682; Box 31, File 976; Box 34, File 1070.
29. Gladys Carr to Patricia Schartle, FRS Box 37, File 1103, 29 October 1969.
30. FRS to Patricia Schartle, FRS Box 37, File 1104, 6 January 1970; Patricia Shartle to Cornelia Wilbur, 16 February 1970, FRS Box 37, File 1104.
31. FRS Box 26, File 694.

CHAPTER 14

1. As transcribed in Schreiber, *Sybil*, 1st ed., pp. 52–53.
2. FRS to Cornelia Wilbur, 23 July 1965, Box 37, File 1102.
3. Barbara J. Nelson, *Making an Issue of Child Abuse* (Chicago: University of Chicago Press, 1984).
4. Ibid.
5. Lisa Aversa Richette, *The Throwaway Children* (New York: Delta, 1969).
6. Cornelia Wilbur to FRS, n.d., FRS Box 37, File 1100.
7. FRS Box 37, File 1093, Tape 66; File 1096, Tape 132; Rieber donation to FRS, Tape 1.
8. FRS Box 37, File 1082.
9. FRS and Melvin Herman, "Should Police Use Hypnosis?" *Science Digest*, May 1966, pp. 17–19. Copy in FRS Box 7, File 166.
10. Cornelia Wilbur to FRS, 4 August 1965, FRS Box 37, File 1102.
11. FRS Box 37, File 1094, Tape 112, 23 July 1970.
12. Rieber donation to FRS, Tape 1; FRS Box 37, File 1097, Tape 24.
13. FRS Box 37, File 1094, Tape 119, "Dr. Wilbur, Sylvia, FRS," 9 August 1970.
14. Ibid.
15. See, e.g., FRS to Mankato Chamber of Commerce, 22 June 1970, FRS Box 37, File 1103.
16. FRS to Gladys Carr, 7 May 1970, FRS Box 26, File 694.
17. FRS Box 37, File 1103.
18. Ibid.
19. Ibid.
20. Ibid.

21. Ibid.
22. Otoniel Flores's death data in records of the Minnesota State Historical Society, see http://people.mnhs.org/dci/Search.cfm; and reminiscences by his daughter Virginia Cravens, audiotaped interview by Mikkel Borch-Jacobsen and Peter Swales 1998, copy in author's possession.
23. FRS Box 37, File 1103.
24. Author telephone interview with the Winseys' daughter Chris Winsey-Rudd, of Sarasota, FL, April 2010.
25. Information and quotations regarding the Winseys' meeting with Flora are taken from FRS Box 37, File 1094. Date of Winsey-Schreiber meeting taken from FRS Box 37, "Tapes of Interviews of Dr. Wilbur."
26. Author interview with Tom Davis, of Yonkers, NY, December 2009.
27. FRS Box 37, File 1095, Tape 119.
28. Ibid.
29. FRS Box 37, Files 1078, 1097, Tape 142.
30. FRS Box 37, File 1089, "Synopsis of Tape 15."
31. STERN.
32. FRS Box 37, File 1089, "Synopsis of Tape 15."
33. All so-called diary material is from FRS Box 37, File 1080.
34. Shirley Mason's so-called diaries in FRS Box 37, File 1080, were viewed and analyzed by questioned-documents examiner Gerry LaPorte, of Reston, VA, in 2010. He concluded that the ink used was ballpoint and the material was written in 1945 or later. In 2009, questioned document examiner Peter Tytell, of New York City, viewed the diaries written in ink, as well as a typewritten set dated 1942. He concluded that the typewriter used to create that set was not manufactured until the early 1960s.
35. Schreiber, *Sybil*, p. 11.
36. Ibid., p. 198.
37. Ibid., p. 156.
38. Ibid., p. 138.
39. Ibid., p. 156.
40. Ibid., p. 160.
41. Ibid., p. 37.
42. Ibid., pp. 80–81.
43. Ibid., pp. 196–198.
44. Ibid., p. 325.

45. STERN.

46. Cornelia Wilbur to FRS, n.d., FRS Box 37, File 1100.

47. For Regnery and Plotnick's work on *Sybil* see Felicia Antonelli Holton, "Philosophy vs. money: a publishing house divided," *Chicago Tribune*, 12 June 1977. About Plotnick rejecting the book at first, see FRS to Abelman, 5 January 1977, FRS Box 30, File 940.

48. Schreiber, *Sybil*, p. 297.

49. Ibid., pp. 339, 344.

50. FRS to Cornelia Wilbur, 24 March 1972, FRS Box 37, File 1102.

51. Dominick Abel to FRS, 24 November 1972, FRS Box 12, Files 294–295.

52. Dominick Abel to FRS, 11 September 1972, FRS Box 12, File 294.

53. Connie Wilbur to FRS, greeting card n.d., FRS Box 37, File 1100.

54. For number of first-edition copies published, see Charlotte Phelan, "Flora has a good friend—'Sybil,'" *Houston Post*, 16 September 1973, copy in FRS Box 12, File 283; for Warner promotional efforts, see FRS Box 13, Files 312 and 315; Box 12, File 296.

55. Patricia Myrer to FRS, 19 April 1973, FRS Box 23, File 634.

CHAPTER 15

1. *Dick Cavett Show*, 14 and 15 May 1973. Copy archived at The Paley Center for Media, New York City.

2. Patricia Myrer to FRS, 1 March 1973, FRS Box 23 File 634

3. "James S. Gordon, "The many selves of Sybil," *New York Times*, 17 June 1973.

4. *Time*, 30 June 1973, available online at <www.time.com/time/magazine/article/0,9171,907646-2,00.html>

5. D.W. Harding, "Crazy mixed-up kids," *New York Review of Books*, 14 June 1973.

6. Nancy Ellis, "Sybil bizarre but true," *Omaha World-Herald*, 15 July 1973.

7. Author telephone interview with Flora Schreiber's cousin Stanley Aronson, in Providence RI, January 2010. For Nobel Prize see FRS Box 13, File 317.

8. Stanley Aronson interview, January 2010; FRS Box 9, File 225.

9. FRS Box 37, File 1098.

10. Reader letters all from FRS Box 12, Files 302, 303, 304.

11. FRS Box 12, File 297, "Sybil Syndrome" film proposal.

12. Sonya Rudikoff, "Of alternative selves and disturbing multiple personalities," *Washington Post*, 20 July 1973.

13. Delphine to FRS, FRS Box 12, File 303.

14. Martin Kasindorf "Primal therapy this year's rage," *Boca Raton News*, 16 June 1971; Ivor Davis, "Scream like a child—Live like an adult," *Pittsburgh Press*, 25 April 1971; Arthur Janov, *The Primal Scream* (New York: Perigee, 1970); Arthur Janov, *The Primal Revolution: Toward a Real World* (New York: Simon and Schuster, 1972); Arthur Janov, *The Feeling Child* (New York: Simon and Schuster, 1973).

15. For criticism of primal therapy, see *Gale Encyclopedia of Psychology*, available online at <http://findarticles.com/p/articles/mi_g2699/is_0005/ai_2699000587/>; J. Cunningham, "Primal therapies—stillborn theories," in C. Feltham, et al., eds., *Controversies in Psychotherapy and Counselling* (London: Sage Publications, 1999), pp. 25–33. For John Lennon, see Jon Weiner, *Come Together: John Lennon in His Time* (Champaign: University of Illinois Press, 1991).

16. For example, Ann McFeatters, "Child abuse found among rich, poor," *Pittsburgh Press*, 25 April 1973; "Child abuse: Doctor says grim figures a national disgrace," *St. Petersburg (FL) Evening Independent*, 26 June 1973. Information about Mondale and child abuse legislation from Nelson, *Making an Issue of Child Abuse*. See also FRS copy of letter to Senator Mondale et al.; Harvey Plotnick to FRS; Walter Mondale to FRS, all in FRS Box 12, File 294.

17. Reader letters are from FRS Box 12, Files 302, 303, 304.

18. *Publishers Weekly*, 23 September 1974. Copy in FRS Box 1, File 3.

19. FRS Box 26, File 703.

CHAPTER 16

1. Patrick McGilligan, *Backstory 2: Interviews with Screenwriters of the 1940s and 1950s* (Berkeley: University of California Press, 1977).

2. Ibid.

3. STERN.

4. Ibid.

5. Ibid.

6. Ibid.

7. Ibid., and *Examining Sybil*, from *Sybil: 30th Anniversary 2-Disc Special Collection* (Warner Brothers DVD, 2006).

8. *Examining Sybil*.

9. Author telephone interview with Stewart Stern, of Seattle, WA, February 2009.

10. STERN.
11. Stewart Stern to Cornelia Wilbur, 14 May 1974, in STERN.
12. *Examining Sybil*, and author telephone interview with Stewart Stern.
13. Cornelia Wilbur to Stewart Stern, 28 September 1974 and 4 October 1974, in STERN.
14. *Sybil: 30th Anniversary 2-Disc Special Collection.*
15. Ibid.
16. Stewart Stern to Connie Wilbur, 11 November 1974, in STERN; "Comments of a Petathal [sic] Session December 1958," FRS Box 37, File 1089.
17. Cornelia Wilbur to Stewart Stern, 7 November 1974, in STERN.
18. Stewart Stern to Cornelia Wilbur, 11 November 1974, in STERN.
19. Cornelia Wilbur to Stewart Stern, 15 November 1974, in STERN.
20. *Sybil* teleplay draft script, in STERN and in FRS Box 26, File 699.
21. FRS to Peter Dunne, 11 September 1975, FRS Box 23, File 637; FRS to Lawrence J. Friedman, 17 January 1975, FRS Box 12, File 283.
22. FRS to B. Franklin Kamsler, 24 January 1975, FRS Box 23, File 637.
23. *Examining Sybil*, and author telephone interview with Stewart Stern.
24. *Scholastic Voice* and *Scholastic Voice Teacher's Edition*, 24 February 1977 (Vol. 61, No. 12), copy in FRS Box, 1 File 4.
25. Ibid., p. 7.
26. *Saturday Night Live*, 18 March 1978, available in *Saturday Night Live, The Complete Third Season*, 1977–1978, DVD (Universal Studios, released 2008).

CHAPTER 17
1. Anita Weeks Bird to SAM, 20 August 1975, FRS Box 37, File 1099.
2. Schreiber, *Sybil*, 1st ed., pp. 183–184.
3. SAM to FM, 9 May 1973, DE.
4. Author telephone interview with David Eichman, of Roseburg, OR, January 2011.
5. Author telephone interview with Muriel Odden Coulter, of Tracy, MN, April 2009; author interview with Daniel Houlihan, of Mankato, MN, May 2008.
6. Dolores Katz, "Sybil today: Brilliant and witty," *Detroit Free Press*, 25 July 1973 (copy in FRS Box 12, File 283).
7. SAM to FM, 30 May 1972; SAM to FM, October 1972, both DE.
8. Schreiber, *Sybil*, pp. 264–265, 290.
9. See FRS to Dominick Abel, 26 September 1973, FRS Box 12, File 294; B.

Franklin Kamsler to FRS, 28 September 1973 and 15 April 1974; all in FRS Box 30, File 939; FRS to Nancy Wechsler, 9 August 1973, FRS Box 37, File 1103.

10. FRS to Dominick Abel, 26 September 1973, FRS Box 12, File 294; FRS to Nancy Wechsler, 9 August 1973, FRS Box 37, File 1103.

11. Schreiber, *Sybil*, pp. 11–12.

12. Author telephone interview with Albert J. Paris, Bullhead City, AZ, May 2008; FRS Box 24, File 686.

13. FRS Box 30, Files 939 and 944; Box 24, File 686.

14. Katz, "Sybil today."

15. Author interview with Jean Lane, in Portland OR, May 2008.

16. Author interview with Dianne Morrow, in Lansdowne, PA, July 2009; Shirley Mason to FM, 16 December 1974, DE.

17. All details about Shirley's life with Connie in Lexington during this period are from author telephone and personal interviews with Dianne Morrow.

18. See FRS to Nancy Wechsler, 13 March 1974, in FRS Box 13, File 315; Box 24, File 686; Box 30, File 944.

19. Author telephone interview with Keith Brown's niece Deborah Brown Kovac, of Bushnell, IL, November 2008.

20. Dianne Morrow, interview.

21. Author telephone interview with Monty Norris, of Oakley, CA., August 2009.

CHAPTER 18

1. Information regarding Monty Norris is taken from author's telephone interview with him at his residence in Oakley, CA, August 2009.

2. Monty Norris, "Sybil: A shocked Dodge Center thinks she grew up there," Minneapolis *Star-Tribune*, 27 August 1975.

3. Ibid.

4. Ibid., and handwritten book club report on *Sybil* by Pearl Lohrbach, n.d. but per contents written in summer 1975. Copy at Dodge Center, MN Public Library and in author's possession.

5. FRS to Lee Canning, 2 September 1975; "Author of Sybil defends reporter's right of confidentiality against the press" (press release by FRS, n.d.). Both in FRS Box 37, File 1103.

6. Harold Severson, "Dodge Center 'mum' over similarity to Sybil," *Rochester (MN) Post Bulletin*, 24 September 1975. For date of Dessie Engbard's death see Minnesota Death Certificates Index: <http://people.mnhs.org>

7. Cornelia Wilbur to Stewart Stern, 19 September 1975, in STERN; Cornelia Wilbur to FRS, 6 April 1976, in FRS Box 13, File 315.

8. Author telephone interview with Charlotte Gray, of Ottawa, Canada, May 2010.

9. Charlotte Gray to FRS, 29 September 1975, FRS Box 12, File 297.

10. FRS to Charlotte Gray, 15 October 1975, FRS Box 12, File 297.

11. Author telephone and in-person interviews with Dr. Stanley Aronson, Providence, RI, January and May 2010.

12. FRS to Patricia Myrer, 14 November 1977, FRS Box 23, File 635. See other, similar letters in Box 23, File 63. Obituary for Frederick Keith Brown, *New York Times*, 19 October 1976; "Stuart Long dies at 63; ran Texas news service," *New York Times*, 4 February 1977; author telephone interview with Flora Schreiber's research assistant during the late 1970s, James McLain, of Milford, PA, May 2010.

CHAPTER 19

1. Author telephone interview with Flora Schreiber's research assistant during the late 1970s, James McLain, of Milford, PA, May 2010.

2. FRS to Patricia Myrer, 30 October 1975, FRS Box 23, File 635.

3. FRS Box 15, File 407, Joe Kallinger to FRS, 8 August 1975.

4. FRS Box 15, File 407, FRS to Joe Kallinger, 8 September 1975.

5. Patricia Myrer to Harvey Plotnick, 26 March 1976, FRS Box 30, File 941; Patricia Myrer to FRS, 28 June 1976, FRS Box 8, File 197; FRS to Eugene Winick, 7 September 1985, FRS Box 8, File 197; Box 2, File 38; Box 18, File 521.

6. Flora Rheta Schreiber, *The Shoemaker* (New York: Simon and Schuster, 1983), pp. 19, 347.

7. Linda Matchan, "Stalking a killer's evil demons," *Boston Globe*, 30 October 1983, Living section, p. 1; FRS Box 3, File 54; Box 5, File 88.

8. Author telephone interview with Flora Schreiber's good friend Ben Termine, of Clearwater, FL, February 2010.

9. Interview with Peggy Polumbo, FRS Box 14, File 402.

10. Schreiber, *The Shoemaker.*

11. Pat Myrer to FRS, 10 September 1975, FRS Box 23, File 635.

12. *Kirkus Reviews*, 1 May 1983; Chris Wall, "Looking for answers to a psycho killer," *Los Angeles Times*, 2 August 1983; Paul Robinson, "Demon in the Little

Bird," *Psychology Today*, July 1983; Shirley Horner, "About Books," *New York Times* (New Jersey Section), 31 July 1983.

13. FRS Box 2, Files 21–25 and 27.
14. FRS Box 1, File 15; FRS Box 8, Files 222 and 223.
15. FRS Box 5, File 103, FRS to Eugene Winick, 20 August 1985; Evva Pryor to Sydell Albert, 20 November 1986; "Part Two: Mistaken Identity Sequences"; File 295; FRS Box 8, File 197, FRS to Eugene Winick, 15 July 1986.
16. For Rudolph Hess see FRS Box 5, Files 100, 100(a); for age misstatement see "Contemporary Authors (copy for revision)," FRS Box 8, File 207.
17. FRS to Cornelia Wilbur, 14 March 1987, FRS Box 1, File 5.
18. FRS Box 3, File 88, FRS to Joe Kallinger, 27 August 1988.
19. FRS Box 3, File 88, September 23, 1988, John Shapiro to Joseph Kallinger.
20. FRS Box 3, File 88, FRS to Joseph Kallinger, 4 October 1988.
21. FRS Box 3, File 88, John Shapiro to Joseph Kallinger, 20 October 1988.
22. Author interview with Flora Schreiber's cousin Stanley Aronson, in Providence, RI, May 2010.
23. FRS Box 8, File 223.
24. Andrew Yarrow, "Flora Schreiber, 70, the writer of 'Sybil' and of 'Shoemaker,'" *New York Times*, 4 November 1988.

CHAPTER 20

1. Information about the founding of the Open Hospital from author personal interview with Dr. Rosa K. Riggs, in Lexington, KY, July 2010.
2. Author personal interview in October 2009 with a former nurse from the Southwestern United States; and from the 1979 diary of the mother of an Open Hospital patient, who has requested anonymity.
3. Letters from Heather (since deceased, last name withheld at family's request), a newly admitted Open Hospital patient, to her family: 13 January 1979 and n.d., copies in author's possession; diary of Heather's mother.
4. Heather to "Mom and Dad," 13 January 1979, copy in author's possession.
5. Heather to her family, 4 July 1979, copy in author's possession; Lucy Freeman, *Nightmare* (New York: Richardson Steirman, 1987), p. 223.
6. Heather's medical background from her family and from author personal interview with Dr. Billie Ables, in Lexington, KY, one of Heather's therapists after she left the Open Hospital.

7. Cornelia Wilbur to Heather's mother, 16 January 1979, copy in author's possession.

8. Author interview with Dr. Billie Ables; author telephone interview with Heather's mother, May 2010.

9. Rosa K. Riggs, interview.

10. Ibid., and Heather to her family, 15 September 1980, copy in author's possession.

11. John Van, "Multiple personalities put creative talents to profitable work," *Chicago Tribune*, 29 May 1979, Tempo section. For further evidence that Connie asked literary agents in New York to help publish her MPD patients' work, see Anita Diamant to Cornelia Wilbur, March 1980 and 3 July 1980, copies in author's possession.

12. *DSM-III (Diagnostic and Statistical Manual of Mental Disorders)* (Washington, DC: American Psychiatric Association, 1980), p. 257.

13. Sandy Pearl, producer, and Jane Wallace, reporter, "Multiple Personalities: People in Pieces," WABC-TV *Eyewitness News*, 11–14 November 1980; Diary of Heather's mother, early 1979.

14. Author interview with Dr. Robert Kraus in Lexington, KY, July 2010.

15. For Mason Arts, see FRS Box 9, File 225.

16. Author interview with Brenda Burwell Canning in Ancaster, Ontario, Canada, April 2009. She is the source for the subsequent account of life in Connie's house.

17. List of audiotapes for sale from ISSMP&D conferences: 1984–1988, copy in author's possession.

18. Dr. Cornelia B. Wilbur, "MPD & Child Abuse: An Etiologic Overview" (Plenary Session, First International Conference on Multiple Personality/Dissociative States, 1984). Tape in author's possession.

19. Lawrence Pazder and Michelle Smith, *Michelle Remembers* (New York: St. Martins, 1980).

20. Wilbur, "MPD & Child Abuse."

21. Ibid.

22. See Debbie Nathan and Michael Snedeker, *Satan's Silence: Ritual Abuse and the Making of a Modern American Witch Hunt* (New York: Basic, 1995).

23. Audiotape list, see note 17.

24. *DSM-III*, p. 258; *DSM-III-R* (1987), p. 271.

25. G. K. Ganaway, "Historical versus narrative truth: Clarifying the role of exog-

enous trauma in the etiology of MPD and its variants," *Dissociation* 2:4 (1989): 205–220; Bill Moyers, "The Chemical Communicators," in *Healing and the Mind* (New York: Doubleday, 1993).

26. P. M. Coons, "The differential diagnosis of multiple personality," *Psychiatric Clinics of North America* 12 (1984): 51–57. Colin Ross et al., "Dissociative experiences in the general population: A factor analysis," *Hospital Community Psychiatry* 42 (March 1991): 297–301. Richard J. Lowenstein, interviewed in Ilan Flammer and Sherrill Mulhern, *La mémoire abusée* (Paris: Eva I Communication, 1993).

27. Lowenstein, in Flammer, *La mémoire*.

28. George B. Greaves and George H. Faust, "Legal and Ethical Issues in the Treatment of Dissociative Disorders," in Larry K. Michelson and William J. Ray (eds.), *Handbook of Dissociation* (University Park: Pennsylvania State University, 1996), p. 600.

29. "Evening with Cornelia B. Wilbur, M.D.," Cornelia Wilbur address to the Eastern Regional Conference on Multiple Personality and Dissociation, 23 June 1989, Alexandria, VA. Audiotape in author's possession.

30. See, e.g., John Lindenbaum et al., "Neuropsychiatric disorders caused by cobalamin deficiency in the absence of anemia or macrocytosis," *New England Journal of Medicine* 318 (30 June 1988): 1720–1728; A. D. M. Smith, "Megaloblastic madness," *British Medical Journal*, 24 December 1960, pp. 1840–1845; Pernicious Anaema Society Symptom Checklist, at www.pernicious-anaemia-society.org/; "Pernicious Anemia and Other Megaloblastic Anemias," in Robert E. Rakel and Edward T. Bope, *Conn's Current Therapy* 2009 (Philadelphia: Saunders Elsevier, 2009), pp. 394–397. For further psychiatric symptoms in pernicious anemia, see Paul W. Preu and Arthur J. Geiger, "Symptomatic psychosis in pernicious anemia," *Annals of Internal Medicine* 9:6 (1 December 1935): 766–778. For psychiatric symptoms and early twentieth-century use of liver extract to treat anemia, see Lawrence Kass, *Pernicious Anemia* (Philadelphia: W.B. Saunders, 1976).

31. Author personal interview of Roberta Guy, of Lexington, KY, July 2010. Guy was Connie's nurse in the late 1980s and early 1990s.

32. Cornelia Burwell Wilbur death certificate, on file with Kentucky Department for Health Services Registrar of Vital Statistics.

33. Richard P. Kluft, "Cornelia B. Wilbur, M.D.," *Dissociation* 5:2 (1992): 71–72.

34. Last Will and Testament of Cornelia B. Wilbur, on file in Lexington, KY. At Fayette County Probate Court.

35. Author personal interview with Dianne Morrow in Landsdowne, PA. She is the daughter of Jeannette Morrow, who died in 2009.

36. Ibid.

CHAPTER 21

1. Jeanne A. Heaton and Nona L. Wilson, *Tuning in Trouble* (San Francisco: Jossey-Bass, 1995), p. 134.

2. C. Gorney, "The many women on the witness stand," *Washington Post*, 8 November 1990.

3. "A Star Cries Incest," *People*, 7 October 1991, pp. 84–88.

4. Gloria Steinem, *Revolution from Within: A Book of Self Esteem* (New York: Little Brown, 1992), p. 318.

5. For Mulhern's work during this period, see, e.g., "Satanism and Psychotherapy: A Rumor in Search of an Inquisition," in James T. Richardson et al. (eds.), *The Satanism Scare* (New York: Aldine de Gruyter, 1991), pp. 145–172.

6. Joan Acocella, *Creating Hysteria: Women and Multiple Personality Disorder* (San Francisco: Jossey-Bass, 1999).

7. *False Memory Syndrome Foundation Newsletter*, 5 February 1993, available in March 2011 at <www.fmsonline.org/newsletters.html>

8. Author telephone interview with Jeanette Bartha, of Denver, CO.

9. Glenn Kessler, "Mining gold in memory business," *Newsday* (Long Island, NY), 28 November 1993; Rosie Waterhouse, "There'll be the devil to pay," *London Independent*, 17 October 1994; Bonnie Gangelhoff, "Diagnosis," *Houston Press*, 6 July 1995.

10. *Diagnostic and Statistical Manual of Mental Disorders, Fourth Edition (DSM-IV)* (Washington, DC: American Psychiatric Association, 1994), pp. 485, 487; *DSM-IV Guidebook* (Washington, DC: American Psychiatric Association, 1995), p. 304.

11. *DSM-IV*, pp. 843–849; Yolanda Kays Jackson (ed.), *Encyclopedia of Multicultural Psychology* (Thousand Oaks, CA: Sage, 2006).

12. Walter Goodman, "Television Review: Who programmed Mary? Could it be Satan?" *New York Times*, 24 October 1995.

13. Pam Belluck, "She recovered memories, then millions in damages," *New York Times*, 9 November 1997.

14. Acocella, *Creating Hysteria*.

15. Helen Kennedy, "Devil doc a crock," *New York Daily News*, 13 February 1997.

16. *Geraldo Live*, CNBC, 12 December 1995.

17. Acocella, *Creating Hysteria*, p. 106.

18. Harold Merskey, *The Analysis of Hysteria: Second Edition* (London: Royal College of Psychiatrists, 1995); John F. Kihlstrom, "Dissociative disorders," *Annual Review of Clinical Psychology* 1 (2005): 227–253; Timo Giesbrecht et al., "Cognitive processes in dissociation: An analysis of core theoretical assumptions, *Psychological Bulletin* 134:5 (2008): 617–647; Rafaele J. C. Huntjens et al., "Inter-identity amnesia in dissociative identity disorder: A simulated memory impairment?" *Psychological Medicine* 36:6 (2006): 857–863; Rafaele J. C. Huntjens et al., "Procedural memory in dissociative identity disorder: When can inter-identity amnesia be truly established?" *Consciousness and Cognition*, 14:2 (June 2005) :377–389; Martin J. Dorahy and Rafaele J. C. Huntjens, "Memory and Attentional Processes in Dissociative Identity Disorder: A Review of the Empirical Literature," in American Psychiatric Publications, *Traumatic Dissociation: Neurobiology and Treatment* (Arlington, VA: American Psychiatric Publishers, 2007), pp. 55–76.

19. Eleanor A. Maguire et al., "Navigation-related structural change in the hippocampi of taxi drivers," *Proceedings of the National Academy of Science* 98:8 (2000): 4398–4403; Christian Gaser and Gottfried Schlaug, "Brain structures differ between musicians and non-musicians," *The Journal of Neuroscience* 23:27 (2003): 9240–9245.

20. Janet Malcolm, "Trouble in the Archives," *The New Yorker*, 12 December 1983, pp. 110–119.

21. Mikkel Borch-Jacobsen and Herbert Spiegel, "Sybil—the Making of a Disease: An Interview with Dr. Herbert Spiegel," *New York Review of Books*, 24 April 1997.

22. Account of Swales's and Borch-Jacobsen's investigation into Shirley's identity is from author telephone conversation with Mikkel Borch-Jacobsen, of Paris, France, September 2010.

CHAPTER 22

1. Author interview with Roberta Guy in Lexington, KY, July 2010.

2. Last Will and Testament of Cornelia Wilbur, on file in Lexington, KY, Fayette County Probate Court.

3. Roberta Guy, interview.

4. Author telephone interview with Lexington, KY, antiques dealer Mark Boultinghouse, August 2010.

5. Shirley Mason to Eddice [*sic*, actually Edice] Barber, 10 February 1998, copy sent from Peter Swales to Daniel Houlihan, copy in author's possession.

EPILOGUE

1. Anita Weeks Bird letter to FRS, 20 August 1975, and Bird to SAM, 20 August 1975, in FRS Box 13, File 315, and Box 37, File 1099; Mikkel Borch-Jacobsen, *Making Minds and Madness* (New York: Cambridge University Press, 2009).
2. Mark Miller and Barbara Kantrowitz, "Unmasking Sybil," *Newsweek*, 25 January 1999, pp. 66–68; Reuters, "Tapes raise new doubts about 'Sybil' personalities," *New York Times*, 19 August 1998, p. A-21.
3. Harrison Pope Jr. et al., "Attitudes toward *DSM-IV* dissociative disorders diagnoses among board-certified American psychiatrists," *American Journal of Psychiatry* 156:2 (1999): 323–323; Numan Gharaibeh, "Dissociative identity disorder: Time to remove it from *DSM-V*?" *Current Psychiatry* 8:9 (2009): 30–36.
4. Flora Rheta Schreiber, *Sybil* (New York: Hachette Book Group, 2009).
5. Ibid.
6. Richard K. Baer, *Switching Time: A Doctor's Harrowing Story of Treating a Woman with 17 Multiple Personalities* (New York: Crown, 2007); Robert B. Oxnam, *A Fractured Mind: My Life with Multiple Personality Disorder* (New York: Hyperion, 2005); Herschel Walker and Jerry Mungadze, *Breaking Free: My Life With Dissociative Identity Disorder* (New York: Touchstone, 2008).
7. Jeanne Dorin McDowell, "The four (at least) faces of Tara," *New York Times*, 9 January 2009.
8. Alfonso Martinez-Taboas, "Multiple personality disorder as seen from a social constructionist viewpoint," *Dissociation* 4: 3 (1991): 129–133.
9. Lina Hartocollis, "The making of multiple personality disorder: A social constructionist view," *Clinical Social Work Journal* 26: 2 (1998): 159–176.

INDEX

protecting anonymity of, xii, 151, 172,
186, 189–91, 192, 193–94, 196,
197, 200–201, 202, 214, 228, 231
psychiatric treatment of, *see* Wilbur-
Mason therapy sessions
psychiatry career of, 58–59, 63, 76,
77, 88, 96, 98, 105, 127, 133, 137,
139, 149
reclusiveness of, xxi, 18, 122, 174,
194, 201, 214, 230, 231, 236
schooling of, 9, 12, 13, 15, 55–57,
61, 62, 75, 76–77, 78–79, 87, 88,
89, 96, 98, 99, 100, 110, 122, 127,
137, 159, 191, 193, 199
Schreiber's investigation into
childhood of, 160–64
Seventh-Day Adventism of, 3–4,
7–8, 9–11, 12–13, 14, 15–16, 19,
54, 55, 57, 58, 59, 60, 75–76, 93,
102, 103, 105, 111, 126–27, 129,
133, 134, 135, 164, 198, 231
Spiegel's hypnosis sessions with, xvii,
130–32
stepmother's warm relationship
with, 129, 133, 190
suicidal leanings of, 100, 104, 131,
134
Swales's investigation into identity
of, 228–29, 230, 232, 233
teaching jobs of, 61, 65, 75, 76,
77–78, 87, 106, 137, 149, 191,
193–94
as underweight, 61, 62, 76, 77, 87,
123, 195, 215, 236
West Virginia move and, 139, 140,
141, 143, 145–46

Wilbur's aiding in career ambitions
of, 88, 98, 127–28, 137, 140
Wilbur's financial assistance to, xviii,
97, 98, 111, 124, 128, 129, 137,
145, 214, 230
Wilbur's improper relationship with,
xviii, 62, 65, 75, 97, 103, 124–26,
128, 146, 164, 182, 194–95, 197,
202, 205, 212, 214, 215, 221
Wilbur's visit to Dodge Center with,
135–37, 189
Mason, Walter, 6, 7–9, 12, 13–14, 15,
17, 18, 54, 55, 59, 60–61, 64–65,
75, 76, 77, 79, 87, 88, 92, 94, 108,
109, 123, 127, 162, 164, 198
death of, 128, 190
as depicted in *Sybil*, xiv, 170, 171
"recovered memories" of abuse at
hands of, 110, 132, 157
Wilbur's meetings with, xiv, 104–5,
170
masturbation, 10, 19, 54, 66, 102
Maxwell, Maureen, 79
Mayflower Shop, 159, 168, 192–93, 194
Mayo Clinic, 8–9, 60–61, 165–66
Meduna, Ladislas von, 45
mental hospitals, 38, 39, 41, 59, 64, 80,
82, 84, 88, 92, 137, 138, 139, 189,
210
barbiturates used in, 47–49, 50,
51–52, 53, 80, 83, 219
"hopeful wards" of, 43–44
lobotomies performed at, 49, 50
MPD wards in, 218–19, 225
Schreiber's articles on, 117–18
shock therapy used in, 45–50, 80, 209

mental hospitals (*cont.*)
   substandard conditions at, 46–47,
      138–39, 140, 210, 219, 225
   see also specific hospitals
Metrazol convulsive therapy, 45–46, 47,
   48–49
Michigan, University of, 24, 27, 37, 41,
   43, 83
   Psychopathic Hospital at, 46, 126
military medicine, 50–51, 80, 81
Miller, William, 4–5
Michelle Remembers (Pazder and
   Smith), 216
Mondale, Walter, 156, 178
Morris, Dick, 115–16
Morris, Terry, 115–17
Morrow, Dianne, 195–97
Morrow, Jan, 195–96, 221
Moulton, Robert, 14, 135–36
Mulhern, Sherrill, 223
multiple personality disorder (MPD),
   xv, xvii, xx, 41, 46, 66, 86, 107,
   122, 136, 139, 151, 193, 237
   childhood trauma's assumed link to,
      xv, 40, 211, 216, 217, 218, 235
   as depicted in *Sybil,* xiii–xiv, 169–70,
      172, 175
   die-hard believers in, 227–28,
      234–35
   DSM-IV's new name for, 225–26,
      233
   DSM's official recognition of, xv,
      213, 218
   epidemic rise of, xii, xv–xvi, xvii, 210,
      211, 216, 218–19, 222–23, 224,
      225, 233, 236

"Eve" case study in, 84–86, 91–92,
   142, 143, 148, 230
as feminist metaphor, xix, 85–86,
   177–78, 179, 233
hypnosis in treatment of, 40, 66, 148,
   212, 224, 227, 236
hysteria patients and, 39, 40, 58
"integrating" of personalities in
   curing of, xiv, 86, 104, 122, 140,
   172, 211, 218
ISSMP&D conferences on, 215–17,
   218, 219, 230
"Jonah" case study in, 148, 211
lawsuits for misdiagnosing of, xvi,
   223–25, 226
Lexington's high-rate diagnosing of,
   146–48, 209, 210–11, 212
medical community's marginal-
   ization of, 226–27, 233,
   235
"memories" of abuse uncovered in
   treatment of, xv–xvi, 148, 211,
   213, 216–18, 222, 223–25, 226,
   235
Open Hospital treatment center for,
   209–12, 213, 219
popular media depictions of, 234
prevalence among women of, xv, 39,
   41
skepticism over, xvi, 142, 175–76,
   201, 224–27, 228, 233
specialized wards for, 218–19, 225
Wilbur's zealous treating and
   promoting of, xxi, 91, 107,
   147–48, 195, 209–14, 215–17,
   218, 219, 221, 227, 234

Wilbur, Cornelia "Connie," (*cont.*)
 Mason's financial dependence on,
  xviii, 97, 98, 111, 124, 128, 129,
  137, 145, 214, 230
 Mason's improper relationship with,
  xviii, 62, 65, 75, 97, 103, 124–26,
  128, 146, 164, 182, 194–95, 197,
  202, 205, 212, 214, 215, 225
 Mason's protected anonymity and,
  151, 172, 186, 189–90, 200–201,
  214
 Mason's psychoanalyst ambitions
  encouraged by, 88, 98, 127–28,
  137, 140
 Mason's unhealthy attachment to,
  xviii, 62–65, 75, 88, 97, 108, 110,
  111, 125, 131, 134, 137–38, 140,
  214, 215
 maternal approach to patients of,
  xx, 44, 84, 97, 100, 101, 110, 126,
  147, 183
 Mattie Mason demonized by, xiii,
  65, 95, 97, 101, 106–7, 108, 110,
  133, 158
 media promotion by, 173, 174–75,
  193, 209, 213
 mental hospitals run by, 138, 140,
  146, 209–12
 MPD zealously treated and
  promoted by, xxi, 91, 107,
  147–48, 195, 209–14, 215–17,
  218, 219, 221, 227, 234
 Open Hospital opened by, 209–12,
  213, 219
 parents' lack of encouragement for,
  20, 22, 26–27, 62, 219

 Pentothal administered by, 47, 48,
  50, 51–52, 53, 63, 80, 83, 93–96,
  97, 98, 99, 100–101, 102–4,
  107–8, 109, 110, 111, 136, 157,
  158, 163, 183, 184, 191
 physical appearance of, 22, 119, 135,
  141, 183, 215, 221
 private practices of, 52, 75, 83–84,
  195
 professional ambitions of, 20, 22,
  24, 26–27, 44, 46, 53, 62, 63, 66,
  79–80
 professional notoriety and fame of,
  25–26, 37, 50, 52, 118, 148, 151,
  213, 219, 221
 Roddy McDowall as patient of,
  118–20, 125
 schooling of, 22–23, 24, 26–27, 37,
  43, 44, 46, 83, 88
 Schreiber's first collaboration with,
  120–22
 Schreiber's strained relationship
  with, 175, 202, 207
 sexism faced by, 20, 22, 24–25, 37,
  52, 63
 shock treatments administered by,
  44, 47, 48–49, 80, 99–100, 101
 Stern's list of *Sybil* queries for, 181,
  183
 Sybil legal action and, 192, 193, 194,
  206
 at University of Kentucky Medical
  School department, 146–48, 171,
  195, 211, 213–14, 227
 Walter Mason's meetings with, xiv,
  104–5, 170

ABOUT THE AUTHOR

Debbie Nathan has been a journalist, editor, and translator for over three decades. She specializes in writing about immigration, the U.S.–Mexico border, sexual politics, and sex panics, particularly in relation to women and children. Her work has won numerous national and regional awards.

In the late 1980s, Debbie was the first journalist to do in-depth critical work for the national press about the "ritual sex abuse" panic that peaked in the United States in the mid- to late 1980s. Her writing about these sex-abuse scandals helped free some falsely convicted defendants, including day care aide Kelly Michaels in New Jersey.

Debbie appears in the Academy Award–nominated documentary *Capturing the Friedmans*, the story of accused child molesters Arnold and Jesse Friedman. She is a board member of the National Center for Reason and Justice (NCRJ). This nonprofit organization advocates for intelligent, humane approaches to preventing child abuse and dealing with accused offenders.

Debbie was raised in Houston, Texas, and currently lives in New York City with her husband, Morten Naess. She has two children, Sophy and Willy.